MW01394006

"Imagine That"

A Spiritual Awakening

by
Joseph Gioffre Jr.

Bloomington, IN   Milton Keynes, UK
authorHOUSE

AuthorHouse™
1663 Liberty Drive, Suite 200
Bloomington, IN 47403
www.authorhouse.com
Phone: 1-800-839-8640

AuthorHouse™ UK Ltd.
500 Avebury Boulevard
Central Milton Keynes, MK9 2BE
www.authorhouse.co.uk
Phone: 08001974150

© 2006 Joseph Gioffre Jr.. All rights reserved.

No part of this book may be reproduced, stored in a retrieval system, or transmitted by any means without the written permission of the author.

First published by AuthorHouse 4/3/2006

ISBN: 1-4259-1928-6 (sc)
ISBN: 1-4259-1929-4 (dj)

Printed in the United States of America
Bloomington, Indiana

This book is printed on acid-free paper.

Dedication

I extend my deepest thanks and gratitude to God and his helpers; even though I ran from You, You never gave up on me. My life has been transformed. I'm all Yours. I love You and surrender to You. Walk with me, guide me, and teach me. To my mother; I forgive you, I love you. Reflecting on the years, discovering the memories you quietly shared with me, let's not dismiss what so few have found. To my mother-in-law; I hardly knew you before your passing but I have learned many things about you since. I appreciate all that you have done for us. We will meet again; I know we will, for it is written on my heart.

Contents

Introduction 1

Chapter 1
    The Big Bang Theory 3

Chapter 2
    Another Country Song 15

Chapter 3
    Letting Go of God 23

Chapter 4
    Time in the Big House 31

Chapter 5
    Hello From Heaven 53

Chapter 6
    Braking for God 63

Chapter 7
    A Family Affair 81

Chapter 8
    Out of the Blue 111

Chapter 9
    Small Medium at Large 125

Chapter 10
    Another Serious Wake-Up Call 133

Chapter 11
- The Bumper Stickers 141

Chapter 12
- Destiny Revealed? 169

Chapter 13
- All About Sharing 181

Chapter 14
- Did You See That? 187

Chapter 15
- What Goes Around Comes Around 215

Chapter 16
- Visiting Hours 225

Chapter 17
- Inspiration, Intention and Interpretation 237

Chapter 18
- Some Assembly Required 251

Chapter 19
- Seeing The Light 299

- Epilogue 315

Introduction

So many wonderful things had already happened by November of 2001, which was only a few months after they began, that I felt a powerful impulse, either internal, external, or both, to record the drama. At that time, my primary reason was to share these experiences with family. I mused, "What else could possibly happen?" What had already happened seemed too strange, too phenomenal, too incredible to continue. How could the story get any more intriguing or inspiring?

But as I typed away at the computer, my developing intuition sensed that the story was still unfolding. Class was just beginning, and I had a long way to go, and a great deal to learn. It seemed too early for the keyboard, as I reluctantly slipped back into life's regular activities while continuing studies of the events surrounding me. And I certainly wasn't aware of the lessons yet to come, lessons that would ultimately change even the reasons for capturing the story. A handwritten journal would temporarily suffice. Clarity, I trusted, would come with time.

The months became years ticking by, as I continued to marvel in amazement, while tenaciously questioning events and the meaning of life itself. I wanted to share what I had discovered, as if I had found the cure for cancer. Surely, I wasn't the first to discover or report these things, but had they ever been told from the perspective of an "average Joe" before? Even if it had been done, I sensed that God wanted it told again. Perhaps He had a new audience in mind.

As you read, I hope you find this story as inspiring as I did while it was transpiring. It is my deepest ambition that some might be awakened as I have become, or at least find themselves intrigued as to what life is really about, and hopefully curious enough to begin their own search for the truth.

As with many stories, to understand the end we must start at the beginning, a long time ago. However, my objective is to include only pertinent information during this look back in time. This is a journey, the story of the awakening of the guy next door, an awakening to a world beyond ours, and to an understanding that is clearly out of this world…for some. I want to share exactly what I was thinking as the journey progressed. I'll transform as the years of inaccurate perceptions and beliefs are chiseled from my petrified brain. It was a long and difficult evolution, assisted by an open mind and a ferocious hunger for the truth.

Chapter 1

The Big Bang Theory

In May of 1965, when I was only five years old, my paternal grandfather passed away in his sleep from an apparent heart attack. We knew him as Pop Pop. He was an immigrant farmer who came to the United States in the '20s with his wife, to try his hand at farming. When asked, Pop Pop claimed they were lonely here in the U.S., thus explaining why they bore seventeen children. My grandmother died about eight months after giving birth to her seventeenth child, my father.

Pop Pop and the children subsequently took care of one another on the eighty-acre farm. Fathering this many children was a testimony to his love of children and family, his kind and gentle demeanor and his extreme patience. The farm became a gathering spot for local children and their families. There were many things to experience on the farm, including animals, pastures, woodlands, trails, barns, gardens, machinery, and a baseball field that kept both kids and adults busy during the warmer months. Pop Pop's presence there would be sorely missed.

"Imagine That"   A Spiritual Awakening

After returning home from Pop Pop's viewing at the funeral parlor, Mom sent me to the babysitter's, several houses down the street of our new suburban community. She was going to prepare food and then return to the services. While at the babysitter's, I became bored and decided to sneak out the back door and do some exploring at the nearby creek. My love for the water began at a very young age.

At the creek, while I was overturning rocks in search of those funny-looking creatures that sometimes lived beneath them, I heard a loud *BANG* that seemed to emanate from my house. I looked in the direction of the sound, now certain that it came from home. It had sounded like a gunshot. My association with the farm, which included hunters, guns, and probably some television westerns, convinced this five-year-old that it was in fact a gunshot that I'd heard. I became concerned but didn't know what to do.

I continued to flip rocks for what seemed like a long time, certainly enough time for Mom to be on her way back to the funeral home, but the baby blue Ford was still in the driveway. My concern escalated. I had to make a decision: check on Mom or return to the sitter's, who still had not discovered I had snuck out. Apprehensive, I approached the house and tried to go in, but the door was locked, so I knocked, all the while sensing that something was wrong.

My mother answered the door. I don't remember who spoke first or what our first words were, probably because I was stunned by the red line running down her face and across her neck. It looked like blood, but I wasn't sure. I was only five. So I asked her if she was okay. She assured me that she was, and told me to go back to the sitter's.

"Are you sure you're okay?" I asked, not really buying her answer.

The Big Bang Theory

She quietly answered, "Yes. Now go on back down to Doris' house."

Somehow, I knew the answer was insincere but I did as I was told. I didn't question her or argue further because I urgently sensed the need to tell someone else, someone who could make an unbiased determination.

I ran to Doris' house and began telling them about the red line on the side of my mother's face and across her neck. I told them I thought it was blood but they assured me that it couldn't have been. I continued trying to convince them that something was wrong with Mom.

More time passed and Mom still hadn't left the house. I brought this to the sitter's attention and yet she did nothing. She continued to insist that there was nothing wrong. Finally, Dad arrived, coming to see why Mom had not returned to the funeral home. The next thing I remember is standing in the driveway with Aunt Anna, both of us crying our eyes out as we watched Mom being rushed to the ambulance.

It was the last time I ever saw her.

Still standing in the driveway crying, believing Mom was going to the hospital to be helped, I asked my aunt—and anyone else who would listen—what had happened to Mom. I didn't get a satisfactory answer. I wasn't even allowed in the house, until I cunningly fabricated a reason and told Aunt Anna that I wanted to go into the house to get a book. She conceded.

But I wasn't looking for a book. Rather, I was in search of clues and maybe even some answers.

I went into the master bedroom and found a stain on the carpet. The full-length mirror on the closet's sliding door was cracked, but the glass was intact. Quickly trying to piece together what had happened, I theorized that Mom had fallen into the mirror while changing clothes, broken it, and been badly cut.

After finding out that Mom died, I began to replay the evidence in my mind and concluded that the clues didn't add up to an injury severe enough to kill her. Part of the problem was the stain on the floor, it wasn't very big and it contained very little red, which I naturally concluded was blood. The stain was more like a wet spot with a gray tint to it. And the mirror wasn't in pieces, so how did she cut herself? And where was the excessive amount of blood; enough for someone to bleed to death? My five-year-old mind didn't completely accept my own theory, but I couldn't come up with a better one, and no one would tell me the truth. After all, what was the *BANG* I'd heard, and why was everyone denying it?

Actually, I don't remember anyone telling me that she died; they just said she wasn't coming back.

I continued to present my evidence of the gunshot and the bloody face, but no one would confirm my eye-witness report. Everyone avoided the subject. The only thing that anyone would tell me was that Mom was badly hurt in an accident while changing her clothes.

I wasn't allowed to attend her funeral because it was thought that I wouldn't understand what was happening. I remember a great deal of sorrow and pain, so I think, at least on a deeper level, that I knew what death was. Even if I didn't, I certainly learned the pain of losing someone very important.

From Green Acres to Golden Pond

Shortly after the tragedy, we moved back to the family farm. I guess Dad didn't want to stay in our new house because of the memories. I have limited memories of the next two years as I'm sure I was trying to cope with the loss. My Dad had lost his mother when he was only eight months old, and had lost several of his brothers and sisters, as well, so he and the family were somewhat numb to death. Losing family members to disease and accidents wasn't unusual in those days. For larger families, such as this one, it was almost expected, an unfortunate part of living that had to be experienced and endured. Life went on.

What I do remember is that I liked the farm, with its creeks, fields, pastures, vegetable gardens, fruit trees, natural springs, old barns and sheds. The open countryside was filled with opportunities to tempt the curiosity of an exploring young boy, not to mention the rotten-tomato fights and eating sour apples until my tummy cramped. The farm was an excellent diversion.

Aunt Toni, Dad's sister, became my primary caretaker and I quickly bonded with her kind, mothering ways. I became very possessive of her. She stayed on the farm and never married. It was as if she was destined to take care of the remaining family who still lived on the farm. Each day before school, I asked her what she had planned for the day, so that I could feel connected to her by thinking of what chore she might be doing. I would think of her frequently during the day and wonder if she was okay. Clearly, I feared losing loved ones when they were out of sight.

My mother's side of the family, my grandparents, aunts and uncles, interacted less and less with Dad and me as time passed. They had previously been through some difficult times of their own, including abuse, divorce and financial struggles. Their family structure and values of love and loyalty to other family members were somewhat lacking. It wasn't until I was in my early thirties that I assessed how unusual it was that this family had apparently "forgotten" a grandson and nephew. Grandmothers are usually very protective of their grandchildren, but not this grandmother. There was probably a reasonable explanation.

At the time, I didn't recognize the disassociation as "strange" because it was all that I knew. Humans, like many creatures, readily adapt to the conditions they are presented. When we're exposed to harsh conditions, such as the cold of the North or the heat of the South, it can become accepted by life-long residents who know no other. We adapt and even conclude that unusual situations or conditions are normal. In this way, it didn't strike me as odd that my maternal grandparents abandoned me. This had become "normal," in my sphere of experience.

When I was seven, my father re-married and purchased a nice house near the family farm. For the next five years, I struggled to get along with my stepmother, but I seemed to be nothing more than a complication to her marriage. She was constantly yelling and backhanding me for the smallest of infractions. I often felt that she invented reasons to hit me. I didn't grow up experiencing the natural, loving relationship that usually exists between a mother and her child. More often than not, a biological parent's love is stronger than a stepparent's love. As a present-day stepparent, I can now see this difference firsthand.

> *Out of love and respect for my parents, who are both still alive, I need to state that our relationship has dramatically improved, over the years. The same overly critical stepmother who was so ready to punish me (probably for my own good and future development) has transformed into a very caring and thoughtful woman who does volunteer and charity work for mentally challenged citizens and others. She leaves birthday presents on my doorstep, prepares my favorite dessert when I come over for dinner and bakes my favorite cookies at Christmas.*

People can and do change as life mellows us. And if the past is no longer evident in the present, then why hold a grudge into the future?

Everything happens for a reason and I now realize that I wouldn't be where I am without the disciplined upbringing that I experienced.

Thanks Mom and Dad! I love you just the way you are.

My stepmother was very critical of my behavior. She wasn't about to tolerate the little things that kids do, like leaving gum and tissues in their pants pockets, ultimately making a big mess in the washing machine. I very quickly learned to clean out pockets or there would be hell to pay. Constantly minding my behavior so that I wouldn't be slapped upside the head was a necessity. I was perpetually on pins and needles, worrying about whether I was doing something that would upset my short-tempered step-mom, always looking at her to see if she was glaring back with that lethal stare that meant I was in for solitary confinement. She wouldn't always punish me in public but would save the lashings for later, when we returned home.

When I was twelve, my dream came true: we moved to waterfront property along a creek that fed the Patuxent River, a tributary on the Chesapeake Bay, near beautiful Solomon's Island. I loved being on and around water. Crabbing, fishing and joy-riding were all I needed to experience ecstasy. Before my parents could unload the furniture I was crabbing off the pier. I was consumed by the call of the great outdoors, especially the water. Dad loved to eat crabs, too, and knew I could catch more for him if I could venture out beyond the end of our shallow creek. Before long, he bought me a skiff that allowed that mobility. The little skiff gave me the freedom to spend a lot of time catching crabs and fish, and learning about nature. It was probably

Heaven-sent, but even with my religious upbringing and parochial schooling, I didn't recognize the gift.

It didn't matter; life was good.

My parents went to church every Sunday but their faith seemed shallow and didn't last much past the service. Attending church seemed more like an unbroken family tradition than a true act of faith. Perhaps it was an insurance policy, just in case there was an actual requirement mandated by God for entry into Heaven. They never quoted bible verses or told parables to illustrate a point, nor did they act especially saintly. We didn't discuss religion at home and it really didn't interest me at school, despite the fact that religion was a major topic.

My parents purchased a children's bible, and together we read it once or twice but not with any accompanying deep discussion that I can recall. I finished my grade school years at *Our Lady Star of the Sea Catholic School* in Solomon's and attended *Ryken High School,* a Catholic High School in Leonardtown, where I graduated. Both schools provided me with an excellent education that prepared me for a successful career, and I'm sure my parents thought I would get enough exposure to religion, as well. After all, that's why they were paying all that money for private-school tuition. I wasn't sure what part of the religion they embraced, however, nor did it concern or anger me. I simply found it odd that all of this association with the church didn't result in a more noticeable religious character. Perhaps their faith was quietly strong.

As a teenager, I considered my stepmother a hypocrite, because she wouldn't let me miss a single Mass during Lent and would decisively let me know if I had by cussing at me, using God's name in vain to drive the point home. This raised serious questions in my mind regarding the value of church and religion. In my youthful opinion, it hadn't done much for my stepmother's Christian development. This included her respect for the Ten Commandments; specifically Number Two, which said not to use God's name in vain. Attending Mass and other services didn't make me a better person, or fool God into allowing me into Heaven, especially if He knew that all I was thinking about during the service was what I was going to do when I got out: *And I sure hope the priest doesn't have a long sermon today because I've got things to do.* I continued to go to church only because I had no choice while I was under my parent's roof and rule.

It Took Two

As the years passed, I finally learned that my mother had committed suicide. Occasionally, I asked Dad and other relatives if they knew why. Everyone had the same response: "We don't know. She didn't even leave a note." The only speculation was that she was upset at my paternal grandfather's passing. But why would she be so upset at the passing of someone she had only known for a few years? It didn't make sense that a mother would "punch out" on her five-year-old child over the death of an in-law. Obviously, something had been deeply bothering her, and no one had seen it. How could that be?

"Oh well, it's not worth dwelling on, now," I told myself. Once again, the hard-nosed view that "life goes on" kicked in; all of that was behind me now. I was young and strong willed, and I had more important things to do than worry about that.

It wasn't until I was twenty-eight years old that I learned the truth. By stumbling across her death certificate, I found that she died from .22 caliber gunshot wounds to her head and chest. I guess that, by the time I had talked with her at the front door, she had already shot herself in the head, thus explaining the one gunshot I had heard. Apparently, she realized that it wasn't going to be enough, so she sent me away, turned the gun toward her chest, and pulled the trigger one last time.

During my teenage years, I got angry once or twice because she had committed suicide. I saw the love and attention that other kids received from their mothers, and I recognized that I didn't have this kind of relationship with my stepmother. There were times when I despised my stepmother for the way she treated me. I remembered very little about Mom, so it wasn't that I was angry at her because I missed her mothering ways. I was angry because of the treatment I was receiving from my stepmother, and I blamed Mom for it. I surmised that I would not have had to endure this wrath if Mom hadn't pulled the trigger. Someone once asked what I would say to her if I saw her after my death. I said that I didn't think she was in Heaven, because she committed suicide, but if I did see her, the first thing I would do is kick her ass for "punching out" on me! I was definitely bitter. Fortunately, the bitterness only bubbled to the surface when the subject came up. Then it would quickly pass, and I'd wonder, *What's for dinner*? I really didn't think it had any effect on me, at the time. I was a teenager with a testosterone-driven agenda of fast cars and women. My emotional and psychological scars were tucked away deep inside, for the time being.

Upon reflection, my childhood really wasn't that bad, all things considered, despite Mom's suicide and my often challenging relationship with my stepmother. Growing up on the farm and on the water was very special, and much of my time was spent outdoors, having fun. I developed a great appreciation for the outdoor world and for nature. I did well in school and stayed out of trouble, which prepared me for a successful career.

Limbo or Purgatory

Right after high school, I left home and got a job working shifts and weekends, which gave me an even easier excuse to stop going to church. Despite my non-attendance, my first wife and I got married in the Catholic Church. It was the wish of the two families that we wed in a church. That was one of the last times I would be seen in one.

As the years passed, it became the family joke that, if I set foot in a church, the walls would implode. My belief in God had not changed; I just didn't get anything out of going to church, so why go? It didn't make me feel better or lift my spirit.

Some of the teachings of the Catholic Church and school, along with some of the verses I had read in the bible, just didn't sit well with me, although I did continue to wonder about a higher power. My impression of God during this time would go something like this: to get to Heaven, you must go to church every Sunday, live by the Ten Commandments, and hope that you are one of the lucky 144,000 that could get into Heaven. I didn't know where the number 144,000 came from, but someone told me that Heaven would only contain that many folks. Everyone else was left in Limbo or Purgatory or, worse yet, cast into Hell. That just didn't make sense.

One of my grade school nuns, Sister Mary Agnes, once told my stepmother that I asked some pretty tough questions during religion class. I found it a little unsettling to think that God could be so cruel and unforgiving over such minor errors. If I had no concrete method of experiencing and realizing that God existed, then how could I be held so accountable? If He were this perfect, compassionate and loving being, then He wouldn't have such strict rules for access to Heaven. Or, at a minimum, I shouldn't have to share the same quarters with serial killers, murderers, rapists and people who drove slow in the fast lane, just because I didn't go to church every Sunday. *Sheesh, give me a break!,* I thought. Because these things didn't make good sense in connection with a loving God, I didn't consider them to be true.

Although I believed that God invoked justice upon evil people when necessary, I believed that he was essentially a loving being.

Chapter 2

Another Country Song

My first marriage was a struggle, right from the start. It didn't take long before I began to question how long it would last. Even though I believed I was normal, I now realize that I had my share of issues to deal with. Further complicating this relationship, my wife also had a less than perfect childhood, with an alcoholic, wife-abusing father. This brought unresolved issues into the marriage from both of us. She had issues with men and I had issues with women. It was a recipe for disaster. We loved each other but we didn't know *how to express* our love to one another. Still, we managed to stay together for thirteen years, trying to figure that out. This is evidence that our marriage wasn't all that bad. We did share many good times and still have many fond memories.

During our marriage, we didn't spend much time with our families because we didn't have many fond childhood memories of times spent with them. There was nothing to draw us back home for a "really good time" with the folks. We both left home directly after finishing high school. We spent time on our own and with friends, and we worked on our careers and our home. We didn't want kids, primarily because I didn't feel ready. We had dogs and cats instead. Neither of us had strong family values that would compel us to devote our lives to being parents and doting on our children. I was more concerned about doing "my thing," after being freed from an overbearing stepmother.

Without getting into the nasty details of our ill-fated marriage, let it suffice to say that we did the usual things that lead to divorce. We just didn't know how to appreciate and love one another. So the tension mounted to a point where we no longer trusted one another. The lack of trust was fatal to our marriage, as it is for many relationships.

I never pictured myself as a divorcee. This symbolized failure. I didn't like failure and had never failed at anything so important. I had been successful at nearly everything I had tried, especially my career. The divorce proceedings would prove to be the ultimate test of my mettle.

In the winter of '94, we separated under amicable terms for a trial period. We *weren't* fighting, the day she moved out. Instead, we were sad. It's as if we knew that what we were doing was wrong, that there was an easier way to mend our differences. I tried to be strong and act like I was going to be just fine, but that only lasted a few months. It was a very lonely, cold and dismal winter, compounded by exhausting twelve-hour shift work and a major ice storm which knocked out power for nearly a week, and before long I became depressed. Ironically, I produced electricity at a power plant but had none at my house, due to the downed power lines.

It was tough, taking care of the house alone. The pipes had to be drained, due to the below freezing temperatures, and I had to constantly run a kerosene heater just to keep the house somewhat tolerable. Fortunately, I was able to pack frozen foods and items needing refrigeration into coolers, and put them outside in the ice and snow to preserve them. Working twelve-hour days, nights and weekends, added to my misery. Shift work is depressing enough in winter, because we often didn't see daylight for days on end, and daylight can be instrumental in maintaining a positive attitude. Working in a room without windows, I never saw sunlight, except on my days off. This harsh winter ordeal added up to a lesser form of solitary confinement. It wasn't long before anger and depression set in.

Throughout this time, the relationship with my wife deteriorated further. We were both angry at the conditions we had forced each other to endure, and this caused us to strike out at each other. She had to move out of a nice home in the woods into the lower level of an apartment complex, while I had to manage everything for myself during a cold lonely winter fraught with one challenge after another.

We argued more in those final months than we had in our thirteen years of marriage. One minute, we fought; the next, we tried to reconcile. Our miserable situation caused us to lash out at each other while, deep inside, we knew we loved one another still. Regardless, we began fighting about who was going to get what, in the divorce settlement. To me, her demands were disproportionately high, and this began to infuriate me, compounded by the fact that the court could decide the case any way it pleased. I was losing control, and I didn't like that feeling one bit. I didn't like being wrong, I didn't like to fail, and I especially didn't like the thought of being a victim.

By May, I was a wreck, uncontrollably losing weight because I had no appetite, and suffering from sleep deprivation. I couldn't sleep for long without waking up to dwell on this miserable situation, constantly trying to figure out a success path, a way out, a way to win, a way to maintain control. Life was unfolding like a country song. I felt like I was losing everything, from control to sleep to material wealth, and now I was losing my wife; she had met someone else and was testing that relationship while keeping one foot in my door. The confusing part was that I finally realized that I really loved her and didn't want any of this to happen. I just wanted to turn back the hands of time and start all over again. But this time I wanted to get it right. I had met several women, but none of them could replace her. She wasn't as fault-filled as I had judged her to be, so I knew we could get through this if I could get her to try, but her new relationship was getting in the way, placing the focus on them, rather than us.

I felt so bad and depressed (primarily from sleep deprivation) that I had myself removed from shift work and began therapy. Unfortunately, therapy didn't seem to help. I wanted answers to why I was feeling the way I did, solutions to get through it and, above all else, to get a good night's sleep. I couldn't understand where my appetite had gone, why I couldn't calm myself into a restful slumber, at least temporarily, and why I couldn't regain control of my emotions. Therapy didn't solve any of those problems but I did learn one answer: I was grieving over my pending divorce and suffering from Post-Traumatic Stress Syndrome. "What the heck is that?" I questioned.

"You probably never grieved over the loss of your mother." the counselor replied. "You are probably grieving for the loss of two people, your mother and your wife."

Well, that's just great!, I thought, *Double Jeopardy!* "Alex, I'll take 'Depression Therapy' for a thousand." All I knew was that I was hurting, and I couldn't talk myself out of that deep dark hole. I was in an Abyss, looking out at a total eclipse of the sun. (Now I understand how powerful depression can be.)

Later that month, I met Janice. I picked her up at the entrance to her community, in my truck, with the boat in tow. Her boss (my old fishing buddy, Dave) had invited her along on a fishing trip that he and I had planned. Since she had recently separated, and mentioned that she liked fishing, Dave thought it would be nice to invite her for a pleasant day outdoors. I'd really like to say the rest is history and that we lived happily ever after, but it wasn't that easy. We did hit it off immediately. Here was an attractive lady who liked to fish and could catch fish, too. Bass fishing isn't that easy to get the hang of, with a variety of rods, reels and casting techniques, and on that first trip she hooked a "limit" of fish, plus one. She hooked me, too!

Even though I knew Janice was everything I was looking for in a (first) mate, I found myself running back home after spending only a few days with her. I needed a couple of days alone to recover. I was tormented by something and required time to figure things out.

My wife found out about my new "girlfriend" and made up her mind to take action. She called me one evening, while Janice was visiting, and told me, "Get that bitch out of my house, because I'm coming over in 15 minutes!" Since it is illegal to change the locks on a house to prevent a separated spouse from entering, we knew that my wife would intrude whether we liked it or not. Janice and I decided to leave and go to her place. I didn't realize that this would prove to be a bad move.

When I got back home, many belongings were gone, including my beloved cat, Nikki. During these dark times, Nikki seemed to sense my misery and snuggled up to me, trying to comfort the pain. When I attempted to sleep, she would lay right next to me, at chest level. If I rolled onto my side, she crossed over and snuggled up to my chest, just below my chin. She knew I needed a companion and now she was gone, too. I had always had animals for pets. My wife and I had recently lost two dogs (one had been hit by a car, and the other was old), so this latest loss of Nikki only injected more agony.

While I was outside, a couple of days later, a scrawny, stray tabby kitten came running up to me and introduced himself. It was easy to see that he was very hungry, because he began chewing on my finger almost immediately. We became fast friends. I found the timely arrival of my new friend welcome, but quite peculiar.

Mentally, I wasn't ready for a long-term commitment with Janice. After about three days with her, I would feel an unusual urge to run away. It was a strange and yet powerful feeling. We dispassionately called it the "three-day push." I didn't understand it, because she had so many good qualities. She was everything that I was looking for in a woman: kind, friendly, athletic, outgoing and fun, with strong family and moral values. But by September she had had enough of the "three-day push," and felt it best to sever the relationship. I had to agree without argument because it didn't seem fair for her to have to deal with my issues. I figured it was one of those psychological things bubbling up, so I purchased self-help books to conduct my own research.

My experience was probably not that different from many folks who have been through emotionally turbulent times, such as death and divorce, but I sure was having trouble with women. From my mother, who didn't care enough to stick around, to her mother (my grandmother "Nanna"), who seemingly dropped off the face of the Earth, to my stepmother, with whom I didn't have a loving relationship, to my wife, who gave up on our marriage. *Sheesh! Women!*

Since neither Janice nor I understood what was happening, we parted as friends, realizing I needed to work through my "women" issues. I wasn't sure of the cause, but there was only one way to find

Another Country Song

out whether the "three-day push" would affect other relationships: I had to continue dating.

Soon thereafter, I began seeing someone else. I hoped and believed that the "three-day push" would go away with someone new, but it didn't. Even worse, after the introductory pleasantries had worn off, this new woman's passive-aggressive behaviors became another nightmare for me. The unpleasant ordeal made me realize how much I missed Janice. While I continued to date the new girlfriend, Janice had managed to stay in touch, and I appreciated that greatly. She wouldn't give up on me, and remained a very good friend. It wasn't her fault that I couldn't figure out the cause of the "three-day push." Even though she tried to date others, she didn't find anyone in whom she was interested enough to continue seeing. Something was keeping her patiently attracted to me, waiting in the wings.

In late October, I received a call, asking me to audition for a singing part in an upcoming children's Christmas musical. One of the show contacts had heard me sing at my sister's wedding, and dropped the dime on me. The audition was about a two-hour drive away, in Delaware. My girlfriend couldn't go, so I planned on traveling there alone. The night before the trip, however, Janice's friend and roommate Cindy called to say that Janice wasn't doing anything and was secretly hoping that I would call to talk to her. *That's odd*, I thought. Cindy wasn't in the habit of calling me. I told her that I was going out of town for an audition, and she suggested that I call Janice and ask her to go. She was sure that Janice would say yes, even on such short notice, which she did. We had a wonderful time just being friends. I felt the pull of my emotions back to her, but I also remembered the "three-day push," and didn't want to press my luck, so we parted company with another fond memory.

In early December, the musical took to the stage in Ocean City, Maryland. My girlfriend attended the two days of shows, and so did Janice. I told Janice she shouldn't come, but she told me I had no control over what she did, and that she would stay out of sight. For a while, I wondered if this was a case of "fatal attraction," but she was too pure for that. She was just offering her support from a close, and yet secure, distance.

I continued to date the other woman, but soon realized it wasn't going to work. She had a passive mean streak, (silent treatment for no apparent reason) that I wasn't fond of. And I experienced the "three-day push" with her, as well, thus confirming that the problem was mine alone and not any woman's fault. Just before Christmas, we broke up. I felt relieved.

Not wanting to spend Christmas alone, I called Janice and asked her if she wanted to attend a Christmas party at my parents' house. And now I can say:

We've been together ever since.

Chapter 3

Letting Go of God

Janice had a strong religious foundation and wanted to continue practicing and deepening her faith, especially for the proper upbringing of her two-and-a-half-year-old son, Alex. I was too busy improving my competitive fishing skills to be bothered with church or religion, but I wasn't about to stop her. It seemed appropriate to provide a child with a foundation in religion; they could later decide if it was right for them. What Janice didn't realize was that my faith in God was almost nonexistent, after all I had been through since age five. If there was a God, He seemed absent from my life. The latest of my ordeals was further eroding what little faith I had left.

In December, 1996, Uncle Dutch died from cancer. He was the perfect role model as a husband, stepfather and grandfather. A carpenter by trade and a farmer by tradition, he had a lot to offer his children and grandchildren. He could build anything out of wood, and his retirement years often found him making crafts that he gave as gifts or sold for additional income. I still have many fond memories of good times on the farm with him, involved in activities like riding the tractor or picking strawberries.

He also made several rabbit traps out of wood for me. The rabbit would have to crawl through the opening of the rectangular wooden box. Inside the box, we placed rabbit food such as a slice of apple. If the rabbit went far enough into the box, it would trip the stick, which was mounted through the roof and tied by string to the front door, causing it to shut behind him—*Ingenious!* I never caught a single rabbit, and perhaps Uncle Dutch knew that the traps wouldn't be very productive for catching rabbits, but he knew that I was excited about baiting and checking those rabbit traps every day.

Finally, I did catch something, something that hissed at me like a cat the entire trip back to the house. I was frightened by the hissing and held the box as far from my body as I could, but I was also excited because I thought for sure that I had caught my first rabbit. But the box was heavy, perhaps too heavy for a rabbit, and, as I found out, rabbits don't hiss. I asked Aunt Toni to help me figure out what was in the trap and how to get it out. We decided it was a possum and it was having the proverbial hissy fit. So I opened the trap door near the edge of the garden and then ran from it as if I was being chased by a tiger to get away from the mad and ferocious creature inside. We never saw the mystery critter exit the trap, as it took its own sweet time to leave, but I was pretty sure it was a "man eating" possum.

The huge loss was apparent at Uncle Dutch's funeral, as I watched his family grieve deeply at his passing. During the service, the priest said that God had called him home. I got angry and began thinking that, if God was compassionate and loving, He would not have called Uncle Dutch home so soon, especially when his family still needed him. I loved the man, too; he was caring and kind, and he helped to raise me on the farm, after my mother died. His passing didn't make sense. It was much too soon. Why would God do something like this? He was only seventy-two, and his family loved him so much. Moreover, the priest claimed that God did this on purpose!

My faith crumbled; God's very existence was now in question. Without proof that He did exist, and with mounting evidence that He didn't, I was finding it easier and easier to draw negative conclusions. I was afraid to admit this, even to myself, so I didn't dare tell anyone in the family, especially Janice. I didn't want to be ridiculed or forced into a debate that couldn't be won for lack of concrete evidence, so I avoided all religious conversations. It didn't even seem worth bringing up, since religion and faith weren't playing a part in my day-to-day life. I was happy to be a hard-working, friendly, reasonable human being, one who didn't need religion or the bible to tell him how to act. I theorized that if someone believed in God, it was because they had faith, not proof. Unfortunately, faith is not proof.

Janice and I got married on Valentine's Day, 1998. Soon after, we built a luxurious dream home and moved in. For about two years, we happily stayed extremely busy, working on the house and yard. I was back to doing shift work, which was definitely not conducive to an abundance of "quality time" with the family, but I sure was getting a lot of fishing time in, on my weekdays off, when I wasn't working on the house or in the yard.

During this time, Aunt Dot, a mother of six, died from leukemia. She, too, was taken long before she was through enjoying her family and her family enjoying her, especially the grandchildren. She was one of those wonderful, kind and caring souls who devoted her life to her children and grandchildren, and recently she seemed to be in the best shape of her life. Between Aunt Toni and Aunt Dot, I was raised in a loving setting on the farm during a deeply traumatic time of my life. Aunt Dot lived next door, with her family, and that provided plenty of cousins to play with and explore the farm. She had lots of fun with me, too. She would catch white-faced bumble bees in her hand and hold them up to my ear, to tease me. She knew they didn't sting but I wasn't convinced of that. A bee was a bee to me. So it didn't matter, I would run off screaming like a little girl anyway. Black-faced bumble bees are the ones that sting, she told me later.

Then there was the time she claimed she saved me from accidentally hanging myself from a tree. My neck had gotten caught in a rope that was tied at each end to a large tree branch. I was trying to do a chin up on the rope, but just about the time the rope reached my chin, I lost strength, falling with my neck across the rope. I thought I had just tilted my head backwards, causing my neck to slide out of the makeshift noose, but she claimed she had to lift me out of it, thus saving my life.

I heard each of these stories over and over again at family gatherings, and every time they were still funny, but much funnier to her than to me. I was glad I was so entertaining as a child.

Once again, the priest said that her death was because "God called her home." This became the final nail, driving the coffin airtight shut concerning my belief in God. God no longer existed in my world. Game over.

When you're dead, you're dead. Ashes to ashes, dust to dust. The only good news in this revelation was that, if God and Heaven didn't exist, then there couldn't be any Hell, either. I no longer had to worry about eternal damnation, if Hell doesn't exist! "Cool, that concern is gone."

But that left me with another dilemma: what was life all about, if there was no afterlife? And maybe that was the way I had been living my life all along—as if there was no afterlife. The concept of an afterlife didn't seem to make sense or pass logical cognitive

Letting Go of God

processes, anyway. And it seemed that many other people were living their lives the same way. Everyone I knew appeared to be caught up in day-to-day life. I saw no signs of preparation for an afterlife. The primary focus seemed to be on worrying about the elements of life that consume our attention, such as finding a mate, developing a career, buying a new car or house, raising children, and saving for college and retirement.

It seemed that even religious folks had the same needs and desires as I had as an atheist. We all wanted the same things: nice homes, cars, relationships, children and a winning football team. Sure, there were men and women of the cloth, and monks in the mountains, but they were a small minority of the population. Logically, I supposed that there must be religious folks around me, but they didn't act any more righteous than anyone else I was encountering. I wasn't familiar with anyone who was adamant enough about God to try and convince me that God really existed. No one talked about God openly. It was as if people were afraid to talk about God, maybe because no one had proof or experience enough to stick their necks out in conversation. I believed that their faith was all they had, and that it had been given to them by their parents and churches. It wasn't something they had acquired on their own, derived from a personal search.

Consequently, I adopted a philosophy to live by the "Golden Rule." At least, that way, I would be remembered as a good person. I certainly didn't want to be remembered as a bad person. That much was clear. I didn't want to be remembered as insensitive, uncaring, controlling, tyrannical, abusive, or any other of a list of negative attributes humans can possess.

I wasn't a bad person inside, and I knew it. I was really a caring and sensitive guy, very sensitive in fact, but that sensitivity had been covered over and suppressed by the School of Hard Knocks. And yet, even with that emotional suppression, I took my divorce very hard. I could find myself getting misty eyed during movies and even some well-done commercials, for cryin' out loud. I couldn't watch a tear-jerker movie with friends because I knew someone might see me and use it to embarrass me later. So I tried to build a harder exterior than really existed. Only I knew my emotional side, and the two sides confused me somewhat. The side I presented to the world was cold and callous. And perhaps my callous character was channeling that sensitivity through anger. Deep down, I wanted to know true love and give true love, but something kept getting in the way.

While my faith in God had dried up like a mud puddle in August, Janice's seemed to be growing. Gradually, I shared my new conviction that God didn't exist. Meanwhile she found a church nearby that was "right" for her and Alex. Before long, she told me that she and Alex were going to be baptized at the church. *Oh, that's just great!* I thought privately, *We're really going in different directions, now*. But I attended, to show my support.

On occasion, Janice mentioned that she was praying for something, sparking discussions about her religious beliefs and my lack thereof. I was adamant that God didn't exist, because I couldn't come up with one good reason why He would take such good people from us when it seemed so vitally important to have them around, if nothing more than for the proper upbringing of the grandchildren.

Furthermore, if God existed, how come I couldn't see Him at work? Couldn't He do something, even something small, every now and then to show me that He existed? It wouldn't take much. Why was this so difficult? And how come I couldn't feel His omnipresence? If God existed, and He wanted me to know Him and love Him, why did He make it so damn difficult to get an appointment with Him to reach this end?

Letting Go of God

I asked Janice if she had seen God at work. Of course, she said she had, but she couldn't substantiate it.

"Exactly!" I exclaimed, feeling both triumphant and oddly disappointed.

Janice kept telling me that things happen for a reason. Since she didn't get any of the recent jobs she had applied for, and she really wanted and prayed for them, I told her it was because God wanted her to be miserable. That way, Heaven would seem like a really great place, no matter what, because it sure was like Hell here. Needless to say, my skepticism had soured a step farther, turning to cynicism.

In addition, I told her that the concept of God couldn't be explained scientifically. As a worker in the electrical utility industry, I knew that there were calculations, engineering, physics, theories, laws, thermodynamics, fluid flow, blah, blah, blah. But it was all explainable! I couldn't explain God, and neither could she. She had faith, and faith is not proof. I couldn't explain life after death, because it didn't make sense. The only way I might understand and embrace the concept of life after death would be if somehow the small electrical energy of our bodies lived on, after physical death. That seemed really far-fetched, but if there was an explanation that I *might* be able to understand, that was it.

People were entitled to their own opinions, so I kept mine to myself, for the most part. If people wanted to believe in God, and it gave them the motivation to be better people, that was wonderful. Perhaps that would create more people who were honest, leaving fewer to rip me off. Our money was for us and no one else. Janice gave to charity occasionally, but I was looking for reasons not to give to charity, such as the United Way scandal of several years before. Every time I could find a reason not to contribute, it quickly became one of my excuses to support my stinginess.

Although she didn't show it, Janice was concerned that religiously we were growing apart. She always wanted to grow together spiritually because that assured her that I would be with her after death. With my recent conviction, I admitted to her that I didn't think it was possible.

What Janice didn't know was that I had one last question for the universe, one last-ditch effort at understanding this "life after death" false hope, if it existed! One day, while contemplating my atheism, I squinted up at the bright, beautiful, blue sky from the bow of my bass boat, shook my pointed finger towards the Heavens, and said, "I'm pretty convinced that You and Heaven, Satan and Hell don't exist, but if You do, You had better show me a sign, because, at this point, You've lost me." I was bold and brazen because, as an atheist, there was no God to fear. If there was a God, then I was sincere in wanting an answer. But I honestly didn't expect one. I challenged God secretly and didn't tell anyone, not even Janice. Still, something made me ask that question. Was it my subconscious, bubbling up to say, "You had better ask this question, and you had better mean it from the bottom of your heart," or was it my intuition, directing this one final effort at the truth?

> I didn't know for sure, but this was the most important question I have ever asked.

Chapter 4

Time in the Big House

Several months passed and, from an outsider's viewpoint, it would have appeared as if life was just perfect. We had a beautiful, big house and yard in an upscale community, the American dream…but we were beginning to question our decisions to take on such a big responsibility. The big house and yard was costing us an arm and a leg to furnish and complete. Add managing two careers, compounded daily by an extremely time-consuming hobby, and we ended up with very little time to realize any "return on investment." We hadn't taken time to enjoy the fruits of our labor, because all we did was labor!

Finally, in the winter, when the fishing season slowed and yard work wasn't required, we hosted a small party and really rolled out the red carpet for our guests. Here was an opportunity to take a break and celebrate the near completion of the interior of our house. Building a luxurious house takes a lot of money to furnish and decorate. I have a saying, "You don't hang fuzzy dice in your Rolls Royce!" We weren't about to put cheap furniture or décor in our home. This required us to pace our efforts to coincide with available funds. We were ready to celebrate, but there was one catch: the guests were required to dress up. The theme was the "Rich and Famous" party; for one night, even though we weren't rich or famous, we were going to pretend that we were. Suits, tuxedos and evening gowns were the rule, so naturally we took pictures. It was truly a wonderful time, sharing our good fortune and accomplishment with members of the family. The event cost us a small fortune, so it didn't take long to realize that, even though we enjoyed doing it, we couldn't do it often.

Then I managed to complicate things further by taking a promotion to a day-shift job that cost me thousands of dollars in salary. Some promotion! Rotating shift workers usually make more money than their equivalent day-shift counterparts, because of shift worker perks and premiums.

On the plus side, this was a good move for an improved family life, which I was slowly getting into. In addition, it got me off shift work, which was taking its toll on me. I now had an office of my own, so I placed an enlarged photo of Janice and me on the desk, from our big party. It was somewhat funny how Janice had just recently asked if I would put a picture of us on a desk, if I had one. It wasn't my nature to display my personal life, but I'd told Janice that I would, if I ever got a desk job. The picture selected was the best picture from those taken. The only problem was that it had a slight golden glowing spot just in front of me. The golden glow was big enough to see but not big enough to ruin the picture.

Fortunately, Janice and I were getting along just fine, but life in general had gotten a little tougher. Being on day-shift was good, but money, time and energy were in less abundance.

I had thought that day-shift would be good for a more "normal" or traditional family life. It *was* good for the family as far as evenings, weekends at home, and holidays off were concerned, but my competitive fishing suffered, and my personality suffered with it. In my mind, if I didn't have enough time to fish, then what was life good for? I worked to live, not lived to work. I was consumed with competitive fishing. I was still trying to make my mark on the local fishing scene. My definition of "quality of life" was being able to fish (a lot) and keep up with responsibilities at work *and* at home. The new job left me too exhausted by the weekend to commit Saturday and Sunday to fishing tournaments.

It required too much time, preparation, focus and intensity to win or even place. My goal was always to place in the top 10 percent, in order to prove consistency, which in turn would promote my marketability with sponsors. The fishing day usually starts at 4 a.m. and doesn't end until everything that was broken during the day has been fixed, the boat and truck are gassed up, the fishing gear is rigged up, and anything else is prepared for Day Two, which again starts at 4 a.m. Then there's the three-hour drive home. I believed that work should not get in the way of recreational activities unless you were a top company executive making mega-dollars for a few years, subsequently retiring to enjoy life. I wanted to sell the house, by a smaller one, save some money, and run off to the professional fishing circuit and give it a try. But even that idea was going to take time to orchestrate, in order to take the leap, had I decided to jump.

In the meantime, I had to settle for a much less active fishing season and consider other, less demanding forms of recreation.

A Summer To Remember

Since I was working "regular" hours and pressed to reduce my fishing involvement, we decided to accept an invitation to go to an outdoor concert. I hadn't been to a concert since the '70s because I didn't like crowds and dealing with large, unfamiliar places, unless I had to. But this particular offer included driving us while we lounged

"Imagine That" A Spiritual Awakening

in the back seat. I had recently told Janice that I would consider going to events and places like concerts, football games, museums or plays if someone else did the driving, and here was my chance. I found it odd that we had just discussed this, and then it happened.

We liked the headlining group's music from the '70s, but they were promoting a new CD with their new lead singer. As usual at concerts, the music was so loud that we couldn't understand the words to the songs. The next time we were in a store, we decided to buy their new CD to offer our support. We listened to the CD at home and liked some of their new songs, too. At least now we could hear the lyrics more clearly than at the concert.

Janice listened to the songs, read the words from the CD cover, and mentioned that some of the songs seemed to have a spiritual overtone to them. She said the songs had words like "faith," "blind faith," and "signs," with lyrics about messages from above. I said, "Uh-huh," while quietly thinking that the rock group had obviously gone south on me. *Well, at least I can still listen to their '70s stuff along with a couple of the good songs on the new CD.*

The summer continued to race by. I'm usually so busy that I don't take time to watch television, especially in the summer. In the winter, or the fishing off-season for our region, I usually catch a movie here or there because it's too cold to fish. This summer was presenting a similar situation in that I was getting home late and tired on many evenings, which provided an opportunity to watch TV. So I decided to sit in front of the tube, vegetate, and do some channel surfing.

While clicking away on the remote, I came across a show where the show's host stood in front of an audience, telling them things about their lives and their departed relatives and friends. He was acting as if these departed folks were communicating with him and he was passing the messages on to the living friends and family.

Time in the Big House

It didn't take me long to realize that this guy was claiming to be psychic. He called himself a "medium." I later learned that a medium is a psychic who acts as the middle man or moderator between the "other side" and those of us here in the physical world. They receive messages and then pass them along to us.

I didn't believe in psychic stuff, much less the concept of being a medium, but he sure was getting my attention. The title of the program was *Crossing Over with John Edward*.

I was mesmerized by what he was doing. Some of the things Edward reported to the audience, or "gallery," as it was called, were vague connections, such as initials and symbols, that the members didn't always understand. Yet some of the information was very precise and specific—indeed, so specific that it didn't seem possible that they were only lucky guesses.

The members of the gallery being "read" seemed equally amazed. Their reactions seemed incredibly real, which compelled me to believe that Edward was really talking with the dead or, more accurately, they were talking to him. I was looking for the smoke, mirrors and sleight of hand, but I couldn't find any. If these were actors planted in the audience, they were more convincing than Tom Hanks. The raw emotion was too powerful and real. They wouldn't be no-names on some fortune-telling Miss Cleo infomercial if their acting ability was this good. And the show was being broadcast back-to-back in prime time.

Wow! I thought in awe, *This is some powerful stuff.* I wanted to know more, and I needed proof. During a break, there was a commercial for one of Edward's books. In an "oh, by the way," fashion, I mentioned to Janice that the book would probably be interesting to read.

The next night, I watched the back-to-back program again. Now, I was even more intrigued by what Edward was doing. Even when he wasn't doing readings and was simply sharing his philosophies, his messages were wholesome, such as his advice to communicate with, and appreciate, our loved ones so that a medium wouldn't be required when they were gone. If folks actually did as Edward suggested, then he would put himself out of business, but his message didn't seem to be driven by financial gain. He appeared genuinely concerned about helping people understand life after death.

Still, I didn't see life after death as possible. Why weren't these spirits in Heaven or Hell? How could they be in the room with Edward? I needed more explanations, evidence or proof.

My Lucky Day

The next day was Friday the 13th of July. My lucky number is 13 and my luckiest day is usually Friday the 13th. Some very good things have happened to me on Friday the 13th over the years. I had always theorized that my luck was so bad that I used this historically symbolic day of bad-luck as a day when good luck would happen to me. Even though I tried to maintain a positive attitude about most things, I considered my luck the opposite of most folks. Any successes I had achieved was due to my determination and perseverance to attain my goals. When I woke up on this particular Friday the 13th, I had a feeling it was going to be another lucky day. I just knew it.

Unbeknownst to me, Janice called around and found a copy of Edward's book, *One Last Time,* at a local bookstore. On her way home, she picked it up. For her to purchase the book for me *wasn't* a surprise, but because she bought it on Friday the 13th *was* a surprise. She could have, just as easily, purchased it yesterday, next week, or next Friday, but instead, it was delivered on my lucky day. I scanned the contents section of the book, with my focus on quickly finding an explanation of how Edward did what he did, and how it was possible for us to live on as spirits. Chapter 6, entitled *The Language*, quickly and clearly explained the answers to both questions, with enough technical detail that I could understand how life after death was possible.

Edward confirmed my half-hearted speculation that our bodies have a tiny electrical field surrounding them, and use electrical impulses to move muscles and make our hearts beat. Our body's electrical field, somehow lives on, even after our physical body dies. Einstein's law, that energy can neither be created nor destroyed, but only transformed, is applicable here. Since our electrical field cannot be destroyed, it must live on. This was a very simplistic explanation but, as a foundation, it held water really well because I understood Einstein's law called, "The Conservation of Energy."

I had only been reading the book for about twenty minutes and was already starting to see the light. I hadn't even gotten out of my work clothes but couldn't seem to put the book down. By the end of that day, I was convinced it had been a truly great day. My faith in the existence of an afterlife had rapidly recovered, because I could now understand life after death and witness evidence to support it through Edward's readings.

Edward's book offered many heartwarming instances of spirits communicating in various ways and doing good things for others. The information Edward brought forth in his readings about these folks was too detailed to be something his staff researched and somehow fed to Edward. It was easy to see that his intentions were pure. When selecting a money-making profession, why would anyone choose to be a medium? It's too controversial, and one would be constantly under fire from critics, non-believers of all kinds, skeptics and cynics. The mental anguish would be enough to scare most people away.

Edward explained that he had a good job and made a comfortable living before he was pushed toward his work as a medium. This fact also led me to believe he was really doing something out of a genuine interest in helping others connect with their lost loved ones, with the byproduct that these folks would begin to understand that life after death does exist. The result might be that people would live better lives and be more prepared for the afterlife.

Edward also explained how spirits communicate, and why their messages vary from fragments of sound to vivid visuals. There is a large gap between our dimension and theirs, and this gap creates problems. Folks on both sides of this divide must train themselves to meet in the middle and find a way to quickly transmit the information in whatever way they have learned, before their energy depletes. Since a picture is worth a thousand words, they may send an image that should mean something to the person receiving the reading, called the "sitter."

I continued to read Edward's book at every chance I got, until it was finished. Edward spoke of spirit guides (or Guardian Angels, as some refer to them) and explained that we all have several or more guides around us who help us live our lives. They very gently nudge us in certain directions and try to warn us of obstacles and problems that they foresee. Out of love, they are there to guide and protect us. They communicate with us by influencing our thoughts, when they can cut through our mind's busy chatter, but we retain complete free will to choose our actions.

All of this was new to me, but it certainly seemed like someone arranged for me to see that television show, followed by the commercial for the book, and then had it delivered on my lucky day. I sensed that something was going on around me, but who was responsible? It definitely was "spooky" to think that someone unseen (a spirit) was

Time in the Big House

watching over us and intervening. Edward stated that our loved ones who have died and "crossed over to the other side" may come back to assist us. In some rare cases, they may even become our spirit guide.

That sparked my curiosity as to who was around me. Could it be Uncle Dutch?

After finishing the book on Sunday morning, I shared my thoughts with Janice. I was almost euphoric because God had not given up on me, and someone was going to a lot of trouble to get this message through to me. I told Janice that I wondered if it was Uncle Dutch. That's when she told me that, the week prior, she visited her mother's grave, which is in the same cemetery where Uncle Dutch is buried. While she was there, she visited his grave, as well. She had difficulty finding it, and persevered for forty-five minutes until she did. Something made this endeavor very important and compelled her to find it. While at his grave, she openly asked that he help get me back on track with God.

I was floored! It seemed as though he (or someone) had truly come through.

That evening, we again sat down to watch *Crossing Over*. About fifteen minutes into the show, the phone rang. When I got up to check the caller ID, it showed that the call was from a travel agency with the same name as my mother's maiden name. I don't answer calls that I believe are from solicitors, so I didn't answer it. It was odd, though, that the name contained my mother's maiden name. However, since it was a common last name, I didn't think any more about it and continued to watch the show.

The next night, the phone rang again, and the caller ID showed the same travel agency, so I figured they were simply trying the usual "calling blitz" routine until someone answered.

The third night, while we were watching the program, the phone rang again, but this time it was from a house line displaying my mother's maiden name. I thought these people were really determined to drum up business because now they were trying to get through on their own personal phone line, so I didn't answer then, either. But this time they were willing to leave a message, and this is what I heard: "Hello. My name is Trish, and I'm trying to reach a Joe Gioffre. I think this is the correct telephone number. I didn't want to leave a message but, since I have not been able to reach you, I will. I am a descendent of your mother's family and, if I have the right phone number, you are the son of Mildred. We know we haven't seen you in many years, but our family is having a family reunion and we would really like to see you there… if I have the right Joe Gioffre."

I was dumbfounded and nearly dropped to the floor because of a rapid onset of weakness in my knees. I quickly sat down next to Janice as we just stared at one other, with our jaws dropped, astonished over what we were hearing. Neither of us had enough composure to answer the phone.

For thirty-six years I had not heard from my mother's side of the family. Up until just a few days prior to this, I would have angrily rejected their sudden interest in me. But now I knew something else was going on, and it seemed clear that someone, not on this physical plane, wanted me to go to this family reunion to learn something.

Being cautious, I called some relatives to see if the two families parted company on friendly terms. I didn't want to walk into a cauldron of bad feelings. But when my questions didn't uncover any reason not to go, I called Trish and chatted with her for awhile. I found out that she was my cousin, and that the family reunion was planned for the coming Saturday. She said that all of my mother's siblings would be there, and Aunt Sissy was bringing two milk crates full of family photo albums, clippings and memorabilia. It was then that I began sensing that someone, somehow, wanted me to get to know my mother.

Could it be that my mother herself wanted me to get to know her? Now I was really getting spooked.

The Reunion

Saturday was a beautiful day for a reunion. Janice and I received a hearty welcome from relatives I vaguely remembered. With the introductions complete, we took some photos and began to talk about the past. It turned out that these siblings had also grown apart by moving to different areas of the country, and the distance separating them had caused them to focus their attention on their immediate family. And due to the turmoil of their childhood, the siblings admitted that they weren't that close to begin with. This hadn't bothered them until the last couple of years, when they began to realize that spending time together was becoming more and more important, before it was too late. They decided to hold family reunions as a way to bring them together.

I probed for clues as to why my mother would commit suicide. I had never been able to ask them before, so here was my chance. Uncle Kenny spoke of their difficult childhood with an abusive, alcoholic father. At first, their father was a decent man, but he became abusive as the years passed. The abuse worsened with time and alcohol. After kicking his pregnant wife (my grandmother Nanna) in the stomach, causing a miscarriage, he abandoned the family and was never seen again.

My mother (Mildred or Millie) was seven at that time. Even though he was often a hostile man, she probably became attached to her father, as most daughters do. More than likely, his loss took its toll on my mother's mental well-being, but no one noticed anything at the time. Her older brother Sonny had to quit high school several years before graduation in order to support and care for the family. He quickly became a father figure for his younger sibling, Millie.

As the years continued, life was probably almost normal…until the day she was beaten and raped while walking home from school. Her teenage years also found her in and out of hospitals to treat plantar warts, heel bone spurs and hemorrhoids. She endured a great deal of trauma.

When she was about fourteen years old, Sonny got married and moved out of the house. Millie was grief-stricken at the loss of another father figure. She poured rat poison onto her sandwich, in an attempt to end her pain. When she got sick, the family rushed her to the hospital, where they pumped her stomach, and she recovered, at least physically. At the family reunion, Uncle Sonny admitted he was not even aware of this attempted suicide until that day.

Interestingly enough, Uncle Sonny was the only sibling still living in the local area. Even if I had located him and asked him for answers, he probably would have drawn a blank. The other siblings had the answers, photos, and clippings that I needed to piece this all together. The only way to get all of the information at the same time was for a family reunion to occur, and for me to attend it. *Hmmm. Imagine that!* I daydreamt. Somehow, they (spirits) had accomplished it.

I also learned that, a few years later, my mother started dating my father and began spending time with his family. Farm life was probably inviting and peaceful to her after what she had been through. The family was friendly and kind to her, including Pop Pop, my grandfather, with whom she became close, apparently establishing him as her new father figure. Soon after, Dad married her and they stayed on the farm, where she was able to establish an

Time in the Big House

even greater bond with a man who truly had a love for, and a way with, children.

Shortly before Pop Pop's death, my mother was in the hospital again for hemorrhoids. A letter she wrote to her sister from the hospital indicated that she was in good spirits at the time, and it said that she wanted to get home to enjoy the spring season and plant some flowers.

Since her suicide occurred the day after my grandfather died, the family had loosely speculated that his death had upset her. Now, I had learned additional information, indicating that this wasn't the first time that grief at the loss of a father figure had prompted her to attempt suicide. After seeing Pop Pop laying in his casket at the funeral home, her grief became overwhelming. She bought a handgun on the way home, with me waiting in the car. She then sent me to the sitter's house and took her life, at home, alone, finally putting an end to her grief and constant struggle. No need for a note; the family would know why, she probably thought. They knew she had attempted suicide before, so they would piece it together, wouldn't they? But it now appeared that they hadn't really talked about it much, perhaps too ashamed about what had happened. Having someone commit suicide meant there were family problems. Denial. Silence.

There were a few other things I wanted to know about my mother. For instance, I was very interested in learning her birth date. For some reason, the need to know it kept gnawing at me, like a puppy with a new shoe, until I finally asked. Her siblings informed me that her birthday was February 1st, 1941 (or 2-1-41). At the time, I wasn't sure why I was so compelled to know her birthday but I really did feel that I needed to know it.

I would soon find out why.

The next day, I sat down at my desk to record some fishing data in my logbook. While doing so, I noticed that the date of the reunion was July 21st or 2-1 just like my mother's birthday. Then the thought occurred to me that I was 41 years old. I was amazed and curiously excited at the seeming coincidence of the number sequence 2-1-41. Did my mother arrange this also, so that I would regain my faith in God with a side dish of learning about her? Did Uncle Dutch help? If the connection I was making was accurate, how did they arrange these events with such precise timing? Did they possess that much control?

I had done a lot of thinking and realized that my mother made a mistake, and that I could even empathize with her. After going through hell during my divorce, and remembering feeling so depressed that I would have considered pulling the trigger myself if life had continued in that awful frame of mind for too long, I could understand her mental state and flawed decision. I was now at the point where forgiving her was possible and appropriate.

It was a welcome emotional release. I felt invigorated to realize that I now had re-established a relationship with my mother across space and time, into eternity, after thirty-six long years. This was gratifying and yet weird. I could hardly contain my excitement. I wanted to tell the world that our loved ones are right here with us, just as Edward says in his book. They want us to know they are here for us and are always trying to help us do the right thing and make the right decisions.

The recent events were happening at a very fast pace. I felt like Ebenezer Scrooge with the ghosts trying to convince me, in a very kind and gentle manner, that I'd been wrong. I was in a whirlwind of emotions, and my mind was now fixated on understanding what that "other world" was all about. And what about this world, what the heck is *it* all about?

Just ten days earlier I had been denying the existence of God, and now I had turned 180 degrees. I embraced the existence of life after death, which also pointed to the existence of God. But my knowledge (and experience) was in its infancy. Even though it was very difficult to undo the layers of my personal experience, that misunderstood God and spirit, it wasn't so painful that I refused to change. Instead, I refused to be hardheaded.

It's not easy correcting, forty-one years of misinformation, misinterpretation, misunderstanding, misuse and mistakes. I was a victim of these "misses." Most of life, as I experienced it, was deeply rooted in the explainable physical world and its experiences. In other words, I primarily experienced or witnessed the pain, the sickness, the suffering, the struggle, the anger, the hatred, the bad relationships and the car that wouldn't start, along with a few good memories. Consequently, my spiritual side became buried, hidden under layers of physical experiences that provided tremendous evidence to support the conclusion that, even if there was a God, He certainly wasn't active in my world. I concluded that the physical world had physical laws that governed its operation, such as "no pain, no gain." My experiences had seemed rationally and logically explainable without the slightest hint of God's intervention…until now.

I was awakening and could see God active in my world. He wanted to wake me up, and so sent His angels to set off the alarm clock in the buzzer mode, with the volume turned up. "It's time for school, Joe!" And I wasn't about to hit the "snooze" button.

I now not only believed in God, I knew He existed because He had answered my plea for proof by sending spirits to break through the barrier to deliver messages and arrange encounters and events that required exact timing. It's as if my plea prompted God to grant permission to the spirit world to help me out. I never thought I would believe that spirits spent time around us, but now the evidence was building.

The Song

On the way to work the next day, I was still in total bliss and amazement at my new discovery about my mother, trying to figure out what it meant on a long-term basis. I was in a state of euphoria and yet somewhat spooked. Edward tells us that spirits can hear us, even though we can't hear them, so all we have to do is talk to them and they will listen. Edward also described the many ways spirits can communicate with us through electronic devices such as flashing lights or songs on the radio, to name only a few. If our guides can influence our behavior, just like the stage image of a little angel speaking into the right ear, while a little devil speaks into the left ear, can they give us a thought in much the same way they communicate with Edward?

I began to speak to my mother aloud, and told her how happy I was that all of this had happened, and that I was happy that we had reestablished a good relationship between us. Then I asked her, "Where do we go from here? What do we do with our newfound relationship and my experience with the spirit world?" I sat quietly and continued driving to work while pondering these questions.

Within a few moments I was humming a tune from the CD we had purchased after the concert in June. Internally, I questioned, *Where did that come from?* The name of the song was *All the Way*. I didn't know the words because I wasn't fond of the song; it was too mellow. But I found it odd that this song came to mind, so I decided to check out the words as soon as I got home, that evening.

Time in the Big House

When I got to work and started my computer, the message on the screen said it was time to change my password. Having used so many other passwords, I decided to use Mom's birthday, along with some other characters, to develop a new password. I entered the number 2141 and whispered that it had a nice "ring" to it.

Within an hour, the phone didn't ring but my pager did go off. I received a message to call extension 2141. The beep was from a guy I had never spoken with. As it turned out, he really didn't need to speak with me, after all, and wasn't quite sure why he had paged me. By now I was thinking, *Okay Mom, I know you're there.* But she wasn't through yet. She didn't want to leave the possible theory of chance coincidence in my logical "doubting Thomas" mind. She was determined to unequivocally rule out the statistical probability of that number in my life.

When I'd received my promotion earlier in the year, I had placed the picture of Janice and me from our "Rich and Famous" party on my desk. I looked at that photo, with its unusual golden glowing spot in front of me, and finally understood where the spot came from. I called my stepmother to see if her camera had been malfunctioning, since this picture was produced from her camera. She said her camera was working fine and had never done this sort of thing before. Edward had mentioned in his book that spirits could affect electronic equipment such as cameras, causing distortion and spots like the one in our photo. I could only conclude that Mom had attended the party and couldn't resist the photo opportunity. She knew I would have the picture enlarged and placed on my desk, to ultimately "see her" later. She also calculated that if the spot was too bright, or if it distorted the picture excessively, I wouldn't have selected it, leaving it to be forgotten.

That night, I forgot to look up the words to the song, and so I found myself humming the tune again, the next day, on the drive to work. This time, I vowed not to forget to read the words when I arrived home. After arriving at work, I received an e-mail from a worker who needed my department number to complete an order. As I typed the response to him, it hit me like a freight train: the number of my new department was 41-41 and I had just been promoted to this department on February 1st (2-1) of my 21st year with the company. Before this I was in department 41-21 for 21 years. As if pre-planned, I muttered quietly in amazement, *Imagine that!* What was Mom trying to tell me?

The first thing I did that evening, when I got home, was to put the CD in the player. I sat on the sofa and began reading the words to the song, *All The Way*, while the song was playing. But the words became blurred as tears welled up in my eyes. It was as if Mom was singing the song to me. The words communicated everything she wanted to tell me. The lyrics resonated sentiments of a love that had become one-sided, caused by mistakes that she had made. It was clear that my mother was telling me that she was sorry for what she had done, and that there was still hope for us if I wanted to continue our new relationship. It also seemed as if she was telling me that she had been watching over me all of this time and would take me "all the way" to my departure from the physical world. To solidify the concept that the message was from the other side, I focused on the lines *Let's not leave behind what so few have found*, regarding this new and unusual type of relationship, and *From the miles that come between us*, symbolizing the apparent great divide between the physical plane and the spirit world.

The part I haven't mentioned is the name of the group and the CD title. Being a little slow at figuring out some of the communications, it took me a while to focus on this aspect. The group is Journey and the CD title is *Arrival*. Mom was saying, "It has been a long journey but I have arrived." She'd been there all along; I just wasn't aware.

Hmmm...so she seems to be telling me that she had been watching over me the entire time.

The department number connections seemed to indicate that she was in my life, assisting my career. Edward says, "There are no coincidences," and Dr. Deepak Chopra claims that "meaningful coincidences" are important to look for. I regarded these as more than mere or chance coincidences; it's as if my mother was making things happen. I did my part and she did hers. I did feel that, through hard work and dedication, I had earned what I had accomplished, but I also recognized that some doors had been opened that otherwise might have remained shut. What a team!

Curious, I started looking for other influences that she might have had a hand in. I began to find too many unusual connections to be mere coincidence. All of these connections were for a reason, to communicate her past presence in my life, to show me that she had been there all along. Some of these connections have been discussed in previous chapters, which was why I chose to highlight those portions of my life:

- When we moved to the waterfront, the name of the creek was Mill Creek. My mother's name was Mildred and she was called "Little Mill" by many family members. She somehow arranged this area so that I could be on the water. She knew it was my dream. I love the water and look upon those years as the best of my childhood.
- When my first wife kidnapped my beloved cat, my mother sent that scrawny stray kitten to give me a companion. I knew

- it seemed odd for a kitten to just wander up at that particular time. Now I understood how and why.
- I met Janice on May 24th, which is the anniversary of my mother's burial. Did she send Janice because she knew I needed someone like Janice to teach me about love and help me develop spiritual growth, to continue where she left off? Janice was a necessity in my development.
- Janice never gave up on me and didn't find anyone else who might take her from me. So was that orchestrated, too? Probably. Most women would not have hung around that long. Someone must have been whispering in her ear not to give up. Thanks again, Mom.
- We signed the contract for our dream home on the 21st of January. Did she help us here, too? I think so, because too many things had to come together to make it happen the way it did. We were given a lot of flexibility while building our house, and dealt directly with the builder himself. Most customers are forced to deal with the real estate company representing the builder, but our builder was in between real estate companies and, due to the complexity of our home, he decided to work with us directly. We were allowed to research subcontractors and select the best, rather than be limited to a pre-selected list.
- Our alarm system bill was $21 a month. Our garbage bill was $21 a month. Our "even monthly" electric bill decreased to $121 a month, shortly after I recognized the number connections. Later it went to $113, which is another fond number of mine.
- The boat I selected to buy in 1998 was a Tr-21.

So she had been there all along, helping in any way she could. She probably helped in ways that I still don't recognize or remember. At this point in my spiritual awakening, I simply concluded that Mom, my spirit guides, and perhaps some other spirit friends and relatives had been taking care of me because of what had happened.

Most religions believe that suicide is not an option, and that the penalty is severe for such conduct. Naturally I wondered how Mom could be doing all of these things if she had been punished or, worse yet, was in Hell. I never expected to receive communications from a spirit, much less my mother. I went back to Edward's book and reread his description of encounters with suicide victims. He stated that most give him the impression that things are okay where they are, but that they are working on their spiritual lessons. Usually they feel great regret for what they did. At this time, I did not consider my mother's involvement in my life as a type of penance. I thought of it as a mother's love for her child, perhaps coupled with a guilty conscience. Having the answer to this question didn't seem that important, because I was too excited and happy to have the relationship we now had. It didn't matter how or why we got there; it just mattered that we got there.

I was so elated about my experiences with Mom and the connection to the 21s that I decided, in her honor, that I would have a birthday party for her on February 1st of the next year.

I still had some doubts as to the "mere coincidence" concept. But every time I began to doubt, I would get another sign or discover another connection. Mom wanted me to get this message, loud and clear. She wasn't about to let the subject drop. I could sense her saying, "It's taken me too long to get through to you. I'm not about to give up now. I'll get help, if I need to, because you ain't seen nothin' yet!"

Thank God for Moms!

Chapter 5

Hello From Heaven

Sparked by the spirits and fueled by my own burning curiosity to understand, I began to research. Like a runaway train, I ran without brakes, not knowing what lay ahead. Would I run out of fuel before too long and end up stranded and lost? Might I derail and end up as nothing more than a smoldering pile of wreckage? Or perhaps I could gain control of this runaway train and coast into my destination, safe and sound. All I knew was, "All aboard! It's time to research metaphysics!"

I started with "After Death Communications" or ADCs. I wanted some corroborating evidence, to show that what I was experiencing had happened to others. I needed to know, to ensure and confirm my own sanity.

Bill and Judy Guggenheim wrote a phenomenal book, called *Hello From Heaven,* which is about ADCs. The research took them seven years to complete, so in my opinion it is an exhaustive and accurate product. Bill Guggenheim had been a stockbroker and securities analyst on Wall Street. Like me, he had been an "avowed materialist," believing the same thing I had come to believe: "When you're dead, you're dead!"

When he sensed a calling to research ADCs, it wasn't without much apprehension, just as accepting God took me forty-one years because of *my* apprehension. I find it interesting and amusing that, once asked by the skeptic, God seems to go after the non-believers with such determination! The book lists the many ways in which our dearly departed will try to make themselves known to us. I have already mentioned a few from Edward's book, some of which had already happened to me. Here are a few others that the Guggenheims list, which are chapters in their book:

Sensing a Presence

Hearing a Voice

Feeling a Touch

Smelling a Fragrance

Partial and Full Appearances

Person to Person: Telephone ADCs

Butterflies and Rainbows: Symbolic ADCs

Our dearly departed want us to stop grieving and get on with life, and they want to let us know that they are doing fine on the other side. The above list illustrates the great effort they will go through in order to get a message to us.

When the Guggenheims began their research, they weren't sure how many people had actually encountered ADCs, but "assumed they were quite rare." But this is what the Guggenheims found:

American Health published the results of a poll conducted by the *National Opinion Research Center* in its January-February 1987 issue. The poll was directed by Andrew Greeley, the well-known Catholic priest and author. The findings stated that 42 percent of American adults believe they have been in contact with someone who has died. Moreover, 67 percent of all widows believe they have had a similar experience.

Most of the ADCs reported to the Guggenheims were quick glimpses or fleeting messages, followed by silence from the loved one. But in my case, the communications wouldn't quit. So why all the attention?

Just Ask

To have all of this attention and energy focused on me really made me feel special and lucky. God, Mom, and my guides hadn't given up on me, even though I had been growing apart from God and had no belief in the spirit world. The divide between us had been like the Grand Canyon. *Ashes to ashes, dust to dust* had been my motto. But I had now come a long way in a very short time.

The notion that spirits were around, doing great things, was exciting but it was quite unnerving, as well. Not knowing whether I was being watched or not was an unusual feeling. It was apparent that "privacy" only applied to privacy from other humans. I had to begin working my way through these concepts and deal with them.

I sensed that the initial flurry of signs and connections should be diminishing, because the "wake-up call" was complete. Now, I wanted to know more about the other side, along with the usual questions, like "What is the purpose of life if there is another dimension? Why are we here?" I wondered how to get information about such a controversial subject like this. One thing I did know was that these spirits were pretty powerful, because they had already arranged quite a few things. So could I just ask them?

Realizing that spirits can manipulate electronic devices, I wondered if they could work with me, using an electronic device I use on a daily basis. The device was a hand geometry reader. I used it to gain access to my workplace. It scans hand dimensions and then generates a number, which represents the closeness of the match to the computer's recorded hand information. Before I used the device, I would ask a question and suggest a number that would mean something as a response. For example, if I got a 13, I knew it was going to be a good day and that something really good might happen.

I was curious about the identity of the spirits around me, so I started to ask these questions. My mother had come through, so I wondered whether Janice's mother would come through for her. Our lost loved ones and friends are dying, pardon the pun, to get through to us. They want us to know they are okay and that there is a Heaven to look forward to. And they don't want us to be saddened over their loss, because they are in such a beautiful place. One reason they are desperately trying to get through to us is because we grieve so long and hard over their loss. We dwell on the pain for far too long, while they are probably on the other side, having a party or at least having a good time, away from earthly problems. They jump at any opportunity to get through to us.

Janice never had a chance to say goodbye to her mother before she passed away, which caused a great deal of anguish for her. Even after many years, she was still upset. I thought that her mother would probably like to get a message through to her, if only to tell her that everything was just fine. I realized that spirit communication did not take the place of a physical relationship, but receiving a happy hello could provide peace of mind and perhaps inspiration. It is not like we can sit down and have a one-on-one conversation, get a hug, and then go out to lunch with them.

Getting a message, however, can require a bit of work and analysis. Most of us have been taught that our dearly departed are in some faraway place and aren't reachable. But now I knew that our dearly departed could hear us and interact with us, to a limited extent. Perhaps this experience would lessen our grief somewhat. I found the knowledge that my mother was around to be energizing and exciting. I was willing to learn how to deal with the complexities of communication and get over the spooky sensation that it caused.

I asked Janice her mother's birth date, and discovered that it was December 21st. "Imagine that!" I said to Janice. "Another 21!"

The next day, before using the hand geometry reader, I posed the question to my mother-in-law, asking if she was hanging around as well. I suggested a response of 12 (representing her birth month of December) if she was.

I got a 12!

The hair stood up on the back of my neck, and I got a chill up my spine. I needed to tell Janice, but she probably wouldn't believe me. She had not been directly experiencing all of these things as I had, and having a direct encounter is far more convincing than hearsay. It seemed rather silly to believe an electronic device but, as I was finding out, "fact is stranger than fiction," and "the truth shall set you free." Could my mother-in-law be assisting in the events happening around me? I definitely believed it was not only possible but probable.

Janice's mother, Jeanne, was a devoted mother of seven, living her life dedicated to her family. Feeding a family of nine on a teacher's income was a remarkable achievement. She had to learn how to squeeze a nickel out of a penny. At the grocery store, dented canned goods would be discounted a few cents. On occasion, when Jeanne found herself alone in the aisle, a few cans may have fallen to their dented discount less than accidentally. Sacrificing the finer things of life became a way of life. Rarely was there an opportunity to indulge, while the children were growing up. So many hungry mouths to feed never left food on the table for seconds. Snacking wasn't an option for Janice and her siblings, because there were no snacks. Perhaps this explains why food became Jeanne's one vice, once it became affordable as her nest emptied. Her strong faith in God, combined with a pauper's life of devout service to others, equated to a very powerful spirit on the other side, as I saw it.

Even though Janice was indirectly experiencing these events through me, she wasn't as convinced by any of it as I was, and she really shied away from the thought of spirit communications. She, too, was mesmerized by Edward's show *Crossing Over* and watched it even more than I did, but she maintained her skepticism. She felt that it was better if these spirit messages were being delivered to someone else, not to her. When I told her about the number 12, she listened but was apprehensive about my conclusion. Janice agreed that something very exciting and unusual was happening, but she credited God more than deceased family spirits. I found it ironic that she had asked Uncle Dutch for help while at his grave but, now that the help had arrived, she wouldn't give them credit. When things threaten our beliefs, it is a natural response to enter a state of denial, become defensive or withdraw. We want to be right in what we believe; it's tough questioning the foundational beliefs that we've embraced for decades. Admitting we're wrong is extremely humbling. Since I had already had a big slice of Humble Pie, I kept asking questions: I simply wanted the truth. This bible verse has been very true for me: "Ask and you shall receive, seek and you shall find." I kept asking and digging…and receiving.

Janice's mother knew she needed to provide more proof of her presence in our lives, but this would take time. Spirit communications are slow, at best, when using an external "sign" system, but the one thing my spirit friends knew was that, if there was anyone who would take the time to figure out the message, it was me.

Fishing with "The Moms"

In August, on our last fishing trip of this year, we were struggling to find fish for an upcoming tournament. We stopped at one spot and had just begun to fish the area when a pretty little brown-and-white dragonfly landed on my shoulder and seemed to stare up at me, as if to watch. I've been fishing for a long time, but I have never had a dragonfly land on me and stay put. I commented to Janice that this was sent by "The Moms," as I now affectionately called the dynamic duo of her mother and mine.

I looked at the pretty dragonfly and asked if it was trying to tell us there were fish to be caught from this particular fishing hole. On the very next cast, I did catch a fish. And on Janice's next cast, she caught one, too. Through all of this commotion, the little dragonfly stayed put on my shoulder. In fact, it stayed on my shoulder for about twenty minutes. It wasn't until I gently brushed it off that it departed. It was time for us to move to another spot, so I had to say goodbye.

As I pondered more and more about this event, I recalled that Janice's family had grown fond of dragonflies since the passing of their mother. There is a story, by Doris Stickney, using the dragonfly to symbolize the transition from this world to the next. It refers to life below the surface of the water, where the dragonfly "water bugs" swim together until, one by one, the time comes for them to climb above the surface and never return. The rest of the "water bugs" don't know where their friends and loved ones have gone, and are upset by their loss. We know that the "water bugs" climb above the surface and become beautiful dragonflies. This beautiful story is simply a metaphor for life and its transformation into the afterlife, or "life after life."

After their mother's death, family members became quite interested in dragonfly decorations of all kinds. The individual siblings were not necessarily aware that the others had experienced an attraction to dragonfly décor. Every visit to their homes found dragonfly memorabilia located inside and out. Some of the daughters routinely wore dragonfly pins and earrings. Finally, I figured out that Jeanne's symbol to us was the dragonfly.

It was a Saturday when this revelation hit me, but Janice was at work. I didn't want to tell her over the phone because this epiphany was too special for that. I wanted to witness her expression and body language, to see if this news might help strengthen her belief that her mother in fact could be close from time to time. I was nervously bubbling with anticipation, waiting for the first opportunity. We were scheduled to meet at my parents' house for dinner, so I decided to tell her there. Outside their home, I pulled Janice aside and told her of my belief that her mother's symbol to us was the dragonfly. At that exact moment, a dragonfly flew up and landed at our feet. I could reason that a dragonfly might fly by at that moment, but for it to land at our feet at that exact moment simply defied statistical probability. It was now "as plain as day" to me, that not only was Jeanne's symbol a dragonfly but that someone unseen was arranging and controlling these events. In this case, it seemed apparent that it was Jeanne.

The Sting Operation

I was having some difficulty with the air conditioning system in my truck and decided to call my cousin, David, who was a heating and ventilation specialist. We discussed my options and potential solutions for the unit. Once I had a repair plan outlined our conversation changed to thoughts of the family.

David's mother, my Aunt Dot, had recently passed away so I asked him how the family was recovering. Her passing was visibly difficult for some immediate family members. When a family suffers a great loss, such as this, it can take a long time to heal. And her passing *wasn't* without impact on me, as I discussed in Chapter 3, *Letting Go of God*. Her untimely loss was the final straw that broke what little belief I still had in God.

We talked about the family and Aunt Dot for awhile, and then I mentioned that our loved ones can send us signs to let us know they are okay, if they choose to, but *we* have to recognize the signs. I shared a little information about what had been happening to me, but was cautious because I didn't know what David's beliefs in the afterlife were, and I didn't want him to think that I was a nutcase, suggesting that spirits might come back to give us a sign.

We continued to chat as I recounted one of Aunt Dot's favorite stories about the white and black-faced bumble bees. David was often around when she taunted me by catching one and tried to get me to listen to it buzzing in her hand, by putting it up to my ear. She may have teased him as well, although I don't remember those details because I was too busy running away, screaming. Like me, David couldn't forget those traumatic, and yet hilarious, episodes of our lives. David then told me that he had recently seen a white-faced bumble bee flying around him. He said that he definitely took notice because he had not seen one in about twenty years. I told him that this was probably his sign sent by Aunt Dot.

Another "Hello Form Heaven" had been delivered.

Chapter 6

Braking for God

I continued with my mission to understand more about the other side and God. Since answers from spirit were slow, I purchased books, audio tapes, and anything else I could get my hands on, in an effort to learn as much as possible. I knew that, while purchasing these things, I would be guided by my spirit friends to select the right books and tapes. My first purchases at the bookstore added up to $121. There was that 21 again. More and more frequently, I found myself murmuring, "Imagine that," in amazement.

Janice began to see the connections, also. Unusual yet beneficial things occurred, prompting intrigued speculation from both of us. Many times, we would simultaneously recognize the uncanny coincidence and how we benefited from it. Often, we found ourselves turning toward one another in awe, with a smile gently growing across our faces as we proclaimed in stereo, "Imagine that!" We were witnessing the power of God and spirit.

I literally stopped doing anything else nonessential in my life, in order to conduct research. I quit tournament fishing and confined myself to the house for studies. One evening, Alex asked us to play a card game with him. I didn't feel like playing because I had so many books to read, but I also knew that I needed to spend some time with him. While playing the game, I also played music on the CD player. Since I was preoccupied by my mission to understand the other side, I was somewhat disengaged from the game. Theories and ideas raced through my mind in an effort to piece together this puzzle of life, afterlife, and God. A few moments later, the CD player stopped for about four seconds, and then the song continued. The CD player had never acted up before and, knowing what I knew about spirit communication, I paid attention to the song that was playing. The song was titled *Livin' to Do*. The theme of this song is that you never know when your time is coming, so live your life to the fullest; you've got livin' to do! As I pondered this event, searching for its meaning, I concluded that I was being instructed to continue researching but without letting it interfere with living a normal life. In other words, I wasn't supposed to become a hermit. There were lessons to learn, things to accomplish, and a normal life to live.

Or had the CD player just been acting up?

The next morning, I woke up, got a cup of coffee, sat in my chair, and began to read more. It was turning into a beautiful day, and staying inside on another pleasant day was really starting to bug me. Being an outdoor person, I found that all of this indoor research was taking its toll. I hadn't been outdoors much or on the water in a couple months, so I was going through hook set withdrawals. On the other hand, I wanted to continue studying, because "God and Company" (as I was now referring to them) shouldn't be ignored anymore. (I define God and Company to include God, the Holy Spirit, angels, ascended masters, saints, spirit guides and departed loved ones.)

After about an hour, I couldn't take it anymore, and figured it was okay to take a little break from my quest. I asked Alex if he wanted to go fishing, and of course he said an emphatic "Yes!" As we pulled out of the garage, I turned on the cassette player, and the first words from the tape were: "These are the best times of your life." I smiled from ear to ear and fought back the happy tears, as I had just learned another valuable lesson. We are expected to live our lives and do the normal, wholesome things that bring us joy. We're not expected to bury ourselves in studying God just because we finally find Him. Our evolution takes time, and God has plenty of time and patience, especially when we are sharing good times with another person—and especially if that person is a child.

It was a beautiful day, but the fishing was slow. I told Alex I would be happy if I just caught a perch. A couple casts later, I did catch a big perch. Time was running out for this trip, and Alex was getting bored with the lack of fish-catching, so I decided to fish just a little bit longer and then call it a day. I thought, *Boy, it sure would be nice to catch just one, but make it a big one since I haven't caught a fish in so long.* A moment later, a dragonfly flew in front of me and then hovered over the water, about a cast away. It was as if the dragonfly was inviting me to cast to that spot, so I did. I caught a good one on that cast; a beautiful four-pound bass! *Awesome! If I could just get you guys to help me with tournaments!* I requested with a sly grin.

Out of Thin Air

I had a lifetime of questions, along with many new ones that comprised a serious burning platform (inferno in my case) that drove my quest for answers. At some point in each of our lives, we begin to ask these questions, and probably never get many satisfactory answers, if any at all. Here are some of the questions I came up with:

- If Heaven exists, what is it like?
- Are there levels to Heaven?
- Are we punished for bad behavior, and does Hell exist?
- Are there varying levels of Hell, or do all bad people have to live with murderers, serial killers, psychopaths, rapists and people who cut in line?
- It doesn't seem fair that I would spend eternity in Hell just because I didn't do so well during the seventy or eighty years I was here on Earth. Is this true?
- If God loves me so much, wouldn't He give me a second chance? Attending Catholic school taught me that, in order to go to Heaven, you have to go through some of the Catholic rituals, such as baptism, and love God, and accept Jesus as our Lord and Savior. The burning question came to me: What happens to a child who dies young in some foreign land and never has the chance to know God or Jesus? Do they go to Hell for eternity? I've actually had some Christians tell me that these children go straight to Hell, do not pass "Go," and do not collect their figurative $200. Not even a "Get Out Of Jail Free" card for their innocence. They claimed that even these innocent children were not worthy of God. If they hadn't gotten a chance to know and love Him, too bad; they deserved Hell for it. I could hardly believe my ears. Hearing this actually upset me for several days. I couldn't fathom how a devout Christian, who certainly knew of the importance of forgiveness to Jesus, could believe such an atrocity.
- Do spirits have a physical body, and what do they do "over there," anyway?

- What do I have to do, and how should I live, to get into Heaven? And what about the higher levels of Heaven, if they exist?
- Why is there so much evil in this world? Why does God let people like Hitler live? Couldn't God have given Hitler a heart attack to eradicate him from the face of the Earth? Who would have known? The Old Testament speaks of an angry, vengeful God that smote his enemy. If this was true then, why wasn't the God of the Twentieth Century doing the same thing? It certainly seemed like we could use some divine "smiting" in our times. It didn't make sense.
- Why is there so much suffering from hunger in poor countries? Why do so many innocent children die from hunger, war and disease?
- Why are there so many religious wars and fanatics who want to kill others just because they believe something a little different? If you really believed in God, wouldn't you embrace peace and love as your primary motivation?

Perhaps the reason we don't get many answers to our philosophical questions is a matter of whether or not we can handle what the truth really is. What if the truth is something that we, especially Americans, would never have dreamt in our wildest dreams? What if the truth goes against the basic concepts that our American society embraces as truth? Would we be willing to defy convention and be different, at the risk of ridicule? We Americans love to be different about certain things, like what we wear, the color of our hair, and what we pierce, but when it comes to our spiritual beliefs, many don't like to talk about it or display it. Even after all of the science fiction movies such as "The Sixth Sense," I don't see people wearing t-shirts that say things like "I'm with My Spirit Friends. Can You See Them?"

or "Do You Know Where Your Spirit Guides Are?" Perhaps it goes back to our five senses; most of us don't develop our spirituality, so we stay locked into the five senses and limit ourselves to physical awareness only. We become so stuck in our physical reality that any thought or belief beyond it is regarded as a waste of time because it cannot be proven. Many live in a "show me" state.

At the top of my personal list of burning questions was: What type of life do I need to live in order to get into Heaven? What behaviors and characteristics do I need to exemplify? I needed to define how I should live to meet God's expectations. I had spent forty-one years skeptical of God's very existence, and now that I knew He really existed, I needed to spend the rest of my life getting it right. If I was being watched all those years (and I now know that I was), I was very sorry for some of the stuff I'd done. Since I now knew that God and Company were watching my every move, I wanted to live the rest of my life as righteously as I could. I also wanted to know more about my new friends from the other side.

By reading Edward's book, I was introduced to many things I'd had no knowledge of. Even though I attended a Catholic school for twelve years, I don't remember being taught anything about the spirit world. It was probably taboo. I don't remember Heaven being discussed, more than in generalized terms. When I was young, I pictured Heaven as a cloud, with God seated on a throne at the center, and with me being terrified to move for fear of doing anything to upset Him. It reminded me of the way I felt as a child when I was around my stepmother. Needless to say, I didn't look forward to that concept of Heaven.

Edward spoke of his life, his introduction to spirit, and what they had taught him about the spirit world and Heaven. I was amazed at the information that these spirits made available and how so many questions could be answered. Through Edward's book, and others by authors such as Sylvia Browne and James Van Praagh, I was able to learn a great deal about the other side. Even though I know a lot more now than I did before, I do believe the spirits guard the information to some degree. We're not supposed to know everything, it would seem, because that would influence our use of "free will." Later, I also discovered these spirits don't necessarily have all the answers anyway. It depends on their spiritual development. The more advanced a spirit becomes the more knowledge is acquired.

Spirits referred to the various levels of Heaven and the absolute beauty thus answering my question. On the more pleasant middle and upper levels of Heaven there is apparently almost no suffering, pain, sorrow or sickness; primarily, there is total bliss. You don't need to eat or sleep, because you never get tired or hungry. You can rest if you like, but you don't need to. They've explained that it's a place similar to our Earth in surface features, such as mountains, valleys, plains, meadows, rolling fields, rivers, streams, lakes and oceans. There are no cars or motorized vehicles, because you don't need them; you just think of where you want to go and you're there. The colors are more brilliant and the fragrances are incredible. Folks live in any kind of house they want. But does everyone go there?

Various religions also embrace the belief that there are various levels of Heaven, and that we will ultimately go to a place equivalent to the level of consciousness we achieve while here on Earth. Hearing a favorite song can uplift one's spirit. The feeling is easily recognizable. Seeing a sunrise or sunset might do the same thing. You might have something good happen to you and have it make you feel like you're "walking on air" or "in seventh Heaven" (a cliché which also points to the levels of Heaven). You might feel "as light as a feather."

These sensations are real because they raise our vibrational level or consciousness, even if it's only for a short while.

By developing the positive characteristics of our personality, our energy field brightens, energizes and elevates. Consequently, our level of consciousness rises. It sounds like a simple recipe, but very few things are "a piece of cake." We might consider a saintly persona such as Mother Theresa's to be the epitome of a higher level of consciousness. This higher level of consciousness may also apply to your Aunt Mary or Uncle John. It's not reserved for canonized saints alone. Unrecognized, quiet saints walk among us. Fortunately, we usually know one or two.

Without getting too technical, let me state that everything is vibrating at a certain frequency. Everything is made up of atoms, which are composed of protons, neutrons, electrons and other subatomic particles. These particles are constantly in motion. The atoms can be positively or negatively charged, which can be affected by other energy forces. Since our bodies are made up of atoms, we carry an electrical field of energy around us, which is called an aura. There are many books on this subject, available for further research. Even though the aura can be seen by some with the naked eye, and photographed using special cameras (called Kirlian photography, as developed in the '30s), the scientific community at large does not recognize this energy field. Our aura, or energy field, can be influenced by positive or negative energy, just as atoms are. Many of us have had the experience of being around someone we were really drawn to and felt comfortable with. This is sometimes referred to as a "magnetic personality," thus confirming or at least comparing this invisible energy to a personal experience with which we are familiar. By the same token, we have been around people with whom we just didn't feel comfortable, and may even have felt a dislike towards, even though we couldn't figure out why.

As stated earlier, Albert Einstein determined that energy could neither be created nor destroyed, but only transformed. The energy field that resides around us and through us cannot be destroyed, but can only be transformed. The human body is electrically and chemically driven. (For example, a pacemaker is used to generate small pulses of electricity to cause the heart muscles to contract and pump blood to keep some folks alive.) So the energy field we possess lives on after our physical body dies. Some people have reported seeing a "glow" of light exiting the room through the ceiling when a loved one dies.

These discoveries could explain how the concept of life after death is possible, as well as how we achieve the various levels of Heaven. In God's universe, fact is stranger than fiction. I've been told that I am a logical thinker who is sometimes more analytical than is strictly necessary. So, just like 2+2=4, an explanation had to "add up" and withstand a certain degree of scrutiny without contradiction or I would (and still will) struggle to understand it and probably reject it. In addition, if there are obvious or underlying reasons supporting why things are the way they are, then that will solidify my theory, to the point where it may become a belief. The above explanation passed my test.

For example, we know that the reporter isn't inside our television, and that *The Rolling Stones* are not inside our radio. We know that audio and video signals are being sent to our televisions, stereos and cell phones through the atmosphere by radio frequencies of various levels. We can't see them, but we know they are there. And they're everywhere! Take your radio or television anywhere and you'll pick up music or the news, and yet the signal is invisible.

Knowing this lends credibility to the possibility that our energy field lives on, even though we can't see it in this dimension. Just because we can't see it doesn't mean it isn't there. Our human senses have limitations that challenge us not to believe more than our five senses can comprehend.

How Do They Know?

I once heard that the answers to all of our spiritual questions lie within nature. God has provided clues to the mysteries of the universe in the world around us. Our mission is to actively look for those clues, in order to unravel the mystery. Some clues are apparent, while others require extensive scientific research. Even Einstein, with his scientific mind, recognized the incredible complexity of the universe and concluded that a superior intelligence or being had to be its designer and creator. He recognized that the universe was too complex to have happened by chance.

Animals reveal one of those clues by using their sixth sense for survival. We all know that animals have extraordinary senses of sight, smell and hearing, to keep them safe from predators and well-fed in wild environments. But ask any hunter and he will tell you that, during the scouting for an ideal location, he will see many deer, including some trophy size big bucks. However, the next day, when the hunting season opens, for some reason the deer have vanished. How did the deer know that the intent had changed into a lethal situation? A universal warning?

Electronic tracking studies showed that bass actively fed along shoreline areas during the week, while a specific lake was closed to fishing. Before the lake was opened to anglers, on the weekend, the bass moved away from the shoreline, into open water, away from where most anglers cast their lines, thus avoiding an invitation to dinner.

Braking for God

These notions simply illustrate that animals can "tune in" to the negative energy of the environment around them, which is very similar to the way we might feel when walking into a crowded room where we either feel comfortable or "on guard" because of the current thoughts and energy in the room. We typically refer to this as "the atmosphere." My point is that there is more to our being than meets the eye. There is a spiritual part to each of us, and it exists here and now. It isn't created when we die. And this spiritual part does not stay confined within our physical bodies, nor does it remain near to us; rather, it is accessible to other beings. Thoughts are "things" that extend beyond us into thin air, and can be received by other objects.

What about jellyfish? They don't even have a brain, so who's driving the boat? How does a jellyfish know what to do? These questions can probably be applied to many similar things, such as sperm, amoeba and even the electron. But you usually can't see these, to wonder at them in awe as you might when watching a jellyfish in an aquarium or at the beach. Something is driving and controlling these things. I can only conclude that it must be God and His universe.

Dogs hear high-pitched sounds that we cannot perceive. Bees see light waves that we cannot. The brainwaves of animals and children remain in the "alpha" state, which is an altered state of consciousness for adult humans. As adults, we remain in the "beta" state most of the time, which is a fully awake and alert state. Alpha brainwave frequency is slower than the beta brainwave state, and is a more relaxed state of mind. Being in this altered state of consciousness makes us more susceptible to the frequency of the other side. We can achieve the alpha brainwave state by simply shutting our eyes. In their "normal" alpha brainwave state, animals are more sensitive to spirit. Perhaps that explains why dogs will sometimes bark at a wall or down the hall. It also explains why children sometimes develop imaginary friends. Those friends may not be so imaginary, after all! Indeed, some psychics reported having been able to see their departed relatives, when they were young.

As we drift deeper into relaxation, we cross through lower brainwave frequencies, such as "theta," and then into sleep (delta). It is in these lower frequencies that we're more "open" to receive a spiritual message. God and Company can more easily slip a message through to us when our brains are quiet. Perhaps the message actually enters in the tiny gaps between our slower thoughts, in our now less-active minds. This explains those thoughts and ideas that come to us "out of the blue."

Most of us have experienced this. We might have been unsuccessful at trying to figure something out, and then we suddenly solve the problem later, while watching television or showering, when our brainwaves are slower and inspiration has a greater chance of success.

The barrier, chasm or divide that exists between us and the other side is often referred to as a "thin veil." The veil is like a brick wall for most of us but, because it is thin, some gifted and talented folks known as "mediums" can breach it. By learning to enter altered states of consciousness, mediums can cut through the veil and access information about and from our dearly departed.

Once we realize the simple notion that the other side is operating at a different frequency around us, we can understand that it is just a matter of tuning in. Part of that "tuning in" is available to most of us as children. In childhood, we are naturally "psychic" but usually don't remember our experiences. As we mature, and because "grown-ups" tell us that these friends don't really exist, we eventually shift over to the beta brainwaves of adulthood. Our imaginary friends then disappear, along with any other psychic phenomena we may have experienced. We soon forget it all.

Some of us though, remember a few "weird" things that happened, but remain hesitant ever to tell the story, for fear of being ridiculed.

Many people struggle with the concept of life after death, and are less likely to embrace the idea of spirits being around, but with research the evidence becomes compelling. Much ink has been expended, by a variety of different authors, which might provide us with the evidence we need in order to understand, or at least consider, the afterlife. Some of the authors I have read include: John Edward, Sylvia Browne, James Van Praagh, Gary E. Schwartz, Ron Roth, Neale Donald Walsch, William W. Hewitt and Bill and Judy Guggenheim, to name just a few of the possibilities for research. Most have fascinating stories to share, detailing how they came to know spirit, and how they work with spirit in today's world. Scientific-minded individuals might find that *The Afterlife Experiments* by Gary E. Schwartz provides particularly compelling scientific evidence of life after death.

Even after doing research, some people probably still won't press the "I believe" button because these things didn't actually happen to them. There's no substitute for personal experience, and I certainly use my own as a foundation for my conclusions. Scientific studies have been conducted on the validity of mediums, the power of prayer, the power of thought, out-of-body experiences, and past life regressions, with results supporting all of them. I highly recommend conducting your own research, along with asking God and Company for assistance. If it's your time to know, God will oblige.

For those who do believe in life after death, many would tell you that Heaven is a faraway place located somewhere in the upper atmosphere or in the stars themselves. Somehow, we have embraced the notion that Heaven is "up." This concept also points toward a theory that Heaven is at a higher frequency than this world of heavy, slow-moving matter. For humans, being depressed equates to feeling "down" or "heavy-hearted," and being happy emanates feelings of "lightheartedness," "upbeat" or "high." The belief that Heaven is far away may have evolved from this feeling of "up," suggesting that one must go higher to reach Heaven. Add to this the fact that we cannot see Heaven, and one might conclude that it is far away. But if Heaven is simply at a "higher" vibration, making it as invisible as a radio signal, then it could be in our midst, all around us. We simply cannot see it.

To compound the difficulty of choosing sides, some scientists, skeptics and cynics spend their lives trying to disprove spiritual matters. Much of the scientific community believes that everything is scientifically explainable. Almost anyone religious or spiritual knows that God works in mysterious ways. Many scientists, doctors, and others have witnessed miracles, but they are too afraid to talk about them, for fear of ridicule from their peers. The more I research, the more I find scientists and doctors who have discovered their spirituality. Individuals such as Joan Borysenko and Deepak Chopra, to name only a few, are making huge contributions to the mind, body and spirit connection.

Spirit Guides

With all of these things going on, I continued to wonder who my spirit guides were. I wanted to meet them, if I could. In Edward's book, he spoke about our guides' desire for us to be aware of them. They're working very hard to help us, and they would like to be recognized, just as we would. He told the story of how he was introduced to his guides through hypnosis. He mentioned that we usually have four to six guides, with the most advanced guide as our "Master Guide." Our guides change to suit our needs as life progresses. For example, if we are trying to become a nurse, we might find that one of our guides has a background in nursing or healthcare, the better to offer advice and help us learn.

As I was drifting off into a nap on the sofa, one afternoon, a large face appeared in my mind's eye. It was like a dream, but I wasn't fully asleep yet. I was in the early stage of sleep where I could still hear the activities in the room. The face was that of an older man, and his expression was neither happy nor sad. His image quickly disappeared as the vision changed to a peaceful view of a winding, single-lane road that traveled slightly uphill through a plush, green forest.

I had never had this happen before. Startled, I fully wakened and assessed it for a while. Was this the face of one of my guides? Did the road symbolize something?

I had been expressing my desire to know my guides with Janice. A couple of days later, she received an advertisement, at work, for an audio program called *Mind Travel,* by Dick Sutphen. It was highly unusual to receive this type of advertisement at work, so I figured that too was "arranged." I read the brochure, which explained that the taped sessions would provide information about meditation, and that it contained guided meditations to create a safe "Higher Self-Sanctuary," where you could meet your guides, among other things.

Wow, what timing! I marveled. This was exactly what I was looking for. I quickly ordered it.

When I got the tapes, I immediately began listening to them. After some basic training on meditation, brainwaves and the various levels of consciousness, I created my "Higher Self-Sanctuary," with Sutphen's guided narration. Once I was in my Higher Self-Sanctuary, Sutphen asked me to visualize a blank movie screen or whiteboard.

On this screen, I was directed to ask my spirit guide to spell his name.

I really didn't know what to expect, because I didn't feel like I was in an altered state of consciousness at all. I felt normal. The sensation was so subtle that I didn't know I had achieved the required altered state. But as I watched the screen, I saw the letters R-A-B-I appear, one at a time, in my mind's eye. When I came out of the meditation, I concluded that my Master Guide was a Rabbi, because a name like Rabi didn't make sense. I reasoned that the B had probably flashed twice, and that I just hadn't caught it, in the dim light of my mind's eye.

I felt a little strange, because having a Jewish Rabbi as my Master Guide didn't seem right for a guy who grew up as a Catholic. Struggling with this, however, is what sealed my conviction that my Master Guide's name was, in fact, Rabbi. Since I didn't think my conscious mind would conjure up something that didn't fit my paradigm, I could only conclude it was the correct name. Surely, I would have accepted another name more readily, had it been something like "Father Luke." Still, since a Rabbi was completely unexpected as my guide, I wondered how he felt about me, if he was a Jew and I was a Catholic.

My schooling as a Catholic taught me not to have much respect for Jews, and now I had to come to grips with the fact that my Master Guide had been a Jew while he was on Earth. This also raised another fundamental question: How could a Jewish Rabbi be spiritually advanced enough to be a Master Spirit Guide, if these were the people who murdered Jesus? I knew very little about Jewish teachings or traditions. Wouldn't God look unfavorably on these people, since they did not accept His son?

But the clues I received certainly didn't support this notion. In Edward's book, he describes his Master Guide as a Native American Indian Chief with a large headdress. This was another clue that Master Guides didn't need to be saints or bishops. *That's interesting,* I thought. *It must not be critically important to have a Christian as a Master Guide. Hmmm. I wonder why not?*

More answers were coming, but it would take time.

Chapter 7

A Family Affair

Don't Tell Your Parents!

What a great message! I surmised. Life after death is true, and our loved ones are never that far away, because Heaven is in our very midst. All we have to do is talk to them and they hear us. Perhaps we could see their helping hand, if we knew how to look. I wanted to tell everyone in the world, but figured I would start with my parents and Aunt Charlotte, the widow of Uncle Dutch, since he was probably involved in my awakening. I wanted to share my excitement and perhaps give them greater hope for what the future might hold.

I put together a presentation, including taped John Edward television shows, to illustrate how spirits communicate. I tabbed specific pages of Edward's book to reference the things that were happening to me. I showed the tape, explained further by using the book, and then I told the whole story of the connections up to that point.

To say the least, my audience was not impressed in a positive fashion. They thought Edward was performing tricks and that our departed loved ones were in some other galaxy and couldn't get through to us, even if they wanted to. They found the connections interesting but coincidental, and they didn't associate any of it with divine intervention in any way. Expressionless faces bespoke disbelief and disengagement.

My sails hung lifeless with rejection at their silent ridicule. Disappointment and frustration flooded over me, followed by embarrassment and a spark of anger. I had failed. Taking a huge chance, I had revealed what I regarded as very exciting, yet controversial, personal information intended to enrich hope, but it served only to alienate me. As a U.S. citizen, I had achieved alien status within my own family.

When I attended Catholic school, we were taught that God sees everything we do and knows all of our thoughts, even before we think them. I had never encountered God on a personal level, so to believe these concepts would have taken a huge stretch of the imagination. Consequently, I didn't take it seriously. I never could understand why humans couldn't experience God. Why was He hidden? Most of us are taught as children that ghosts and paranormal occurrences don't really exist, that television programmers and filmmakers just make that stuff up because it makes money. We become programmed so that if we can't see it, feel it, touch it, taste it or smell it through our personal experience then it's easier to reject it. For many of us, as children we saw things on television and said "It is so true, I saw it on TV." Then our fathers would laugh and say, "You can't believe anything you see on TV because it is all trick photography." Before long, we didn't know who or what to believe, and after being laughed at several times, we became skeptical of everything unless we witnessed it with our own five senses. Our programming was complete. We were now skeptical, if not cynical, about everything.

A Family Affair

But couldn't the same skepticism that we developed about ghosts and other paranormal phenomena apply to God as well. After all, the concept of God is largely paranormal, in and of itself.

My point here is that belief in God suggests one's acceptance of very radical, otherworldly, science fiction-like, and just plain "far out" concepts such as:

- God is around us and can see *us* but we can't see *Him*, meaning He is *invisible*.
- God has angels to assist us, and they are also *invisible* unless they make a rare appearance to deliver a message.
- God is omnipresent, meaning He is everywhere at the same time, perhaps like a vapor or microwave.
- God knows our thoughts, meaning He has ESP and can read minds.
- God knows our future thoughts and actions, which means He is clairvoyant.

To summarize these basic concepts, one could conclude that accepting the existence of God therefore dictates a belief in ESP, clairvoyance and spirit beings. By many standards, this is simply some weird stuff, but I guess it must be acceptable to many, as long as God alone possesses these characteristics.

One characteristic we don't always associate with God is His tremendous sense of humor. While I was typing the above list, my iPOD was quietly playing in another room. The iPOD currently contains 1076 songs in a wide variety of genre, from hard rock to Christian rock to classical. The play mode was set to play the tunes randomly from all genres. The song that played while I was typing about God being invisible was called Visible by 4Him, a Christian

> group. The song is from their Visible CD. The lyric that caught my attention in the background was "I want to make the invisible God, visible." Clever, very clever, as well as very inspiring!

A litmus test for the radical nature of these beliefs could be conducted by presenting them to an atheist while asking for his perspective and honest opinion. The words "crazy," "condemnation" and "fruitcake" rapidly come to mind. Comments about scientific proof, or lack thereof, might quickly follow. And the atheist will probably only consider certain scientific studies which support his beliefs, and denounce as invalid or inconclusive any studies that might provide a shred of evidence for the existence of God.

Perhaps we need this sort of challenge to prompt us to reflect on what we really do believe. We have become so willing to accept the existence of God that the paranormal aspects of such a belief have drifted deep into our subconscious mind (or someplace) and are no longer re-visited or reviewed. We no longer consider what the acceptance of these beliefs truly mean. We don't walk around town contemplating that if we believe in God then we also must believe in ESP, clairvoyance and invisible beings that might be behind us at this very moment. Therefore, our mental model of God finalizes without all the sci-fi aspects being heavily weighted or plainly recognized in our decision to believe.

But some "believers" sure are quick to denounce and disbelieve any talk associated with paranormal subjects not associated with God. And yet the bible even discusses and recognizes mediums, (spiritists and wizards) speaking in tongues, and prophesizing. In the Old Testament mediumship was frowned upon, while speaking in tongues and developing one's psychic ability (prophesy) was encouraged in the New Testament. Actually there are far too many references to these in the bible to list.

Sprucing Things Up

Earlier in the year we decided to re-do some of the landscaping around the house because a few shrubs died or weren't doing well. We had one area, along a walkway, where we couldn't decide which kind of shrub to plant. We considered several types of plants but none really jumped out at us as "the one" for the area. On a Sunday, we went to the local nursery to purchase plants and get ideas for the walkway.

We accepted a young woman's offer to help. For over two hours, she stayed with us, answered all of our questions, and gave suggestions. While I was walking around trying to get ideas about the walkway, a vision stopped me dead in my tracks. I envisioned it lined with Dwarf Alberta Spruce, which look like miniature Christmas trees. The image was lucid and appealing, even though one of our Spiral Alberta Spruces had died recently for unknown reasons, and we had planned to stay away from them, as a result. The Spiral Spruce was specially sculpted in a spiral design; consequently, it was expensive. The frustration of that sizeable monetary loss was fresh in our minds, so I knew Janice would be a tough sell on buying more.

Nevertheless, I quickly found her and shared my vision. Because she thought they would be too tall for the area, it took some convincing, but once I told her we could space and shape them, she was okay with the idea. In addition, I told her the Spruce would look awesome decorated like little Christmas trees. We would do it in honor of her mother, who loved and lived for Christmas and the spirit of giving that it fostered.

Unfortunately, we needed nine of the Spruces, and the nursery only had two poor-quality shrubs left, for $59.95 each. They told us to call back on Tuesday, when they expected to have more.

Despite this minor setback, we had accomplished a lot. Janice and I truly felt as though we had received very high quality service, because we had gotten everything accomplished with the excellent technical assistance of our young woman helper. That's when we found out her name was Angela, which obviously is a derivation of the root word "angel." Then she added that she never worked Sundays but had decided to work that Sunday for a reason she couldn't even remember. On the way home, we discussed our stroke of good luck. Again, we surmised it had been orchestrated by "The Moms." We expressed our appreciation.

Janice forgot to call the nursery on Tuesday, since we were still busy in the yard. The project took longer than expected, but by the next week, we were done. She mentioned her interest in finding Dwarf Alberta Spruce to a co-worker. He suggested a different nursery, so Janice went there after work.

It turned out that the nursery had quite a few healthy Spruces, and they were having an end of year sale. The price tag on the Spruces was $59.95 but they were on sale for $35. Janice told the salesperson she wanted to buy in bulk and asked her if she could do better on the price. Meanwhile, she called me to see what I thought of the deal. I told Janice that $35 was a good price and to make the purchase. When Janice came home, she said, "You'll never guess how much I paid for these plants!" I was thinking total price, so I was confused, and then she said, "$21 each!"

We planted those healthy Spruces and then I trimmed them into shape. As soon as I began trimming them, the fond sweet scent of a Christmas tree filled the calm fall air. I found Janice so that she could share the moment with her Mom and me. It is amazing how a fragrance can bring back such great memories, and this memory was being brought to us courtesy of the "The Moms." Once again, my heart welled up with gratitude for what "The Moms" had done. I told Janice I wanted to have a party to honor her mother at the house on her birthday, December 21st. We would invite the family and ask them to bring their stories and memories to reminisce. She agreed.

Since I was now witnessing the power of Janice's mother, I began to wonder if she had been the main driving force behind "The Moms" all along. After all, she had lived her life in service to her family while being devoted to God. In my mind, this equated to a more advanced and powerful spirit. The things I had witnessed seemed as if they were being accomplished by someone with great influence. I thought that she might have been helping my mother come through to me, somehow. My focus was shifting to Janice's mother because of the signs I was seeing. I just felt as though she was in the spotlight now, trying to tell me something.

The Sevens

During this same time frame, I kept getting a 7 on the hand geometry reader at work. I got the feeling there was something I was supposed to figure out about the 7, but I drew a blank. There was a connection…but what was it? The date of the reunion was 7/21, which also included a 7, but at the time I didn't "feel" a connection.

Trying to recap what I knew: "The Moms" liked to represent themselves with the 21, since it was common to both of them. God's number was 7 and anything divisible by 7, which included 21. Janice's mother also represented herself by using dragonflies, but that wasn't connected to the 7. My mother had not established an animal or other creature with me.

So why did I keep seeing the 7's?

"Imagine That" A Spiritual Awakening

One morning in October, it dawned on me while I was in the shower. When our eyes are shut, such as when we're washing our hair, we are in an altered state of awareness which can be conducive to receiving guidance, especially soon after awakening, as with a morning shower. I've since had many revelations while in the shower. So I got out of the shower, got dressed, and was about to leave the house when I decided, instead, to call Janice and tell her of my discovery.

I told her the 7's represented her family of seven children. Janice's mother wanted me to deliver the message to her seven children. I glanced at the clock on the microwave oven while explaining my discovery; the time was 7:21 a.m. Bingo! My conclusion was confirmed. I was convinced.

Since I already had some experience with this message-delivery stuff, I was definitely apprehensive. I really wanted to deliver the message, but I feared ridicule and rejection again. I didn't know much about the life of Jesus, at this point, but I knew he came here with a good message and yet many people rejected it and ultimately fabricated reasons to execute him as a criminal. Knowing what I knew, and how I felt about God, I decided I would risk rejection to help spread the word. People, especially the family, needed to know. Perhaps a few would welcome the message.

Don't Tell Anyone?

My mind was racing in a different direction now; how should I deliver this message to Janice's family? Maybe I would be bold and draft a letter as if it were written by Janice's mother, describing her introduction to me and inviting the family to her own party. Once assembled, I could tell the whole story, and the rest of the family could tell their stories, too. Or maybe I should approach them one at a time and see how they responded to the message.

A Family Affair

A few days later, we received a surprise visit from Janice's sister, Penny, along with her eighteen-month-old son and her mother-in-law, Rachel. They lived quite a distance from our house, so having them "drop in" was highly unusual. Just before arriving, they called to see if we were home, stating they were in the area for an errand. Before they pulled into the driveway, I asked Janice, "Should I tell Penny about your Mom?" We agreed that I should wait for an appropriate time (or sign) that could lead me into such a conversation. I wanted to tell Penny the story but I wasn't sure if it was the right time.

Rachel wanted me to show her our house. She wanted to pick up some "pointers" for building her next house. Later, I found out that her next house was to support a women's ministry. She was very religious and active in her church. She then explained the project was to be called "Promise Land." The next thing I knew, she was telling me about visions she had been receiving from God of what "Promise Land" was to look like. With all of this talk about visions and messages from above; I knew this was my introduction.

I took them aside and recounted my experiences, while focusing on the message from Janice and Penny's mother. I mentioned that I had finally figured out that 7/21 meant that I was to deliver the message to family members. At the exact moment that I told them that Mom wanted them to know she was doing fine in Heaven and was always around to assist if she could, Penny's eighteen-month-old son, who had been quietly playing on the floor between us, jumped up, clapped his hands above his head and yelled, "Yeah!" for no apparent reason. Did my mother-in-law put the eighteen-month-old up to this? I think so. My recent experiences indicated that spirit could influence our thoughts and decisions.

Once again, the message was heard with a mixed response. On the one hand, the notion that Mom was okay in Heaven was appealing and comforting, but the idea that someone from the other side was trying to get through to us just seemed too "freaky" for Penny. I thought, *Wait a second, this is your mother we're talking about. She's not "freaky!" Most spirits are not "freaky" at all. Spirits are what's real. The physical world is the dream!* Life is usually only about seventy or eighty years long. These fleeting years will seem like a dream after we've been in Heaven for about a million years. These physical years will be a "drop in the bucket" of our overall existence.

Even though Penny readily admitted that she frequently thought of her mother and even asked for her mother's guidance during difficult times, the notion that her mother could actually hear her, and perhaps even help her, just didn't fit Penny's mental model. The action of asking for her mother's help, and then denying the possibility it could happen, was a contradiction in itself. Penny believed that any assistance she received was from God alone. People often find themselves thinking about their dearly departed and even talking aloud to them in times of need. When confronted with the notion that these dearly departed actually hear our pleas, people "freak out" or deny the possibility. Please give the spirits credit; they're working hard to guide and protect us, and they deserve some thanks, too. I frequently thank God and Company, to ensure I don't miss anyone.

Shortly after my testimonial, Penny and Rachel left the house. Telling the story energized me and elevated my spirit. It seemed to draw me closer to God and Company. Perhaps this was because I was trying to spread the great news of life after death and the need to be more loving, caring and sharing. During the story, it was as if God was supplying the energy to keep me going, and when I was done, I was left energized. It would prove advantageous to have some energy in reserve.

A Family Affair

Later that day, we received another unexpected knock at the door. This time, it was my parents, along with some long-time family friends, another couple who had been our neighbors many years ago. About twenty years before, they moved to Florida, but kept in touch and visited from time to time. My parents didn't see them often and I hadn't seen them for at least ten years. Both families went to the same church, and their children and I went to the same school. They had a son named Chip with whom I hung out, from time to time. When they left for Florida, Chip and I did not stay in contact with one another. We were young and too busy chasing girls and building fast cars to be worried about staying in touch.

My parents did update me from time to time about our family friends. About two years earlier, Chip had been diagnosed with brain tumors and was battling them, but they were discovered too late. In the spring, he passed away. The family, including his wife and children, were grieving the loss, trying to pick up the pieces and start healing.

I found it odd that his parents would be on my doorstep, since they usually came to visit my parents. When they did pay my parents a visit, I usually dropped in to see them. I guess a good reason for them to pay me a visit was to see the new house. But what was their reason to come up north in October? Usually my parents traveled to Florida to visit them when the weather was cool. But now they told me they needed a break from the usual issues caused by a death in the family. There is quite a bit that must be placed in order, which can consume any family's time and energy. Moreover, it acts as a constant reminder of the loss. They just wanted to get out of town to see some new sights and try to put it behind them and begin to heal.

I showed them around the house, but all the while I felt the urge to tell them about the other side. I wanted to assure them that Chip was okay and that he probably wanted them to know that. After the tour, we sat down and began to chat, catching up on old times, reliving some of the crazy things we'd done. We had a few good laughs, but I still had the urge to say something, and it wouldn't subside. Finally I did.

I quickly told Chip's mother and father about some of the things I had recently discovered, primarily focusing on the fact that the spirits of our lost loved ones may try to communicate with us, using signs to let us know they are doing well. While not on purpose, I focused my attention on a bare white wall, as if staring into space. I said "You know, Chip may have a sign like…" At that moment I saw birds flying through my mind, in my mind's eye. But these weren't just birds, they were ducks, so I blurted out, "Ducks!"

His parents quickly sat forward on the sofa with a look of amazement as they said, "He loved ducks! Chip loved two things; NASCAR and ducks!"

Every hair on my body stood up. *Uh-oh! What's going on here? What's happening to me? Am I finding out I'm psychic, too! Now I'm receiving visions from spirit!*

Had Chip paid me a visit? I'm sure he had. It gave me the impetus to dig deeper.

I assured Chip's parents that the "ducks" connection wasn't a lucky wild guess and that Chip wanted them to know he was okay. They seemed happier to hear some confirmation, although I didn't know if they really believed me or not. But I did know that I was now on a mission to figure out what my potential was. Was I a budding medium who just needed some development to awaken my abilities? I didn't know but I was determined to find out.

My experiences to that point were a sign of the great power of the spirit realm to make things happen in the physical world. Sending

A Family Affair

dragonflies to greet me, assisting my career, controlling electronic devices…it all seemed rather awesome. Unknowingly receiving a thought or starting to hum (or sing) a particular song didn't seem out of the question, after witnessing these other feats. But to get a vision of "ducks" when I wasn't looking for a vision at all caused me to wonder, *How did I get this?*

Having learned that our spirit guides were meant to gently provide guidance while remaining in the background, undetected, was explanation enough for how I had gotten some of these thoughts. Even the notion of an angel or spirit guide whispering in my ear was a bit unnerving, and to think another spirit had influenced my thoughts was even scarier. But now that I had received a clear vision, I began to wonder if the spirit of the deceased (Chip) hadn't directly delivered the vision. Chip's presence didn't frighten me but the idea that spirits could influence a human's thoughts was cause for concern for all of us. Fortunately, our guides are powerful enough to protect us, in most cases.

The audio program that I had purchased, by Sutphen, gave instructions on how to develop our "birthright" psychic abilities. I never realized that being intuitive was a natural ability that simply needed to be awakened. Of course, until recently I believed that psychic stuff was all a hoax, anyway. With my introduction to Sutphen and Edward, I now accepted and understood that some folks were psychic, which simply means, "power of the soul." What I did not expect to find was that I might be one of those psychic folks, at least to a lesser degree.

I decided to meditate more frequently, using the methods suggested by the psychics, to see what developed. Simplifying the instructions would go something like this: pick a quiet place with no distractions, breathe deeply and relax, close your eyes and visualize going higher and higher, to a safe and pleasant place of your choice. While you are in your "Higher Self-Sanctuary," do whatever you like, such as pray, ask questions and work with your guides. When you ask a question, pay attention to the first answer you get. I found that I could receive bits of information and get a few answers, which I assumed were from my guides. But was I also receiving information from the dearly departed?

Over the next week, I focused my meditations on receiving a message from one of "The Moms."

The Plane Truth

I was standing in the shower, one morning, washing my hair with my eyes closed (as usual), when I got something. I saw an image of my father-in-law's desk, which had a model plane on it. I sensed the focus was on the model plane and that there was something about it that I needed to discover.

The next weekend, Penny and another of Janice's sisters, Kelly, came by to take Janice shopping. It was unusual for the sisters to rendezvous here for a day of shopping, but here they were.

After the sisters departed, I began doing chores around the house. It was mid-October, and the day was sunny and pleasant enough to open the garage doors while I worked. Just after completing an oil change in Janice's car, I was washing my hands when a beautiful orange Monarch butterfly flew into the garage, passed right in front of me and then flew back out. I wondered, *Now who could that be?* I wasn't sure if Mom was trying to represent herself as a butterfly or not, but this butterfly wanted my attention.

Since it was such a pleasant day, I went jogging that afternoon. While I jogged, another orange Monarch butterfly passed directly in front of me. So I asked the question: "If that is you, Mom, would you somehow get together with the dragonfly and reveal yourselves together, so that I will know the butterfly is your symbol?"

The sisters returned home and unloaded Janice's shopping prizes while showing me what they had purchased. Kelly had purchased a yard ornament that had a dragonfly on a metal pole. Janice had only purchased Christmas gifts, with the exception of a gardening hat that she bought for herself.

The hat was unusual-looking, with a wide, oblong rim designed to keep the sun out of her eyes and off the back of her neck. When she put it on, it made me laugh because it seemed more appropriate for a delicate older woman using cotton gloves, a trowel and a small flowerpot. Not that there's anything wrong with that; it's just that the gardening we had been doing was tough physical labor, using leather gloves, work boots, rotor tillers, shovels and rakes. This hat personified a simpler, almost therapeutic kind of gardening, which was far from what we had encountered. She put the hat in the foyer closet for safekeeping until she would need it.

Before we wished Penny and Kelly farewell, I took Penny aside and asked her to check the planes on her Dad's desk, to see if there was anything unusual about them. I specifically suggested that the numbers on the plane might be worth looking at. I told her to call me if she found anything that related to the story I'd told her a week ago. She said she would. Penny and her husband were temporarily staying at her father's house because they were having a house of their own built. This would make it easy and convenient for her to check the planes.

We said goodbye, and the women headed home.

Once back in the house, Janice teased me. "So you don't like my new hat? I got it because it reminded me of the type of hat my mother would wear when she was outside." I told her that it wasn't that I didn't like the hat, it was just unusual and looked funny on her, considering the type of gardening we had been doing. I did get the sense that it was a hat style her mother would have worn. "Did you see what's on the hat?" she asked, and pulled it back out of the closet to point to the butterflies embroidered on the side of the brim.

"Wow!" I proclaimed. They had done it again. The dynamic duo had managed to get the dragonfly and the butterfly together in the car for the ride home. My question had been answered; Mom chose to represent herself as a Monarch butterfly. So both of them really were around! And the butterflies were on a hat that reminded Janice of her mother also confirming my conclusion.

During the next week, I heard no response from Penny regarding the plane. On Monday, I saw it again during meditation. I knew there was something about the plane. Why hadn't she given a report?

Janice and her three sisters were scheduled to gather for their annual sabbatical in the mountains the next week. On occasion, Janice stayed at her father's house the night before the trip, in order to hitch a ride with a sister rather than drive separately. She wasn't planning to stay at her Dad's this year because she was meeting a closer sister and leaving from there. I told her that, since we had not heard anything from Penny, the situation would probably change and she would have to stay at her father's house, thus giving her a chance to check the plane herself.

Sure enough, things did change. A kink in the plan surfaced, requiring Janice to stay at her Dad's house and leave from there.

As it turned out, there were two planes on her father's desk. One had the number 777 on it. There were those 7's again, screaming at me to pay attention and to take note that three 7s add up to 21! Janice figured that out before I did. This again linked the family of 7 children to the 21 which was my mother-in-law's way of representing herself numerically. The other plane had the number 737-400 which, when added together, also equaled 21! Janice added the numbers in the row because that's how numbers are added when using Numerology, which I had recently studied. Evidently, Janice had learned a little about Numerology from my studies, as well. I imagine I was prompted to purchase and read a book on Numerology in order to recognize these clues, even if Janice was the first to employ it. And it wouldn't be the last time this sort of communication was used.

Penny told Janice she was too "freaked out" by the numbers on the plane to give me a call. Nonetheless, when God and Company are on a mission, the necessary arrangements will be made "behind the scenes." In this case the objective was to get Janice to her father's house to investigate. Janice's mother (Jeanne) wanted me to continue my quest for the true meaning of the 7's.

Finding the 7

Upon returning from her trip to the mountains, Janice brought home another interesting and important bit of information. Another of Janice's sisters (Cathy) had approached her about using our house for a party. The reason she wanted to use our house was because it was big enough to contain the entire family and it had an open floor plan which allowed everyone to be together.

Cathy had given birth to the family's only granddaughter about six months before the mother of seven passed away. Jeanne, now the grandmother of her first granddaughter, had purchased two rings while on a trip to Korea. The plan was to present one ring to the granddaughter on her 7th birthday and the other on her fourteenth birthday! Now I understood another meaning surrounding the 7. Somehow, Jeanne knew that I would plan to have a party in her honor, but now she was asking me to host the birthday party for her granddaughter instead. It just so happened that the granddaughter's birthday was in December also! This was coming together nicely.

In addition to all of the 7's relating to the family of seven, it was now clear that a lot of the focus was directed toward the granddaughter and her 7th birthday. I still felt the message was meant to be communicated to at least some of the family members, so I didn't give up in this area.

We agreed to host the party, since we owed so much to Mom. I couldn't help wondering whether the message was supposed to be delivered to the family on that particular day or not. I kept trying to come up with a delivery method that wouldn't scare or offend anyone but Janice warned me that talking about "the dead" in this fashion, to a family of disbelievers, wouldn't go over well.

The family members had various beliefs about life after death and certainly didn't believe the deceased would hang around to talk to us. Even though I had accepted these concepts, I had to step back and recognize my perspective from just a few short months ago. I asked myself a sobering question: "What would I have done if I were presented with the same information back then?" I knew that the answer lay somewhere between laughing and kicking them out of the house, so I had to re-think the entire approach.

I found it funny and yet sadly appropriate that, all of my life, I've had truthful messages to deliver to people who just wouldn't believe. It started at age five, when I told the babysitter that Mom was hurt. The disbelief and rejection I encountered was manifesting itself in my determination to reach someone with this message. There had to be someone who was searching for the same answers that I was.

I became very frustrated and disappointed by the potential rejection I knew I would have to grow accustomed to. I decided to pour my heart into a poem. I had never seriously written a poem before and knew nothing about poetic style or mechanics, but this is what I came up with:

Finding Your Way Home

Feeling so fortunate, given understanding to grow
To find the meaning, the truth, everyone should know
The meaning of life, so simple, so pure
This had to be the way Home, I felt so sure
My hope that this message might set us all free
So you'll share the same joy that you see is in me
But everywhere I turned screamed deafness and fear
Taught not to believe, they choose not to hear
So I searched and I pondered, both long and hard
All day and all night as I paced in the yard
When our journey traverses blue skies and calm seas
We may not recall our hidden realities
My hope is that you don't run half of your life
To be brought to your knees then from pain or from strife
Some struggles are destined; that comes from the source
But constant pain means you've gone way, way off course
And thus it is written: dark precedes the light
For in the dark we discover inner sight
Enemies cause failure, suffering, pain, too
Forgive them as Jesus, for they know not what they do
Do not pass judgment, there surely is reason
Let your Soul grow wisely to its next season
Every failure, all pain has meaning from above
Seek the lesson and I'm sure you'll find only Love
For the Soul cannot grow without suffering and pain
We must see the perfection in the fire and the rain
Value the lessons and the wisdom they give
For it is through wisdom we joyfully live
Don't wait for the darkness to blind your own way
Open your heart; let Him lighten your day
The treasure inside you, hidden so well,

We exhaust our whole lives, not able to tell
God is within you; He waits to assist
Relax and be quiet, close your eyes, don't resist
The guidance received will lift and enlighten
Understanding and knowing will follow and brighten
Your course will now change, an ocean of glass
Through the eye of a needle you will easily pass
Be loving and caring, compassionate, forgiving
Pleasant journey to Home from this wonderful living

The 11th at 11

Since I knew Janice's mother was very close, somehow arranging events, I asked her specific questions while looking for the answers through external signs. During meditation, "mind chatter" would interfere, so I didn't want to take the chance of my analytical mind guiding me incorrectly. I wanted to get the word out but needed to be patient and accurate as to who needed the information. I asked for external signs to confirm whether I should approach the family members one at a time or present the message at the party.

One of Janice's brothers and his wife had just given birth to the second granddaughter of the family. They sent out invitations to their daughter's christening. Using numerology, I noticed that the zip code of their home address added up to 21, and that the zip code of the church, where the christening was taking place, added up to 13 (my number). Someone gave me the idea to add those numbers, because I had never done that before. Janice had added the numbers on the plane, when I had not considered it. But once I saw the results, I had a "knowing" that, at a minimum, I was supposed to deliver the message to this brother-in-law, John. The numbers conveyed the message that I (represented by the 13) needed to speak to John about his mother (represented by the 21). This may have been a stretch on the use of signs but I still felt the need to communicate to John and thought he would be receptive.

We called John and managed to set a tentative meeting date, due to potential schedule problems. We also needed to iron out the details and schedule the party, so we attempted to arrange a meeting with Cathy at the same time.

Two days in a row, I saw the time 11:11 (eleven-eleven) on a big digital clock as I passed it at work. Both times, I got the sensation that it meant something that I was supposed to figure out. In addition, I kept seeing 11's nearly everywhere I looked. I knew something was up but I had to figure out what.

Cathy decided to meet us at our house on November 5th to discuss the party. On that day, I received an external sign which signified that some sort of trouble was going to occur. I had developed a simple numbering system with God and Company for receiving information when necessary. Certain numbers meant certain things. I called Janice and told her to be careful because I suspected trouble. Later that day, she beeped me with the news that Cathy's house had been burglarized, which also meant that she wouldn't be coming over that evening to discuss party details. She said that she would get in touch with us later to re-schedule.

John was also having trouble with his schedule and had to figure out a new date and time to meet with us. Finally, it dawned on me that the meeting date would be November 11th, at about 11 a.m. I told Janice not to worry about trying to schedule the two of them because it would end up being November 11th anyway. Being curious, Janice called and simply told them to figure out a convenient day and time based on their schedule, and we would make ourselves available. As predicted, they both decided to meet us Sunday, November 11th, at about 11 a.m.!

Cathy arrived early so we had the opportunity to speak with her first. She, rather naturally, led the conversation into a spiritually based discussion about Jeanne, which I considered a sign to deliver the message. Judging by the tears of joy and amazement, she seemed to take it reasonably well and with an open mind—but then again, so had Penny. I wasn't sure. Were the tears because we graciously agreed to open our home to a party for her daughter? Or perhaps it was the kind words about her mother's assistance which brought back memories of her mother's kindness. At least for now, I wasn't sure. Cathy couldn't stay long and left about the time John showed up.

I started my story and message again for John and his wife, once our introductions subsided. I told John about the connection with the zip codes and how they gave me the sign to deliver the message. In addition to the usual message, I felt a need to tell John and his wife that his mother recognized and probably witnessed the birth of their child and was happy for them. I also mentioned that Mom was probably assisting in any way she could to make things go smoothly. He also seemed to take the message well but it appeared a more genuine acceptance, rather than insincere lip service.

As I continued to detail the number connections, I hadn't had a chance to discuss our November 11th meeting arrangement, when John told me that all of his life he had frequently seen the numbers 11 11 (eleven-eleven) and strongly felt there was some significance to these numbers but wasn't sure what it was. The look on his face was priceless when I told him the date was November 11th or 11/11. I told him that perhaps this day was the day he had been waiting for, and to take this message of love and hope and use it wisely.

Two weeks later, we attended the christening of John's daughter. Afterwards we went back to his house for a celebration. Since I had delivered the message to Penny, Cathy and John, I was interested to

A Family Affair

see how the message had ultimately sunk in. Did they still embrace the message with joy and wonder, or had they gone into denial? As I spoke with Cathy about the upcoming granddaughter's party, I again inquired about the possibility of sharing fond memories about her mother. The reply: let the dead stay dead, no need to bring up the memories. *Holy mackerel*, I screamed out in my mind, *Who has turned her off?* Later, I found out that she had spoken with her husband and with another of her sisters. The other sister also spoke with her husband, and the men told them that "No one can talk to the dead," and that this was a bunch of baloney best left quiet.

I now felt that all eyes of the family were focused on the "fruitcake" (me) for what I had dared to share with them. I wandered around the house wallowing in dejection and disappointment again, and ended up in the baby's room. It was decorated from ceiling to floor with dragonflies. Dragonfly wallpaper, dragonfly picture frames, dragonfly sheets, dragonfly blankets, and even a dragonfly mobile. I asked John what gave him the idea to decorate with dragonflies. He said he didn't know why, he just thought it was nice. I was pretty sure I knew where his inspiration came from!

Fortunately, John didn't go into a state of denial regarding the message, and actually considered it interesting enough to tell his brother, Jack. He suggested to Jack that he talk to me. Jack and I did get a brief opportunity to speak but it didn't do the message justice. Nonetheless, Jack was also intrigued and mentioned that he had heard his mother's favorite song, *What A Wonderful World*, by Louis Armstrong, "a lot lately," which caused him to think of her frequently. I smiled from ear to ear as I said, "Hello from Heaven!"

Party Time

It was now beyond question that the party was *not* to make mention of my mother-in-law in the spiritual aspect I had intended. The party would focus on the presentation of the ring to the granddaughter and limit the conversation about Jeanne to this event and its history. Even so, I was still concerned about the success of the party, in light of my new persona as the family oddball, so I expressed my concerns to Janice. Shortly after, while looking in Edward's book for a reference explaining how spirits communicate, I randomly opened the book to a page to begin my search, and the first thing I read was a statement where Edward's mother told him, "The party will be great." I temporarily stopped my search and showed Janice the passage that calmed my growing fear. From that moment forward, I knew everything would be just fine. My concerns diminished, and I thanked Jeanne for another lesson in how spirits communicate. They're so clever!

The party was great, if not excellent, and everyone was able to attend, which was very unusual for a family of this size. But since this was very important to Jeanne, I knew she would pull all the strings she needed to get everyone together. I never doubted her ability, even for a moment. One of my brother-in-laws even managed a dirt-cheap round-trip airfare that happened to be going back to his hometown exactly when he needed it. This was important because he had just started a new job and hadn't accrued any leave, so he needed to be home Sunday night in order to return to work on Monday morning. If the travel arrangements had not worked out he would not have been able to attend the party.

I was wondering how Jeanne would reveal herself to me during the party. I knew she would be present, even if she didn't reveal herself to the family.

We had decided to do one of those gift-exchange games where each player chooses a gift from a pile, one at a time, and then can "steal" a gift from someone else if they don't like the gift they

A Family Affair

opened. It can be a very fun game. The game has been given names such as "Chinese Christmas," "Yankee Gift Exchange," or "Thieves Christmas," to name a few. Someone bought a very nice picture frame with a dragonfly carved into it. I wanted it and I knew I would end up with it because it was meant to be. But I didn't have it yet. Someone else had grabbed the gift so, when it was my turn, I exchanged my gift for it and just hoped no one would steal it. Realizing that almost everyone in the family liked dragonfly decorations, I worried that I would lose my prize, but I didn't. Jeanne probably pulled some more strings and let me keep the treasure.

As funny as it might sound, I didn't have a picture of my own mother mentally stored in my mind. In the past, as far as I was concerned, I hadn't felt any need to remember her, since she had abandoned me. But when my experiences with "The Moms" began, I naturally wanted to know who I was dealing with. I found some pictures of them, to help me remember what they looked like and to visualize who I was talking to when I called out to them or thanked them.

I had a picture of my mother from her youth but I didn't have a youthful picture of Jeanne. As I sat looking at a picture of my mother-in-law one day, taken just before she died, I found myself thinking that she wasn't very attractive. She was overweight, with thinning hair, and just didn't take good care of herself in her latter years. It seemed odd that one of the "angels" in my life didn't look more angelic. I caught myself having these thoughts and accidentally muttered the words aloud. I quickly tried to stop, but it was too late, the damage was done. The unflattering words had escaped my lips. I apologized and scolded myself for my superficiality.

I should have known my mother-in-law would find a way to have a word with me.

Before the festivities were over, Penny got everyone's attention because she had something to give us. She explained that she had been going through some old photo albums and found a flattering picture of her mother from her college days. Penny had thought it would be nice to have the photo enlarged and give us all a copy of a younger, healthier-looking Mom.

Penny handed me the picture, and once again my jaw dropped. She was beautiful! As I sat there, fighting back the tears of embarrassment, joy and love, I knew Mom had gotten through to Penny to arrange this little ribbing. I could almost hear her say, "What do you think now?" She was also telling me that this was the appearance she had chosen on the other side. I whispered, "Thanks Mom. You're beautiful!!"

So, not only did she make her appearance...she was stunning!

The Gift

Janice and I were not supposed to exchange gifts, that Christmas. During the course of the year, we purchased what we wanted when money was available, so there was no need to exchange gifts. We joked that it was always Christmas at our house.

A couple of weeks before Christmas, Janice brought home shopping bags full of gifts for the family. She pointedly told me not to look in one bag, so I knew it had something in it for me. Naturally, I didn't want to feel like a heel on Christmas morning by not having a gift for her, so I planned to get her something.

We enjoyed having outdoor fires in the yard on cool nights but we didn't have a fire pit or fireplace. We simply had a burnt spot in the grass. Sitting around the crackling warmth, while gazing up at a crystal clear starry sky or staring into the orange, red and yellow flames as they danced over the logs, was inviting and serene. Roasting marshmallows was another treat we enjoyed. The campfire

A Family Affair

atmosphere brought back fond memories from Janice's childhood, when her family frequently camped.

There are many types, sizes and shapes of outdoor fireplaces. We had discussed buying one in the future, rather than leaving a charred spot in the yard. I thought this would be the perfect gift so I began to research the market.

Since we liked seeing the flames and not just feeling the heat, we didn't want the kind that looked like a chemistry beaker. These have a round base with a chimney, and the flames are hidden, so these didn't interest us. We wanted one with an open base long enough to accept big logs and display the flames.

Finally, I found exactly what I was looking for, in one of the many mail order catalogs that we receive. Of the many I had viewed, only one fit our criteria. I called the company and placed the order. They said it would take three to four weeks for delivery so, unfortunately, it wouldn't be here by Christmas. "Oh well, it's the thought that counts anyway, right?" So I cut the picture of the fireplace out of the catalog and sealed it in an envelope to present to Janice on Christmas morning.

She was thrilled.

Later Christmas morning, my parents and sister came over to spend the day with us. They arrived bearing gifts, which included a rather large box. I didn't pay much attention to it, other than noticing that it was large.

Janice showed my stepmother and sister her present, the picture of the fireplace. I didn't see the look on their faces when they saw it, but later they admitted they had looked at each other with wide-eyed curiosity and bafflement.

After dinner, we opened the gifts. Again, my jaw dropped in total amazement: my parents had bought us the exact same outdoor fireplace that I had purchased for Janice. Of all the fireplaces to choose from, how did they manage to pick the exact one? It seemed to defy chance. I was speechless.

The reason my stepmother and sister had such unusual looks on their faces when they saw the picture was because they thought I had used some psychic ability to guess what their present would be, and that I was playing a joke on them. They were somewhat aware of my developing intuition.

We continued to celebrate the day as I walked around in amazement. Something was tugging at me, prompting me to continue pondering this surprise.

Later that evening, after the family departed, we cleaned the house a little and then prepared for bed. I was still marveling at the gift. Janice was in her walk-in closet and I was standing in the doorway of mine, which is directly across from hers. To my right was the bedroom and to my left was the bathroom. In my peripheral vision, I could see them both.

As I was unbuttoning my shirt, a revelation rocked my consciousness! "Janice! I figured it out!" I said as I tried to gain composure. "The fireplace was a gift from your mother, from the other side!" At that exact moment, both one hundred-watt lights in Janice's closet went completely out and then turned back on. It wasn't a power loss or spike because the lights were on in the bedroom and the bathroom and they didn't dim a single watt. I could see these rooms in my peripheral vision. I asked Janice if she saw the bedroom or bathroom lights flicker, along with her closet lights. She said they did not flicker a bit. This was confirmation from Mom that she had planted the idea in my stepmother's mind, to buy the exact fireplace we were looking for.

A Family Affair

With weakness in my knees and tears of amazement and joy in my eyes, I sat on the edge of the bed, gazed upward and sweetly whispered "Thanks Mom, and a Merry Christmas to you, too."

Chapter 8

Out of the Blue

The Crystal Ball

From time to time, during meditations, I would get images of equipment at work. At first I found this annoying, because meditation time was "my time" to forget about work. I'd ask myself "Why are you bugging me about this stuff?" Sometimes I also picked up thoughts that these components were going to break or become a problem. I'd jot these down on the pad on my knee and keep them in my records.

A few days, weeks, and sometimes months later, these pieces of equipment would cause trouble. Sometimes these equipment problems would cost the company a great deal of money in plant down-time.

During one meditation, I received a glimpse of the letters CWP with a number in front of it, but I wasn't sure of the number. On my pad, I wrote 11 CWP. CWP is an acronym which stands for Circulating Water Pump. We have twelve of these pumps at the plant, six for each unit. I sensed the pump in question was associated with Unit One but wasn't sure which of the six. Three days later, an electrical component in 12 CWP burned up, causing the pump to shut itself down. When this happens, a certain amount of personnel-scrambling occurs, due to the minor plant problem that it can cause. In addition, electrical output of the plant decreases, costing the company revenue due to the lost generation. If I had been able to warn of the pending problem, we could have used a Thermal Imaging Camera (thermography) to detect the overheating component and replace it in a controlled fashion.

Once I realized the messages were associated with equipment that did break, I wondered how I could report these things, prior to them happening. Who was going to understand what I was experiencing?

Even though I was very familiar with the plant, conducting my own investigations wouldn't reveal the problems that were about to happen anyway. Many of the problems were deep within the machinery and not detectable by the naked eye, or they were in parts of the plant that were not accessible while in operation.

But if we knew something was about to become a problem, perhaps we could prepare for it. Everyone wants a crystal ball, and I was that crystal ball, but who would believe me? How do you tell a bunch of left-brain, linear-thinking engineer types that you had a vision? I figured they, too, would "freak out" and call me a fruitcake, like I'd heard a few times before. So I just kept quiet.

All I Want for Christmas Is

I continued to use the *Mind Travel* tapes to enhance my ability to meditate properly, in an effort to help me relax and create a stronger connection with my guides. I had borderline high blood pressure and this was an excellent way to lower it. It worked. By sitting quietly, using the whiteboard method, I could silently ask questions during meditation and wait for the first thought or image that came through. Unfortunately, many of the answers were created by mind-chatter, which was simply my own analytical mind providing answers and random thoughts. It's difficult to get through but nearly everyone experiences it.

Then, one day, I sat down to meditate and as soon as I closed my eyes I saw an image of a stick being swung toward my head. It didn't seem like an ax or a bat but a stick. I opened my eyes to ensure there was no one in the room, even though I knew there wasn't. *Man!* I fretted, *Someone doesn't want me to meditate today!* I shut my eyes and it happened again. I was a little spooked by it but, as taught, I acknowledged it and let it pass.

The next afternoon, Alex was playing street hockey at a neighbor's house and got both of his front teeth knocked out by a hockey stick in the mouth. The teeth were badly broken. One tooth was broken off horizontally at the gum line, with pink pulp showing. The other tooth was broken diagonally from the middle to the gum line, with pulp showing. The accident occurred right at dusk, and the kids all ran into the house, crying and upset over the accident. By the time the kids and parents regained composure and controlled the bleeding, it was dark. The kids went out to the cul-de-sac with flashlights and actually found both pieces of his teeth, fully intact. They weren't shattered and in pieces as we'd expected. Finding the pieces in the dark was phenomenal enough; to have them intact too was beyond phenomenal! But would this matter to the dentist? I believed the teeth were damaged beyond repair.

We called the dentist to inquire. He asked if the pink pulp was showing. We told him it was. He said that the teeth would probably need root canals and crowns, but recommended bringing the pieces anyway. The next day, Janice took Alex to the dentist with the broken teeth, just in case. The dentist checked his teeth and found no damage to them, even though the pulp was showing. He glued the teeth back on, and they have been fine ever since. We could hardly believe it. We believed we had witnessed a miracle. Even the dentist was surprised that the roots of the teeth were not damaged.

In retrospect, the vision of the stick seemed to be an apparent warning that someone was going to get hurt. Even if I had known I was supposed to figure out the vision's meaning, it still would have been difficult to put the pieces together (pardon the pun). I didn't realize it, at the time, but this was my indoctrination into one of the methods God and Company intended to use to communicate needed information. I had already experienced external signs and a few thoughts that didn't seem to be my own, but now I was receiving visions as I began to meditate. What I didn't consider at the time was that the vision came before I was deep into meditation; I had just shut my eyes. Perhaps my guides were working with me. And it didn't require deep meditation, just quiet.

I'm Sorry

Janice and I had just had a pretty severe argument regarding religious matters. My fast awakening and her immersion into traditional religion left huge differences in our beliefs. Much of our daily life was spent discussing spiritual and religious topics because it was such a huge part of our lives. We tried to make our discussions just that, discussions. But this discussion went too far, and we started to yell at one another. I was furious with her apparent ability to mentally block the truth, and I'm sure she was just as furious with me for my inability to accept her bible as the inspired word of God.

That night and the next day, we didn't speak at all. The next night, I decided to meditate, to clear my mind and release the tension. Shortly after I reached a deep meditative state, I heard Janice say to me, in an emphatic, apologetic voice, "I'm sorry!" It was as if she was announcing it to the universe. It was also as if she was near me

Out of the Blue

when I heard it. It was her voice, and it was very discernible, but she wasn't near the room I was in.

After the meditation, I went to her and asked her if she had something she wanted to tell me. I know that may sound stiff and pompous, but I didn't know how else to ask the question without giving away what I'd heard. She told me that, on her way home, she'd been agonizing about our argument, and had yelled out in the car "I'm sorry!"

Well, the message got through, loud and clear.

I also apologized for my behavior. We have since learned to accept our differences, which is another reason why Janice is in my life. And I reasoned that if I could learn to accept the differences within my own home, then I could surely learn to tolerate the differences I was bound to encounter in my travels.

Another concept revealed itself through this experience; the message always reaches the intended party. Janice's cry "I'm sorry!" reached me. And because of the power, energy and conviction she put into it, I was able to hear it, loud and clear. Even if I hadn't been in meditation, the energy of her feelings would have reached me and had some affect on me. The important thing to learn from this is that our thoughts, whether loving or destructive, reach the person for whom they are intended. Studies have been conducted where individuals were placed in rooms alone, with electrical measuring devices attached to their skin. The electrical device measured skin electrical activity while the subject sat quietly, allowing baseline data to be collected. In another room, other study participants were given a picture of the subject and told to direct angry thoughts toward the subject. The measurement devices immediately registered increased skin electrical activity in reaction to the angry thoughts.

What Were You Thinking?

In the same way that we can feel the energy or atmosphere of a room, we can pick up pieces of information about someone, including what they are thinking. By attempting to tune in, you might be surprised by what you can pick up. Janice and I do this all the time, as I'm sure many couples do. Just when I'm thinking about something totally unrelated to the current conversation, Janice will bring that exact subject up, or vice versa. I've heard this referred to as "psychic twins," which simply means that two people are basically on the same wavelength, making it easier for them to telepathically communicate.

Janice and I were in a hardware store buying supplies when I picked up a specialty light bulb that we needed for a Curio cabinet. I was shocked at the price and held it in my hand while I got Janice's attention in the next aisle and asked, "Do you know how much this little stinkin' bulb costs?" She paused a moment, as if tuning into the universe, and said, "Three twenty-nine." I just put the bulb in our basket, smirked and shook my head at her ability to read my mind.

I was sitting at the kitchen table editing a résumé for a friend while Janice cleaned up after dinner. I wrote the words "detail oriented" on one of the pages when Janice said, "Make sure you add that he is 'detail oriented.'" I just laughed and told her to stop reading my mind.

A guy asked me to pick a number from one to ten, in order to figure out who was going to go first. The closest one would win. I looked into his eyes and just listened for a moment, and then said, "Three." He said I was right and so I went first. Now, there is a ten percent chance of guessing correctly, but this is an example of just one of many times that this sort of thing has worked.

Out of the Blue

City of Fear

The Washington D.C. area was gripped with fear when a sniper was on a rampage during the fall of 2002. Ten people were killed and three seriously wounded, in over a month-long killing spree. I remember it well because we live in the D.C. area, not far enough from the heart of the shootings to have felt safe. Everyone was constantly looking over their shoulder when they were outside in a public place. No one felt secure.

An early clue pointed to the possibility that a white van was the vehicle used by the sniper. Everyone became wary of white vans of any kind. I don't think we realized, previously, how many white vans were on the highways. When I stopped to fill my car with gas, I was definitely checking out any white van nearby.

One evening during meditation, I asked for clues regarding the sniper case. The word "Tacoma" flew into my consciousness, so I raised my awareness just enough to record it on my pad so I wouldn't forget it. After the meditation, I sat quietly and assessed what the clue might mean. My analytical mind now took over and came up with Tacoma Park, which is a town in Maryland that is also considered a part of the D.C. area.

Because I didn't receive any other information, I didn't know what the connection was. Would there be a sniper attack in Tacoma Park, or were the snipers from that area? I didn't know.

Finally, two suspects were arrested, charged and eventually convicted. During the investigation it was determined that one of the suspects had recently lived in Tacoma, Washington. Once again, my clue was accurate, less of course my analytical mind's input. This isn't to say that the analytical mind isn't necessary or valuable; we just have to be careful when listening to it.

Now I more fully understood how psychics could be useful to law enforcement agencies. The information is accessible from anywhere not just at the crime scene. However, it is probably more powerful at the scene.

A Stock Tip

If you ask the universe for lottery numbers, you probably won't get them. But William W. Hewitt relays a story about investments, in his book *Psychic Development for Beginners.* Hewitt, before he was an accomplished psychic, was sitting in his office at the computer-equipment engineering company where he worked. With no one else in the room, he heard a voice instruct him to sell his company stock. He looked around to ensure the room was empty, shrugged it off, and continued working. With increased authority, the voice again told him to sell his stock. He thought it was foolish, since his company stock was performing well, and so he ignored the request. The voice then commanded him to sell his stock and offered proof for making the request.

Hewitt called his broker and told him to sell all of his company stock. The broker tried to talk Hewitt out of it but, after twenty minutes, conceded to Hewitt's demand. The broker then wanted to know what to reinvest the money in. The voice didn't offer an immediate reply but waited for Hewitt to ask the broker for suggestions. When the broker named a certain very high-risk investment, the voice said, "Buy that." The broker again tried to talk Hewitt out his decision, but failed again.

Two days later, the bottom dropped out of the company stock, and the reinvested money went on to perform extremely well until six months later, when the voice said, "Sell." At that time, Hewitt promptly listened and sold the stock.

Out of the Blue

Once I realized I had developed a psychic connection of my own, I decided to ask God and Company for a personal stock tip. While meditating one evening, I posed the question, *What's a good...* Right then, I heard the word "horizon" before I even had a chance to finish the question. Previous experience taught me that anytime an answer came through before the question was completed ruled out analytical mind as the source of the response and pointed to spirit as the source. I knew this tip was definitely worth paying attention to, so I got on the internet to search for a stock titled "horizon." I wasn't successful.

Bewildered and now questioning the validity of what I had heard, I shared my experience with Janice. It didn't take her long to chime in with "New Horizons, that's a mutual fund in our 401K plan at work." I felt so stupid. We already had some money in this fund.

The stock market had been doing extremely well in recent years but was now going through a significant market correction and reduction for many stock prices. I thought the stock tip was meant to preserve our investments and perhaps grow them significantly, while other portfolios suffered. I transferred thousands of dollars to the New Horizons fund and also set up additional pay-period contributions to the fund.

Over the next year, the fund went from approximately thirty dollars a share down to somewhere in the teens. Our whole portfolio was hurting, as was most everyone else's. I should have taken this as a clue but, out of frustration with the whole stock market game (which I wasn't good at), I decided to transfer a significant portion of our money to a much more secure "guaranteed rate" low-risk fund that performed more like a savings account. I vowed not to play the game again and to settle for the steady performance of the low-risk funds.

After another year had passed, I stumbled across some of my co-workers discussing the stock market. I told them about my bad luck with stocks and that I was tired of "rolling the dice," because I didn't have time to thoroughly investigate what stocks to buy. Then one co-worker said, "I don't like telling people what to do with their money, but if there was ever a time to get back into the market this is it." The suggestion was sincere and I sensed I should heed the advice.

That evening, I went to the company 401K retirement plan website to check on the performance of the various mutual funds offered to employees. Boy, was I upset when I saw that the New Horizons fund had been the best-performing fund in our available portfolio for the last six months, at nearly a thirty percent return on investment.

This was yet another lesson in patience and thorough, complete communications. I should have asked more amplifying questions and let the money sit safely where I was told.

Mechanic On Duty

The engine coolant temperature gauge in my car stopped working. Being the shade-tree mechanic that I am, I set out to fix it. I broke out the repair manual to determine the problem and then locate the part that needed to be replaced. The repair manual listed two components associated with the engine temperature: a temperature switch and a temperature sensor. The sensor, which sends an analog electrical signal to the gauge at the dash, was supposed to have two wires coming out of it, while the switch only had one wire. According to the manual, the two-wire sensor was the fix.

I was having trouble finding either of the devices under the hood, due to the massive tangle of wires, vacuum hoses, cables, turbo and other metal machinery. I referred back to the repair manual to see if it had a decent picture or description, but it only listed a general area for the sensor.

Before continuing the search, I grabbed a flashlight and said, "Okay, guys, how about a little help finding this sensor?" As soon as I turned the flashlight on, it shone into a dark area around the engine that otherwise would not have been visible. The light shone directly onto the one-wire temperature switch. With a chuckle and a smirk, I said, "Nice try, guys, but I'm looking for the two-wire temperature sensor. I guess you guys aren't great mechanics, anyway." I continued to search for the two-wire sensor until I found it. I removed it and took it to the auto parts store to match up a replacement.

I installed the new two-wire sensor, only to find that my temperature gauge still didn't work. "Hmmm...how could that be?" I muttered in disgust and confusion. I scratched my head some more and re-checked connections and re-reviewed the repair manual. This should have been the correct part. It still didn't make sense to me that it wasn't.

With only one option left, I purchased the one-wire temperature switch and installed it. The temperature gauge worked fine after that. So, my friends were right after all; I had to eat a little crow. They're better mechanics than I gave them credit for being, after all.

I later learned that Archangel Michael (a.k.a. Saint Michael), from whom I always requested spiritual protection during meditation, is also known for his assistance with mechanical or electrical-component problems. This might explain the invisible guidance I received in shining the flashlight on the exact part that needed to be replaced.

These days, whenever I'm troubleshooting or fixing something, I ask Saint Michael for help. I find it very comforting to know that I've got additional help. I just have to pay attention and tune in.

Hey Joe

I had read and heard about mediums who could hear the voices of spirits external to their bodies just as we hear another person during conversation. An internal voice that seemed to be heard inside one's head was much more common. I had experienced this several times, if not many, but had not heard an external voice and didn't know if I was capable of it. Not being sure of the requirements, or level of psychic development, I didn't know if I could bridge the gap to spirit or spirit to me. Since I had often felt that someone was trying to tell me something, I kept asking for them to just talk to me. I was curious as to what they would sound like. Would it be close or distant, loud or weak, whispered or yelled, garbled or clear?

One sunny day, while meditating, I got my answer. Just before coming out of the meditation, I very clearly and very closely heard someone say into my right ear, "Hey, Joe," and that was it. Immediately, I came out of the meditation and assessed how audible and close those words had been…but then I became skeptical. Had my subconscious created this voice out of my desire to hear spirit externally? It seemed too discernible and external not to be authentic, but why would a spirit just say, "Hey, Joe," and not something more convincing like, "Hey, Joe, this is so-and-so, and we're with you."? This fueled my skepticism.

Back at work, I was reviewing some archived voice mails, looking for a specific message. I pressed the "skip" button after listening to the first few words of each message, searching for the one I wanted. I stopped for a moment at the fourth message and wondered, *Did all of these messages start with "Hey Joe?"* I reviewed the introductions again and, indeed, each of the four messages began with "Hey Joe," spoken in a casual, informal and friendly tone. The unusual part was a message from a guy that I didn't even know, from company headquarters. Usually, when voice-mailing someone we don't know, our introduction is more formal than "Hey Joe." I concluded that this was confirmation that I had in fact heard someone from the other side speak to me, and they were using this reference as the convincing coincidence.

This communication meant much more than a simple "hello," though. I had read about spirits coming through in times of need to "regular" people (not mediums or psychics), so it was apparent that this was possible. It was also obvious that it is not normal and is usually limited to special situations or emergencies. I don't believe that spirits can communicate whenever they please or we would hear their voices all the time, constantly warning us about our actions. Mediums wouldn't be needed. I theorize that a certain level of permission must be granted by a higher authority before these spirits are given the permission—and perhaps the tools—to communicate across the divide. Another complicating factor might be our inability to tune in. If our psychic abilities are too underdeveloped, spirit may not be able to get through.

Another interesting aspect to this "hello" was that the spirit obviously knew I would review the voice mails and find the connection. As with other stories I have shared, the spirits knew the future before it happened: further confirmation that time is not linear, as Einstein theorized.

Chapter 9

Small Medium at Large

I was moving forward in as many venues as possible, in an effort to determine my strengths and/or God's will for me, knowing my strengths would allow concentration on their development. And as I developed my strengths, then perhaps my destiny or purpose might become clear. I could only hope.

Previous encounters with spirit compelled me to develop my psychic abilities using exercises as prescribed in the different books and tapes I'd reviewed. But I needed test subjects willing to let me attempt "readings" on them. *Well, where the heck do you find them?* I thought. I even asked God to deliver a couple so I could practice on them. If I practiced performing readings and was successful, then that might be my calling, to be like John Edward, giving people hope of life after death. But the knocks on my door didn't happen—at least not as I expected them to happen.

Despite all the books I'd read about developing psychic abilities and mediumship, it seemed that I was missing some key pieces. The psychics or mediums I'd read about had psychic experiences as children, such as being able to see auras, knowing things before they occurred or talking with dead relatives. It was as if they were born pre-programmed for their profession. I had not experienced any of this as a child. Many of these folks also began developing these skills very early in their lives. I definitely felt that I was behind the eight ball here. Since I hadn't had these experiences, I figured I was probably meant to develop something else, but what? Since I didn't know, I simply continued to develop my psychic skills until pushed in another direction. For all I knew, I might have experienced a breakthrough at any time.

I had read that one of the best ways to develop our innate psychic abilities was to join a "development circle." A development circle is a group of like-minded people who gather to develop their psychic abilities. Just as the name suggests, these folks sit in a circle and meditate on the same subject or desire to connect with someone from the other side. Like-minds focused on the same purpose can amplify the ability to connect to the other side, thus training the mind to "tune in" more rapidly. It's like getting a jump-start to the advanced class. Searching for a "circle" locally, I ran into a dead end. On the internet, however, I stumbled across a website called *The Seeker's Circle*, which was a site for "intuition development." It had a message board where someone could ask for a reading or give one. *Excellent! That's exactly what I'm looking for!* I could do practice readings and not feel uncomfortable, since they weren't paying customers waiting patiently in front of me for a message to come through. Receiving information or a message could be painfully slow, like watching grass grow.

I scanned the requests for readings and just followed my intuition as to which ones to try. My intentions were to help others in need of answers or closure, if I could, and along the way improve my skills as a medium. It didn't occur to me that what was about to happen would help me beyond psychic skills.

Because the sitter was nowhere in sight when the reading was conducted, I was skeptical. I couldn't understand how these long distance readings would work. I theorized that I had to be near the person's aura to pick up the "energy" of the person. I believed the information was contained within their spirit or aura. Then again, if another spirit such as a guide or a deceased loved one was providing the information, then I guessed I didn't have to be physically close at all. Another reason for skepticism was the fact that many people on the internet didn't use their real names, and I didn't think focusing on an alias would work.

I performed readings for several people and found that I could pick up meaningful information for them. The information was too specific to be a stretch of the imagination, no matter what their alias was.

While meditating and focusing on the person's name or e-mail request, I would receive images, get feelings or have thoughts "out of the blue." As an example, I saw the Eiffel Tower as part of a reading for one woman. I didn't know where she lived; therefore I didn't know what it meant. I just passed it along to her. She told me, "Oh, that's easy. I was in Paris last week and went into the Tower." Psychics and mediums call this a "hit." A direct hit as far as I was concerned.

Many more "hits" would come through for different folks, but most were what I considered low-level connections of past events or of things to come. No earth-shattering revelations came through. An occasional warning to be careful while driving did prove valuable for Janice, who brushed a deer rather than slam it. And one other person narrowly missed an accident by being cautious at an intersection after my warning.

There are two types of information a psychic can receive for or about someone. They might receive general information, such as their birthday, a significant date or anniversary, their favorite color, or a recent or future trip. This information comes from the sitter's energy field or spirit. Then there is the information that comes from the spirits of departed loved ones, friends or guides. Since communication across the veil is difficult, they don't simply walk up and start carrying on a conversation, unless the medium is very gifted and well developed. They'll do the best they can to give the medium meaningful clues that they can pass along to the sitter, who will have to put the pieces of the puzzle together and find meaning in the metaphors.

I performed readings while I meditated, with no one waiting around for information, so the pressure to quickly deliver messages wasn't on my shoulders to interfere with the results. The first step was to protect myself from harm (negative energies and spirits) by praying and requesting the Divine Light of Love and Protection to surround me, while also visualizing It's presence. I would also request Saint Michael to send the Archangels to form an impenetrable barrier around the meditation room. I would instruct my protectors to only allow invited and welcome positive spirits into the area. After protecting myself and praying, I would sit quietly, waiting for whatever information came through for the sitter. If the information was very general, then so be it. If a spirit decided to pay me a visit and get a message through, then that was okay, too.

Uncle Patty

It is important to receive permission from the sitter before performing a reading. A reading should not be purposely conducted against someone's will. I received permission from a friend to do a reading, so I conducted a meditation that evening. I picked up a few bits of information, which I passed along to her the next day. Most of the items didn't mean anything to her except the name "Uncle Robby." She just chuckled and said she had an Uncle who mentioned how he felt like "the odd man out" because all of his brothers (and perhaps other relatives) had names that ended in "y" or "ie," making them all Uncle Bobbies, Uncle Billys and so on. But his name, Patrick, wasn't conducive to this ending. I found it interesting that I had picked that up, and suggested that I try another meditation. She told me that Uncle Pat had died from a drug overdose. I quickly stopped her and told her not to tell me any more. I didn't want to influence the reading by having more information. This could have caused my own analytical mind-chatter to fabricate information based on what I was told.

That night, I meditated and invited Uncle Patrick to pay me a visit, provided he was willing and met the criteria of my guides and protectors. I was a bit concerned because he had died of a drug overdose, suggesting he may have been involved in corrupt activities. I didn't want to open myself to a negative energy for whatever harm they might intend. I trusted my guides and protectors, and settled into a deep meditation. During my information collection, I received a vision of an ambulance and later heard someone yelling the word "oxygen" at me. The yelling seemed off in the distance, the way you might hear someone yelling from down the street. It was clearly audible, but distant. There was no doubt I heard someone putting power into their voice to bridge the gap from their dimension to ours.

Later in the meditation, I saw an image of a woman I knew whose name was Patty. Patty was walking toward me, her arms folded across her chest, with the serious, authoritative expression of a grade school teacher facing an unruly student. I was looking up at her as if

I was that student, seated at my third grade desk. When she reached me, she looked down and said, in a stern voice, "This is the way it should have been!" I started to laugh when I sensed that Uncle Pat was telling me he should have been called Uncle Patty.

Spirits definitely have a sense of humor and their personality is generally much like it was while they were on Earth.

The next day, I passed the information along to my friend and said that it seemed to make sense that I saw an ambulance, since Pat died of an overdose and probably was in an ambulance. I figured my analytical mind had fabricated that information from the fact that he died of an overdose. "No" she said, "He was asthmatic and spent a lot of time in ambulances." I then told her that would explain why I heard him say "oxygen."

Thanks for stopping by, Uncle Patty.

Andy's Cap

Another reading for a friend went like this. I received an image of Andy Capp, the cartoon character, and sensed a connection to either his character in general or to his cap, which is traditionally recognized as a train conductor's hat. During the entire meditation, I felt as if the right side of my face was lightly burning and tingling, all the way over to my ear. I sensed there was someone who had suffered facial damage such as burns or bruises. When I passed this along to my friend, she wasn't sure, so she discussed it with her mother, who confirmed that she had an uncle who died before she was born. He worked for the railroad and was killed by a train. The right side of his face was crushed in the accident.

Spirits did visit and deliver images, thoughts, and feelings that I could pass along to the sitter. I couldn't always feel their energy or presence in the room as some psychics can, but I could tell when they were connected with me because my visions, thoughts and feelings would come through more quickly and then stop. Their energy is limited, so they could only be connected with me for a short time. They probably remained close until a window of opportunity opened, allowing them to get through. And knowing that my vibration/connection was probably not that highly developed, they had to expend more energy to get through. I appreciate their effort and hope the sitters did, too, because they come to us out of love for us, to give us hope and a reason to believe in what lies ahead.

We all possess this innate psychic ability that simply needs to be awakened if we so choose. I'm not unique or special. I just took the time to develop these abilities and discover a little truth along the way. And, like any skill that requires practice to remain proficient, it will diminish when not used, as I have found due to a lack of practice.

I discovered that I required a fairly significant time commitment to maintain my psychic abilities. Other priorities and commitments emerged, such as my career, spiritual studies, and trying to get back into a regular family life, which pulled me away from performing readings and regular meditation. The decision was easy because my capabilities were weak, at best. I couldn't bring forth enough information to cause a skeptic to question his skepticism, and a 50 percent "hit" accuracy wouldn't impress an intermediate level psychic. At least for now my energy was best focused elsewhere. The one mistake I did make was stopping regular meditations as they are very therapeutic.

Chapter 10

Another Serious Wake-Up Call

Up to this point, I have been highlighting my developing relationship with "The Moms" and my budding psychic skills. But while this part of the story was unfolding another path was "under construction" as well.

When I first began meditating, one of my objectives was to lower my blood pressure. I used visualizations and soft music to eliminate negative energy, negative emotion and tension from my body. By relaxing in my own special place, created in my mind, I could unwind, think, pray and ask a question or two. Overall, it was very relaxing and did reduce my blood pressure.

On occasion, an image or thought popped into my conscious awareness that eventually came true. Most of these things were of no consequence when they occurred. I had developed a limited expectation of what could happen while meditating.

While I was meditating one evening, however, my expectations were far exceeded. I had no idea that what was about to happen could actually happen during meditation. After completing my usual relaxation techniques, I simply remained quiet, trying not to focus on anything in particular. All of a sudden, I saw Jesus coming toward me in my mind's eye! It was very vivid and it was very him! Unfortunately, I was so startled that it scared the be-Jesus out of me. I knew it was Jesus but what did he want with me? Sure, I now believed in God, but I wasn't religious and I wasn't calling on Jesus for assistance of any kind. Why would he come to me? On one hand, I was honored that he came to tell me something; on the other, I was upset that I had become so startled that I ejected out of the meditation. I had ruined the chance for Jesus to get a message through.

The rest of the evening, I was dizzy. The kind of dizzy that makes you put your foot on the floor to keep the bed from spinning. The kind of dizzy you get from too much alcohol but without the double vision and the drunken effects. Since I told God and Company that I was forever indebted to them for bringing my faith back, I would do whatever God wanted me to. "Where do we go from here and what do we want to accomplish?" I asked. I sure was happy to know that Jesus thought enough of me to pay a visit. Now I needed to figure out what his message and intent was.

A few weeks later, Janice and I went to her sister's house for a birthday party of one of the grandchildren. Word was starting to spread about my reported encounters with the spirit of Jeanne. Penny and Cathy obviously were discussing my story with other family members, who were becoming uneasy about all of it, including their attitudes toward me.

At the party, the mood towards me was undoubtedly distant. No one wanted to strike up a conversation with me and inadvertently wind up in a spiritual discussion about Mom. I was very frustrated; I had such a heartwarming story to tell involving their mother that I couldn't understand why they wouldn't be delighted to hear it.

We left late in the evening. Alex was tired and fell asleep soon after we began our fifty-minute trip home. Janice was tired as well and just sat peacefully. In the darkness of the nearly-barren highway, I quietly reflected upon the evening. I agonized over how it was such a shame to have been brought such great understanding of the other dimension and its relationship with ours, and no one in the family wanted any part of discussing "the dead." I remember thinking, *God, I really appreciate all that you've done for me, and you know I'm not the type of person to keep good news to myself, but nobody wants to hear it.* Then I pleaded with God with an elevated internal voice, *What am I supposed to do with this message? What is it that you want me to do?*

About thirty seconds later, a sport utility vehicle (SUV) drove by in the left lane. The SUV had a vanity tag which read GODS SON on it! There are probably still smudge marks on my driver's side window from where I pressed my face to the glass to make sure I was reading it correctly. Blown away by the tag, I must have taken my foot off the gas, so I hurried to catch up again and re-read the license plate, to make sure I had read it correctly. I told Janice what I had been thinking, and then the tag went by. I made sure she saw the tag, to confirm I was not seeing things. She confirmed the tag.

So, just a few weeks earlier, Jesus approached me in a meditation and now here was a tag referring to him, at the exact moment I asked for an answer. Something was brewing!

Later, I had an unusual vision while meditating. I had not yet worked out a deal with my spirit guides or God to communicate with me in unique ways while I meditated, but of course, they already knew to do this. Since it is difficult to distinguish between your own thoughts (mind-chatter) and a thought from spirit, there are several ways to determine if the thoughts you are receiving are from spirit:

- You receive the answer before the question is completed.
- The answer is quick, clear, and stated with perfect or what might be called elegant, proper, old-style English.
- The image is symbolic or metaphorical and contains the answer.

God and Company knew this, of course, so they delivered messages to me symbolically whenever possible. In later meditations, I asked for creative answers so that I could be assured they were real and not from my own subconscious creation.

The unusual vision I had was of an outstretched arm pointing toward me but over my head. There was no body, just an arm. I remember thinking, *What are you pointing at?* because I sensed that I needed to know. I changed my vantage point to see what the arm was pointing at. My vision shifted to behind the arm so that I could see the object of interest. It was the sun. As soon as I recognized the light was the sun, I sensed that this message was about me. Then I heard the words, "It is again time for another one." I immediately began trying to figure it out. I knew this message was for me and it wasn't something my subconscious created. It was too ingenious. My mind raced with concern, *Am I destined to be like Jesus, in regards to having a message to deliver that's difficult for many to accept? A message that could ultimately encounter the rejection and ridicule of many modern-day Pharisees and Sadducees with closed minds, forged by their own religious doctrine, egos, and upbringing, that refuses to yield or consider another perspective. I can accept differing opinions because I believe "there are many rivers leading to the sea," but many religions feel there is only one way...theirs! And some are convinced and adamant about their beliefs, to the point they are willing to attack any "heathens" they encounter, in an attempt to convert or discredit the non-believer.* If I was to continue this path I had to mentally prepare myself for what might lay ahead.

Obviously, I knew that I wasn't another messiah, but this was a powerful vision and message that had me perplexed. Perhaps it meant I was destined to be another "bringer of the light:" a messenger for those searching for the truth with an open mind. I had encountered many people that fulfilled this role; perhaps I was meant to be another. Even if what I was learning, and preparing to write, wasn't 100 percent accurate, its fundamental principles centered around love, *with harm to no one.*

Why Me?

I was definitely starting to question my destiny now; why was all of this stuff happening to me, and around me? After all, ADC's (After Death Communications) are usually to help a grieving person heal from the loss of their loved one, but I hadn't been grieving. My mother died thirty-six years ago, before I even knew her or could remember much about her. When I became aware of her spirit presence, I wasn't grieving at all.

Then my mother and mother-in-law teamed up. Both revealed their presence and did wonderful things for us. Now that I had forgiven my mother (which I believe was necessary as part of my healing and spiritual development) and I knew she was near, why did the communications continue to come, singularly from her and jointly from "The Mom's"? ADC's usually don't continue this long. The song *All the Way,* suggested that she would be with me until my physical death, showing me the way. This was comforting to know. But the communication had shifted from a "Hello, we are here for you" to "Now that we have awakened you, we will turn you over to a higher authority." I did promise I would do anything that God

"Imagine That"   A Spiritual Awakening

wanted me to do, to spread good news and good will. But what did God want me to do?

Easy Does It

My experiences to date had taught me that God could certainly get a message to me if He wanted to. Of course, I wondered why an angel (or someone else) didn't just materialize before me and tell me what I was supposed to do. I realize now that everything happens in its proper time and way. For someone to simply materialize before me with a message might have altered the path of discovery that I needed to walk. An angel with a direct message might have violated the law of "free will"...although an agenda, with a suggested list of books and audio programs to study, sure would have been time saving and appreciated!

We choose what we want to become because of "free will." God then provides the resources along the path to meet our needs and develop our talents. If we wander off course, resources and assistance might be in short supply, gently nudging us back on course toward our greater, perhaps yet undiscovered, strengths. As in my case, this path might include a lot of training through experience.

I do believe, however, that there are limitations to what we should choose. For example, it wouldn't be prudent to choose professional basketball if you are four-foot-two inches tall. We all have certain talents and gifts that are waiting to be awakened and developed. We need to discover them. Unfortunately, this can take a lifetime. And herein lay the challenge facing me at the time; what were my talents and what might be my destiny? Notice I didn't say "What is my destiny?" but rather "What might be my destiny?" It was easy to see that I didn't have to do anything at all. No one was holding a gun to my head. I wanted to do something out of sheer desire. So I continued to look for the signs and guidance.

Another Serious Wake-Up Call

Every now and then, I reviewed my meditation notes and other notes from the day-to-day occurrences that I thought were associated with this path. I made notes while meditating because I was so "deep" in the meditation, right on the edge of sleep, I didn't always recall everything that I had experienced. I would raise my awareness just a little, jot down a note on a pad in my lap, with my eyes closed, and then continue. In an early meditation, I thought I heard Uncle Dutch's voice say, "Stick with it. People are counting on you." So here was another clue, telling me that I needed to persevere. I continued to meditate frequently and asked for signs and clues. My experience was teaching me to be patient. God doesn't always answer immediately. The answer has to be put into motion, and it could take some time to get the right players into alignment.

I wanted to deliver this message to as many people as possible, and had envisioned conducting lectures on my experiences. Since Jesus had paid me a visit once, I wanted to connect with him again, to see if he had a specific message. Before starting my meditations, I would ask Jesus to attempt to get a message through, if he could. My specific question was: how should I deliver this message about life after death? One evening, while meditating, I got a glimpse of Jesus, and I thought I heard him say, "One soul at a time," but I wasn't sure.

A couple of days later, I was listening to an audio program entitled *Thirsting for God,* by Mother Theresa. Mother was telling an audience that after her *Mission of Charities* organization had grown, she was still helping the poor and "dying destitutes" in the streets daily. A government official asked her why she wasn't trying to help the poor on a larger scale, such as by influencing governments to assist. Mother explained to the official that when she prayed to

Jesus about how to minister to these folks, Jesus told her "One soul at a time."

When I heard this, I was once again astonished. I concluded that I had heard Jesus correctly, and that "One soul at a time" was my mission, at least for the time being. I still had much to learn, and it was appropriate *not* to "tell the world" just yet. My schooling was just beginning.

I still asked God and Company to send individuals who needed to hear what I had to say. From time to time, this happened, but it happened more from the angle of explaining life after death to doubters, which was within my understanding.

Chapter 11

The Bumper Stickers

After Christmas, Alex brought home a DVD movie that surprised me. His father gave him the movie *Jesus of Nazareth,* which was filmed in the '70s. This was peculiar because Alex's father didn't strike me as being very religious. Perhaps I misjudged him but he didn't seem the type to buy his son a movie about Jesus rather than hunting equipment. I wouldn't have blinked an eye if it had been a DVD about turkey hunting. His dad loved to hunt, and Alex was getting old enough to partake in the sport, so the boy needed some gear. I understood this from my own "bass fever" mentality of wanting him to have all the necessary fishing equipment, so that he had his own and didn't need to borrow mine. And why would Alex bring the DVD to our house and not watch it with his dad, who bought it for him in the first place? I didn't see it in the '70s because it didn't interest me then.

The two families have joint custody of Alex, meaning he spends an equal amount of time in each household on a week-here, week-there basis. Arrangements like this are usually very challenging, but this one works well because of the cooperation and genuine concern for his wellbeing from both homes.

Alex just as easily could have kept the DVD at his dad's house, but something prompted him to bring it to ours. That DVD was meant as a basic starting point and another clue to inspire and motivate the next leg of my journey.

It is also interesting to note that a message or sign can be delivered by anyone, regardless of their religious or spiritual beliefs or background. It was clear once again that if God wanted to get a message through using someone else or several people, then so be it.

Even though I attended Catholic school for twelve years, I couldn't remember much about the life of Jesus, other than the big stories such as feeding the multitudes, turning water into wine at the wedding in Cana, walking on water, the healings, and his death and resurrection.

As my studies helped dust off the cobwebs in my mind, I recalled more of what I had once learned in school and in church. In addition, I began to uncover more information about Jesus, through the other books I was reading. These studies suggested that Jesus was an enlightened master and not God Incarnate. This didn't bother me much because my Catholic upbringing had taught that Jesus was the "Son of God" and not God Incarnate. At least, this was my understanding of the relationship, whether accurate or not. The nuns would tell my parents that I asked some tough questions about Jesus during religion class. I honestly don't remember what they were. This was another clue that I didn't accept doctrine just because an authority figure in a classroom declared it as truth.

I regarded Jesus as a special person sent by God to deliver an important message—an ambassador for God with "power of

The Bumper Stickers

attorney," so to speak, able to back his words with miracles to prove his point and purpose.

I was okay with this concept, but Janice was not. She kept telling me that if I didn't accept Jesus as my Lord and Savior, I couldn't be saved. I valued her words then, as I still do today, because I know that she is one of those people who can be inspired by spirit to deliver a message to me. On a number of occasions, she had been compelled to read passages or quotes from a book, which just happened to be an answer or clue for which I'd been searching. I had witnessed this enough to realize that her spirituality had strengthened her "connection" to receive and act upon inspiration. This allowed her to deliver messages when I needed them. As a result, I listened to her intently, while trying to figure out if God was working through her.

I wasn't sure about the source of Janice's convictions, and thought it best to give the matter some consideration by reading the bible, at least in part, because she was so adamant and strong in her faith. Add to that the vision of Jesus during meditation, along with the timely sighting of the GODS SON license plate and the uncanny delivery of the movie *Jesus of Nazareth,* and I was certain that I needed to keep an open mind.

It was about this time that I first recognized another clue that had been placed in my path. Sometimes things are so "conspicuous" in our lives that they become "inconspicuous." We forget we have them and no longer notice them, I guess. The only object that I possessed (and still do) that belonged to my mother was a ceramic figurine of Jesus praying against a boulder in the Garden of Gesthamany. I've had it since after her death. Why this was the only keepsake I was ever given, I don't know, but because it *is* the only item I have, it magnifies its importance. And perhaps this, too, was Divinely orchestrated,

"Imagine That" A Spiritual Awakening

providing me with another convincing reason to continue studying the life of Jesus.

I began reading the Gospel of Matthew and was incredibly touched by the teachings of Jesus and the simple purity and kindness of his heart. More than once, I wept with Jesus at his struggle to spread his message. The words, simple and pure, such as "Do unto others as you would do unto yourself," touched me deeply. In the bible commentary book that I read, the verses were printed first; followed by the author's explanation of the verse as he understood them. Bible verses are sometimes hard to understand, which may explain why many of us never try to read it. It's easier to let someone else do the work for us. Therefore, we rely on our Sunday sermons to teach us the way, the truth and the life. We put our trust in parents, priests, pastors, and pulpits to interpret the bible accurately and deliver us guidance.

Much to my own amazement, after completing the Gospel of Matthew I concluded that Jesus was, in fact, God Incarnate. There was a ton of evidence, in all of the miracles and exorcisms, that he had the power of God. I didn't know that Jesus had performed so many healings and exorcisms (nearly 3300). And the demons even knew who he was and were frightened of him. Some things still didn't make sense to me, but I just continued to ask God for clarification, and I knew He would deliver the answers in time.

For now, I was nearly certain that Jesus was God Incarnate, and I was comfortable with that new belief. I still felt that I needed to continue studying the life of Jesus, because I had a few unanswered questions that bothered me.

I felt a huge void because none of these sources (especially the bible) gave a detailed chronological account of Jesus' life. It was fragmented and didn't explain the culture of the time. It was very difficult to understand some of Jesus' teachings without understanding the Jewish customs and culture of that era. A much greater understanding could be gained by learning some of the history of the area and the religious differences between the various people of the time. Some of my studies had introduced these things but the surface was barely scratched. I asked Jesus for better guidance, a better book or video. I wanted the truth, just the truth, so help me God. My mind was wide open and hungry, but how would I know if I was getting the truth and not a message from Satan?

I devised a method to prepare for messages and judge the information or lessons I was being taught, as follows:

One of the first things I learned when my sensitive psychic side began to awaken was to protect myself from negative entities and the dark side. By praying for protection and visualizing being protected by God's Divine Light of Love and Protection, I would remain safe. I would also ask Saint Michael to surround and protect me with the Archangels. I have never had a bad experience while meditating, whereas I have heard of others who have. The protection really worked, and I used it all the time, even for routine prayer.

I incorporated a "righteousness" test: if what I learned was of a pure nature and would not cause harm to anyone then, at a minimum, it could be a concept worth considering. When the Pharisees saw Jesus casting out demons, they tried to charge Jesus with using the power of Beelzebub, the prince of the devils, to accomplish this. Jesus told them that if Satan was casting out Satan, then his house was divided against itself and would soon destroy itself. I would employ this same notion to evaluate what I had learned. If I put into practice or taught what I learned, would it strengthen Satan's house or destroy it? Naturally, I wanted to destroy his house and strengthen God's house.

- If the concept had a logical fit into the process of creation or explained reasons for life, then it also had a chance.
- If my personal experience clarified the concept, then it definitely had value, especially if it was a direct answer to a question that I asked God.
- If I was led to read a book, listen to an audio program or watch a video, then it was much more powerful if I could corroborate the concept/idea with a separate source. Corroborated information from separate sources, perhaps from different eras, became quite convincing.
- If the source of the information or supporting evidence was someone who was not paid to tell their story or share their knowledge, then I regarded the information as more compelling. In other words, these folks willfully shared information when they didn't have to. If the information or experience was shared at the risk of ridicule, then I considered it even more compelling. Most people avoid condemnation, so to report something that might invite it suggested a strong conviction.

The final check was the gut check. This was a tough one because lifelong beliefs can interfere with our intuition and sixth sense, which come from spirit. In many cases, it took quite some time to internalize what I had learned. But once I found the logic and how the concept fit into the process of life and creation, I was content with my conclusion.

God knew that I wanted the truth. He also knew that I was going to test things to be sure that I wasn't being fooled. I didn't like being a sucker or being gullible. I just wanted the truth.

The Challenge Reciprocal

I was now comfortable with the concept that Jesus was God Incarnate. Embracing Christianity's fundamental principle of accepting Jesus Christ as my Lord and Savior was accomplished. A sense of calm had entered my life. I was quietly happy, with an air of satisfaction and contentment that I had reached the same conclusion that millions of Christians had. Now I belonged somewhere; I could be categorized and binned with millions of other like-minded worshipers; these were people with whom I could share my beliefs, and who could share their beliefs with me. I felt good about it.

I wasn't convinced, though, that following Jesus was the only way to Heaven. There were still too many people who had never heard of Jesus. It didn't seem logical that they could be held accountable for not knowing the teachings of Jesus, when global communication still didn't reach everyone. How could it be their fault? It couldn't be, in my mind. God had taken the time to get through to me. God did not forsake me when He could easily have let me continue driving this life right off the cliff and straight into Hell since, after all, I had turned from Him. If He was willing to rescue me, an atheist with an axe to grind against God, then why would He turn His back on innocent children who would have loved Him from the start, if they had only known of Him? There had to be other spiritual teachers sent by God to deliver a similar message, for those other cultures that Jesus' word wouldn't reach for centuries, if ever. I knew that this belief wasn't in line with some Christian doctrine, but I didn't consider this minor difference of opinion enough to preclude my acceptance in a Christian church or faith.

I was driving to work, one beautiful sunny afternoon in May, when God delivered a unique message. I was temporarily assigned to the evening shift, so I was on the road at about two o'clock in the afternoon. At that time of day, and on this stretch of highway, vehicles were few and far between. The road gently wanders through Amish countryside with many farms along the way. The shoulder is quite wide, to allow the horse-drawn buggies to trot along, with plenty of room for passing vehicles. Since the farm houses are back off the main road, the area is wide open with fields of tobacco, corn, soybean and pasture. It is a pleasant, low-stress drive.

Along the way, I managed to catch up to a car traveling slower than I was. As I got closer, I noticed there was a bumper sticker in the back window of the car. I thought it odd that the bumper sticker was in the back window and not on the bumper. It's not unusual to see stickers in the back window of a car but I hadn't seen too many bumper stickers in the back window. Here is what the bumper sticker said:

Have You Been Saved? If Not, Why Not?

I had heard the phrase "Have you been saved?" a thousand times, so I didn't find the phrase unusual, but the location was. I backed off a little and considered the question for a moment as I thought about it out loud:

"Well, I think I have been saved, so to speak, because Jesus is a huge part of my life and I do accept his teachings as something to strive towards. I love Jesus and have a phenomenal respect for his purpose and the suffering he endured to complete his mission.

Yes, I do accept Jesus as my Lord and Savior. So, yes, I do believe I am saved."

I continued cruising along, smiling rather smugly, content with my answer to the question. Shortly thereafter, I decided to pass this

The Bumper Stickers

slower-moving car and continue on my way. About a half mile farther ahead of the car I had just passed, I caught up to another car. The two cars were not within sight of one another and did not appear to be traveling together, but this car had a bumper sticker in exactly the same place on the back window.

I remember chuckling as I approached the car, knowing that I needed to get close enough to read the bumper sticker. I knew there was a message for me but I didn't know what to expect. Here is what the bumper sticker said:

> You'd Better Be Right!

I was shocked and confused. All I could think was, *What does it mean?* and, *What am I doing wrong that I'm not saved? Obviously, I must be missing something! But what?* This really upset and disturbed me. I was being challenged. And how appropriate, and yet ironic, that I should be challenged after challenging God.

The one thing I could be sure of was that God and Company would ultimately provide an answer. Now that they had my full attention, I would be sure to recognize it when it arrived.

Being impatient, however, I wanted an answer right away. The weeks it took to get the answer wore on my nerves.

I had recently listened to audio programs by Joan Borysenko and Mother Theresa. Listening to Mother Theresa made me realize what a wonderful, caring and kind person she was. I could feel the love in her gentle voice.

Mother taught simple things that were easy to remember. Of all the tapes, books and videos I had studied, I can still easily remember her simple teachings:

- Be all for Jesus (embrace Jesus' teachings and do everything you do for Jesus)
- Do something beautiful for God (whatever it is you do, put love into it)
- Give until it hurts (give to the needy to the point where it causes you to sacrifice something, like dining out)

These simple phrases were very easy for me to understand and remember. I was deeply moved by Mother's devotion to caring for the sick and needy. I began to question what my role in missionary work should be.

Maybe I should quit my job and become a missionary so that I could serve God in a better way? But that didn't seem right for me, and Mother even mentioned that it was very difficult work. Even some of the most well-intentioned nuns couldn't tolerate the harsh conditions of some impoverished countries for long. I wasn't the volunteering type, especially in the horrific conditions Mother worked through. I had to concede that missionary life wasn't for me. Still, I had to help out somehow.

Jesus didn't own a thing, and Mother didn't have much either. Jesus told some to give everything they owned to the poor and follow him. Was this what I was supposed to do? That didn't feel right for me, either. I was a recovering materialist, and the idea of selling or, worse yet, giving away everything I had worked so hard for only invoked sadness and depression.

I liked my "stuff" and enjoyed the things I could do with it, like going fishing. I enjoyed the outdoors a great deal. To keep me away from the water would eliminate one of my reasons for living. Yes, the house was big, but I liked a lot of space to help me feel unrestricted and unconfined. The niceties of the house helped comfort a long day at the office. The beauty of the house helped soothe the pain and stress of work, by reminding me that my efforts were not in vain.

I wanted to do the right thing, but to live a life of poverty, as Jesus or Mother had done, just wasn't me. I would be miserable. There had to be another way, I hoped. I theorized that many religious figures and leaders lived very comfortably, while fully understanding that Jesus said it "was easier for a camel to fit through the eye of a needle than for a rich man to get into Heaven." If this was absolute truth, then weren't all of those well-to-do religious people going to go to Hell with the rest of us? I must have been missing something.

To compound the issue further, it seemed that if anyone knew the formula for Heaven, wouldn't it be the religious leaders? If they didn't live like paupers, then why should I? Had religions twisted the meaning of the bible to somehow elevate material wealth to an acceptable status? It just didn't make sense that we all had to live like beggars. On the other hand, I wasn't about to blindly trust religious leaders; Jesus was unambiguous in his words about needles and camels! This became a big worry bead for me. Was it okay to have nice things?

God knew that I was familiar with what the "good book" said, and my beliefs taught me that He wasn't going to accept my request for leniency when I begged, "Lighten up on the sentence, will ya, God? How was I supposed to know I needed to sell my stuff!" The passage was blatant and unmistakable.

Most people could claim that they had never read the bible or hadn't been exposed to the teachings that dictated a more pauper-like lifestyle, so they might be able to get away with it, but not me; I was doomed because I knew what the bible said and chose not to comply. It's like owning a car with power windows and door locks; once you've experienced the luxury, it's hard to go back to window cranks. We easily grow accustomed to the niceties, conveniences and luxuries of life, because they raise the ever-important "quality of life" to the point where they become our minimum expectations.

Well, at least I could come back and get it right in my next life, maybe. But I didn't want to come back if life was going to be this tough again. I'd rather get it right this time, so I didn't have to do it again.

At a deeper level, I felt that it was okay to have nice things as long as they didn't consume me and become something I worshiped. As it says in the bible, one cannot serve two masters. I didn't worship my stuff but I liked the convenience and beauty. Regardless, I continued my search for an answer.

Since the plans were already in place, Janice and I decided to do something beautiful for God, instead of giving stuff away. We wanted to beautify our yard.

The previous fall, we had done landscape work around the yard, and we were preparing to plant flowers in the new beds now that it was spring. We spent quite a bit of money on the flowers, shrubs and other landscaping supplies to complete the project. We managed to exhaust our budget and then some. We didn't have any extra money to "give until it hurts," because we were already hurting.

One night, just after crawling into bed, Janice got a little teary-eyed, so I asked her what was troubling her. Earlier in the week, she had listened to the Borysenko audio program, *The Power of the Mind to Heal*. A story Borysenko told was weighing heavily on her mind. Borysenko had traveled to a poverty-stricken country and, while walking the street of a poor village, she realized that she was probably wearing enough jewelry to feed the entire village for a month. The villagers were busy preparing the evening meals outside of their primitive homes, while children happily played in the dusty surroundings. Despite their poverty, everyone was happy. Borysenko met a village woman who recognized her as a westerner. The woman asked if it was true that western parents left their children with strangers daily while they went away to work so they could afford to live. When Borysenko confirmed this, the woman expressed pity towards westerners for having to separate from their children.

The story revealed interesting concepts about the human condition. On one hand, Borysenko's observation delivered a sobering reflection on the wealthy lifestyles in the west in comparison to this village, while a poor village woman expressed pity for the enslaved westerners. Two cultures had collided, each feeling sorry for the other, and neither seemed aware of their sacrifices. Adaptation and justification rendered both situations acceptable and tolerable, if not desirable. The poor woman was comfortable with, and had adapted to her world of lack, while westerners were comfortable with, and had adapted to their world which required them to leave their children with strangers. If hindsight is 20/20, then perception and beliefs must be nearsighted. We rarely look beyond the immediacy of our own world for a different perspective.

Janice, comfortable with her western lifestyle, focused on the world's poor. After spending a lot of money on our yard, which exhausted our cash reserves, the story tugged at her heartstrings. She was upset because we had "broken the bank" and did it in a selfish way. At the time, we'd thought we were doing something beautiful for God, and that it would make us feel good, but something was missing. Janice explained that she felt the need to help others. She relayed a story about a friend's daughter, a missionary who needed donations to pay for an upcoming mission trip to Russia. The missionaries had to generate their own donations in order to serve God around the world. I sat straight up in the bed and emphatically declared, "That's it! That's what we need to do. If I can't be a missionary, then at least I can help support one." Interestingly, a few days later, a very late heavy frost severely damaged our newly planted flowers, as if God and Company were suggesting that beautifying the yard wasn't that important after all.

I wasn't comfortable with giving money away, so this was a huge first step. I had donated money to the local fire department and my old high school, but this was different. This money was going far from home into a foreign country, with a religious message traveling with it.

I spoke with Christina, the missionary, and got the details about her organization's target audience and message. She worked with poor, deprived children, some of whom lived on the streets because they didn't have caretakers for various reasons. She shared a story of two brothers who lived on the streets of Russia after they watched their parents' execution during a war. The boys had been hardened by their experience, so it took Christina considerable time to break through with her Christian message of love and hope for the children. I was heartbroken after hearing the details. She was kind, compassionate and caring. I knew I was destined to support her.

Christina also taught me that it was okay to be a contributor because that was part of the mission's process or network. Some people do the fieldwork and some raise the money to support the field workers. "That's where I fit in," I figured, and so Janice and I made regular contributions to support Christina's work.

This made it clear to me that it *wasn't* by coincidence that I had chosen to listen to Mother Theresa's audio program. Mother taught me several things, but the most significant thing I learned was a valuable lesson about giving and sharing. Mother educated me about the harsh conditions and tough lifestyle of a missionary and the

The Bumper Stickers

dedication and commitment required to stick with it. This changed my perception of mission workers at just the right time for Christina to come into my life and receive our help when she needed it most. God has a plan, and it often makes me smile and laugh to see it Divinely orchestrated.

The message behind the bumper stickers was coming into view. God and Company were telling me that *there was more to salvation than the concept of simply accepting Jesus as my Lord and Savior.* I had to admit that my intuition felt that it couldn't be that easy. Believing that I could accept Jesus and he'd get me out of jail free was overly simplistic. A negative number, (behavior) plus a negative number, plus another negative number equals *a very negative number indeed.* The equation couldn't be filled only with negative behavior values and equal a positive experience in Heaven if the only positive value was hoping for Jesus' saving grace; that didn't add up correctly. It seemed that the equation should have more positive values than that. Perhaps Jesus was powerful enough to bail someone out, but why would he, if they really hadn't tried to be a good person? He would know the content of their heart and judge saving them accordingly, should they turn to him. At least for now, I was content to know that the equation or recipe required more than blind reliance on Jesus to save me, especially if I wasn't worthy. I had to earn it.

I had now been introduced to another significant ingredient: sharing.

I believed living a good life elevated our spiritual vibration, which equated to a higher level of Heaven in the afterlife. The completion of the recipe for salvation wasn't about the minimum criteria for salvation but, rather, about maximizing spiritual potential. I expected more ingredients to follow.

The burning question about the appropriateness of material possessions still perplexed my credit card. I now understood the need to give until it hurts; but can we have too many possessions and should we live more modestly? It wasn't long after this that I decided to read a little of the Old Testament, beginning with Genesis. Soon I reached the story of Abraham. God bestowed great wealth upon Abraham because he kept the laws of God and listened to God's instructions.

But there seemed to be a contradiction between what God did for Abraham and what Jesus taught about rich people. I then learned that the Jewish people of Jesus' time, including his disciples, believed that having wealth was a blessing from God and signified that they were pleasing in the eyes of God. The disciples also hoped they were due some great reward for following Jesus. Jesus was using shock therapy when he told his disciples it would be easier for a camel to fit through the eye of a needle than for a rich man to enter Heaven. He wanted to ensure that his disciples got the message, loud and clear. He wanted to break their mistaken notion of wealth. Jesus didn't say it was impossible, but he recognized that most of the rich Jews didn't have the character they needed to enter Heaven, because they were too caught up in their material wealth.

A short while later, I received the following e-mail list from my best friend, (and wife) Janice. The list of values was insightful in many venues of life and it shed a different light on the positive characteristics of wealth. Wealth could be put to good use. Wealth and sharing could unite, becoming "sharing wealth."

- God won't ask what kind of car you drove, but He'll ask how many people you drove who didn't have transportation.
- God won't ask the square footage of your house, but He'll ask how many people you welcomed into your home.

- God won't ask about the clothes you had in your closet, but He'll ask how many you helped to clothe.
- God won't ask about your social status; He will ask what kind of class you displayed.
- God won't ask how many material possessions you had, but He'll ask if they dictated your life.
- God won't ask what your highest salary was, but He'll ask if you compromised your character to obtain it.
- God won't ask how many promotions you received, but He'll ask how you promoted others.
- God won't ask what your job title was, but He'll ask if you performed your job to the best of your ability.
- God won't ask what you did to help yourself, but He'll ask what you did to help others.
- God won't ask how many friends you had, but He'll ask how many people there are to whom you were a friend.
- God won't ask what you did to protect your rights, but He'll ask what you did to protect the rights of others.
- God won't ask in what neighborhood you lived, but He'll ask how you treated your neighbors.

This e-mail hit home because it helped answer my question about material possession and offered a practical application of values and behaviors. It helped me recognize caring and compassion as additional ingredients for achieving salvation.

Broken Silence

After doing readings for one another with decent success, I shared my experiences with a woman named Lisa from Indiana. She explained that she'd also had similar experiences. She was very knowledgeable about the life of Jesus. After assisting her with questions pertaining to psychic development, I asked her some questions about the life of

Jesus. She went to the library, gathered information, and proceeded to send me seven consecutive e-mails loaded with information about Jesus and the culture of his time. I was thankfully astonished that she did this. I learned about the Gnostic Gospels, the Gospel of Thomas and more—material I wasn't aware existed. I expressed my gratitude.

After a few months of trading e-mails and learning from one another, Lisa decided she needed to concentrate on her spiritual path, and we agreed to stop communicating. She was borrowing a friend's computer and it was becoming a chore to answer e-mails. I couldn't agree more. I didn't type very fast, and long e-mails consumed too much time. We went our separate ways in a friendly fashion.

About a month after Lisa and I stopped communicating, Lisa broke the agreed silence and sent an unexpected e-mail. While she was walking through a bookstore that day, a book had fallen off the shelf behind her as she passed. She said she didn't bump anything; the book just fell on the floor. She immediately sensed the "strangeness" of what had happened, but also knew that things happen for a reason. She reached down to pick it up and saw that the title was *Rabbi Jesus,* and immediately she intuitively knew it was meant for me. She knew that I called my Master Spirit Guide "Rabbi," and that Jesus was becoming a very important figure and role model in my life. She also knew that I was wondering if Jesus was my Master Spirit Guide, since I had learned that he was sometimes referred to as a Rabbi in his era.

I didn't consider it significant that she associated the book to me but I did find it significant that the book fell off the shelf after she passed by. I remembered seeing this book at the store before I had my encounters with Jesus. I didn't purchase it because I wasn't studying Jesus at the time. Now, however, I was certain that I was supposed to read it. I couldn't get it fast enough. I didn't know who wrote the book or what it would say, but I knew it was meant for me.

Before I even finished the introduction, I knew the book was just what I had been asking for, to help me understand the life of Jesus. The author, Bruce Chilton, an Anglican priest and Professor of Religion, explained Jesus within the context of his cultural time. He explained the various cultures, rituals, holidays and beliefs. I hadn't realized all of the different cultures that existed during the period. In my naïve mind, I had thought that everyone was Jewish, Roman or Greek. But there were many different denominations of Jews and, much like today, the different groups didn't get along, so they chose to separate themselves from one another.

Chilton characterized Jesus as a man who tapped into the power of God through his meditative skills, a disciple of John the Baptist who rose to even greater heights than John. I found this a little unsettling because I had convinced myself that Jesus was God Incarnate, and now this was being challenged.

The book made some very good points that caused me to seriously question my belief that Jesus was God Incarnate. The story of Jesus and the Gentile (Syro-Phoenician) woman who asked for the exorcism of an unclean spirit from her daughter offered a prime example. Jesus compared her to a dog (Mark 7:24-28). It struck me as odd that God Incarnate would call another human a dog, and yet the biblical words are very clear and don't require interpretation. He called her a dog!

In Jesus' ministry, he first sought to teach the Jewish people as if the gentile population wasn't worthy. But after the Jews repeatedly rejected him, he took his message to the gentiles. I didn't find it appropriate that God Incarnate would initially consider discriminating against certain cultures in his message. I'm certain that God considers all to be worthy of His word.

Other things that Jesus was quoted as saying didn't make sense to me, either. I figured that either Jesus didn't say these things or that he characterized them through his beliefs as a Galilean Jew. In other words, one sect of Jews didn't always agree with the teachings of another, which built tension and dislike between them.

Jesus may also have been influenced by the Essenes of Qumran in his teachings. The Essenes moved away from mainstream Judaism and settled in a little village away from the influence of the Jewish beliefs of the city, because they didn't agree with them. They believed that all goods were community property. This influence may very well explain why material possessions and social status were the source of much criticism by Jesus.

And why didn't Jesus write down his teachings in his own words? Having the Sermon on the Mount written by Jesus would have been awesome. This would have eliminated improper interpretations, memory lapses or hearsay influences that probably affected the Gospel writers. Surely this would have eliminated or at least reduced the tremendous amount of controversy regarding the New Testament and its authors and accuracy. It wasn't unusual for Jesus to encounter difficulty getting his disciples to understand him, so to assume they fully understood him was a stretch. He covered a great deal of material in the Sermon on the Mount alone, and I find it difficult to believe that a disciple could accurately scribe it twenty, thirty or more years later. It seems to me that if God incarnated as Jesus, then He would at least have taught Jesus to write so that he could accurately record exactly what He wanted to teach, thus eliminating the potential for these errors.

Gathering these data points caused a reversal in my beliefs, causing me to conclude (once again) that Jesus was as I originally thought: an enlightened master who could channel the power of God.

But through his "humanness," he was capable of allowing his cultural beliefs to influence his concern for, and verbal treatment of, certain other cultures. Fortunately, these encounters remained intact in the bible, providing evidence of Jesus' true identity as a remarkably spiritually advanced human.

Through the contents of Chilton's book, I also learned that others throughout history, such as the Old Testament prophets Elijah and Elisha, had performed miracles. Elijah also raised the dead, thus removing that distinction from Jesus alone. This additional research strengthened my belief that Jesus was in fact an enlightened master since he wasn't the first, or only one, to work miracles.

Further evidence to convince me that Jesus wasn't claiming to be God Incarnate is contained in the last sentence from John, verse 14:28, "I go unto the Father; for my Father is greater than I." This communicated to me that Jesus recognized a separation between God the Father and himself. Jesus also said, "Verily, verily I say unto you, he that believeth on me, the works that I do shall he do also; and greater works than these shall he do; because I go unto my Father." (John 14:12 KJV) Jesus appeared to be claiming that believing the same things that he taught could manifest the same powers through the believer. The operative word here is "believeth *on* me," rather than "believeth *in* me," pointing to his teachings and not his personal being.

I couldn't find evidence that Jesus claimed to be God but rather found evidence that indicated he *didn't* claim to be God Incarnate.

For a short while, I had embraced the teaching that Jesus was in fact God Incarnate, but now I had reversed my conclusion. What this *did* teach me was how easy it is to draw the conclusion that Jesus was God Incarnate. My experience with others taught me that we all want to be right about what we believe, and most of us want to believe in something. Furthermore, we like to associate ourselves with objects or deities that possess power. And naturally we want to be associated with the most powerful, especially if we don't possess a great deal of individual power. If we can't be powerful personally then at least we can associate with someone who is. Another way to view this is: everyone wants a hero. And all the better if the hero is the underdog, such as Jesus was. His simple impoverished life is easy for many to relate to in this world of constant oppression. Many can relate to his struggles and find solace in the belief that his triumph can be ours.

It became easy to see how and why Jesus' actions and words had been misjudged, misinterpreted and misunderstood, thus transforming him into a god. Religion had to create a more powerful deity in order to attract parishioners. If deities could be packaged and sold at the local grocery store, we might find an entire aisle, the deity produce aisle, dedicated to the many gods identified throughout history. The Jesus package would undoubtedly be very appealing, not only because he was a god that raised himself from the dead, but because the package comes with a free gift, the gift of salvation for accepting Jesus as Lord and Savior. And to date, marketing has been very successful.

It may seem that I am downplaying or making fun of Jesus' ministry, but on the contrary, quite the opposite is true. What Jesus accomplished in his life is far more impressive if you consider that he was just a man. For God to heal the sick, raise the dead, or calm the sea is all in a day's work for God, so to speak. That's a routine part of God's job description. But for a mere mortal man, such as Jesus, to develop these skills is a phenomenal achievement, indeed.

Kabbalah

Another important item in Chilton's book was the notion that Jesus was an accomplished disciple of the teachings, practices and wisdom of Kabbalah. I had recently seen an advertisement for an audio program about Kabbalah, which was something I had never heard of before. The advertisement talked about the ancient wisdom and power of Kabbalah, which contained the secret to bringing great fulfillment into your life. I studied the literature but decided not to purchase it at that time, but now I was wondering if I was supposed to study this, also.

I took the hint and ordered *The Power of Kabbalah* by Michael Moskowitz. Again, I found myself listening to material that contained unique insights that helped me piece together an understanding of God and the universe. I'll try to summarize the teachings of Kabbalah, describing our beginning and relationship with God in a simplified way.

In the beginning, there was God and one "vessel," which received all of the caring and gifts from God. The vessel contained all beings, and all of these beings had everything they could ever want, because God gave them everything. The beings in the vessel were very happy with their lives and their abundance, and they wanted to share their abundance and good fortune with others, but there was no one who needed anything. All one had to do was think about what they wanted and God made it happen. And, believe it or not, we became tired of the pampering and wanted to be like God, in the respect that we wanted to be able to give and share with others. So we asked God if He could create a way for us to experience this.

Naturally, God wanted us to get what we wanted, so He devised a plan and presented it to us. We liked the plan, so God shattered the vessel (us) into the trillions and trillions of people and pieces of the universe. So the Big Bang Theory was right after all. God created the Earth, the Heavens, the stars, and so on, and devised an environment that would challenge our godlike characteristics. He put upon the Earth a negative force to oppose us, which was called Satan (pronounced Sŭ-tăn).

This negative force was not a fork-tailed entity similar to what we traditionally visualize as the devil; rather, it was the second law of thermodynamics. Here's where it can get technical; the second law of thermodynamics is also called "Entropy," which refers to the natural tendency for systems or things, left to themselves (unattended), to fall apart or experience chaos. Everything will eventually rust, corrode or rot. Another example: leave a two-year-old unattended for long and you will have chaos. We also refer to this law as Murphy's Law. So almost everything we encounter in life is meant to challenge us, through these chaotic measures. We got what we asked for, and we've been crying ever since. At this very moment, nearly everything around us and almost everything we own is slowly rusting, rotting, decomposing or falling apart. The best we can do is tend to these things and perform what's referred to as "preventive maintenance" to slow the process.

When we were just a happy little vessel, we were only programmed to receive, because we had no one to give to. So when we incarnate here on Earth, our natural desire is to continue receiving rather than to give. We can see this reflected throughout our society in the form of greed. Unfortunately, we can also see this in many of our children; they can never get enough, it seems.

Our mission then is to change the paradigm and begin giving and sharing, in order to bring the gifts of God upon us. In addition, we should be compassionate, loving and caring, and we should avoid or defuse negative situations.

I had already been learning some of these things, but God wanted me to hear it from several sources, to ensure I received the message

The Bumper Stickers

enough times to eliminate any doubt. A corroborated message helps to confirm its validity.

Kabbalah contained excellent wisdom and interesting teachings, but at this point in my development I wasn't ready to fully embrace such dramatic new revelations as the vessel theory. My horizons were expanding rapidly and I wasn't prepared to hang my hat solely on the teachings of Kabbalah and stop my continued search for truth. Fundamentally speaking, Kabbalah offered unique insights that were correct in theory and as metaphors for truth.

Kabbalah also claimed that the Israelites parted the Red Sea using a collective consciousness (or will), led by a man named Nachson who walked into the water up to his nose to prove his determination and conviction that the Israelites could part the sea. This was definitely new to me. I had always believed that God parted the Red Sea for the Israelites, but Kabbalah disputes this. Exodus does include a verse where God basically said to Moses, "Why are you crying to me, stretch out your hand and part the sea yourself!" (Ex.14:15 KJV). However, several verses later the bible says that God parted the sea, using a strong east wind. The Zohar, which is a Jewish Kabbalistic text, gives all the credit to Nachson and the Israelites for their incredible will power.

A Kabbalah teaching that confused me was the belief that the more positive, righteous and spiritual one becomes, the more chaos enters into the person's life to challenge them. This seemed counterproductive and hardly a reward for spiritual development; it seemed to me that it might only serve as negative reinforcement for continued spiritual commitment. I theorized that, once I had achieved this lifelong dream of fulfillment, chaotic circumstances would eliminate all of it. It sounded like the story of Job from the Old Testament: attain it only to lose it, a very difficult test indeed.

One morning, on the way to work, I was re-listening to the tapes in an effort to make sure I had some of the concepts straight, and to clear up some confusion. I came across a portion of the tape that still didn't make sense, the second time through. I turned off the tape temporarily, the better to have a heart-to-heart talk with God. I said, "This is very interesting material but some of it doesn't make sense to me. I thought that this was something You wanted me to study, but now I'm not sure. If You don't want me to continue studying this material, please let me know. I just don't want to make a wrong turn."

When I re-started the tape, the first words out of the speakers were "you already have." I was dumbfounded. I continued to listen to the tapes anyway, wondering if that was just a coincidence or if it was a real message. Even I lapsed into weak moments of disbelief at such strong coincidences. I had to keep telling myself, "There are no coincidences!" but I couldn't figure out why I was led to get this audio program if I *wasn't* supposed to embrace its teachings.

At the time, I didn't realize that studying Kabbalah was going to prepare me for future training. God was simply suggesting that it was time to stop studying Kabbalah and forget the confusing pieces. Perhaps some confusion would clear up with further research and experience. I had learned what I needed and was ready to continue moving forward. God was slowly and gently teaching me, at a pace that allowed time to internalize and shift my paradigm. It was particularly hard to change and/or erase those beliefs that had been handed to me since I was a child.

What I did learn from the wisdom of Kabbalah was:
- We are created in the true image and likeness of God, complete with the power to manifest miracles.

The Bumper Stickers

- We can align with others and combine our mental power, known as "collective consciousness," to manifest miracles on a much larger regional or global scale, if we so choose.
- Satan does not exist as we are traditionally taught.
- One of our life goals should be to be more godlike by sharing and caring for others.

Chapter 12

Destiny Revealed?

During the time that I was developing my psychic abilities, I performed quite a few readings for others and had several performed for me. Here is one of the readings which Lisa, my friend from Indiana, performed for me:

I went into a deep meditation and was amazed at what I saw. Like I've told you before, I just get flashes of pictures sometimes, or thoughts in my head. But sometimes, when I'm very lucky or someone really needs me, I get a bigger picture, where I can see a lot of details without all the blackness. Well, this meditation was one of those times. I am very happy for you. Here is what I saw:

First, I saw a big church, the kind with stained-glass windows with pictures of angels, Jesus and different saints. But I knew this was not a regular Christian or Catholic church. I saw that this church was packed full of followers. Then I could see down

> the main aisle up to the podium. Behind the podium, you were standing at the altar, giving a sermon on Jesus. There were several angels around you, and they were smiling and looking toward Heaven. I had a feeling of extreme peace, and also a sense that this was an important quest. It was almost like they were in a hurry to lead you to this path. This was all I saw but I believe your mission in life is to be a spiritual leader, as well as a great spiritual teacher. Remember, though, we make our own destinies!

This intrigued me because I had asked for a reading from another woman named Kathy a month earlier. She was quickly gaining popularity because she was very accurate with her readings. I asked Kathy if she could get a message from "The Moms," since I hadn't heard from them in a while. Her reading was equally as interesting but I didn't know what to think of it at the time. Here's what she said:

> I seem to be getting a complicated message and I'm not sure if I've got it at all, but here goes. I saw a torch like the one on top of the Statue of Liberty, illuminating writing which I couldn't read. I also saw a person writing at a desk fervently. I also saw the Statue of Liberty and the phrase "Children of the world, unite." The feeling I get about the interpretation is that there is a cause, possibly regarding human rights, that you are bringing to light to the rest of the world, or are campaigning against through writing, but not solely. I feel the message was coming from the three "Moms." They were standing back, however, as if they were only delivering the message. They didn't

Destiny Revealed?

have a clear, strong presence. I often receive strong images of people who have a message.

I didn't tell Kathy that "The Moms" that I asked about only referred to two "Moms." She may very well have uncovered a third mom that I hadn't considered. Aunt Toni and Aunt Dot had been deceased for some time now. Both of them had taken care of me after my mother died. They were like mothers to me. So there may have been three moms, but I only discovered two. Aunt Dot's birthday also fell on the 21st (of January) which pleasantly surprised me when I found that out. Her number would have blended with the others, if I had looked for another connection. She, too, may have been there, assisting.

I asked Kathy for further clarification since the information she brought forth rang true regarding my developing aspirations. A psychic will usually provide some initial information and, once validated, will then take the time to elaborate. Here is what she said:

The message felt complicated because I felt there was a lot more to it than I was capable of reading, I think. The torch was symbolic in that it was illuminating, enlightening or making clear. The human rights issue came about from the "Children of the world, unite" phrase, which was my personal association, but even as I was writing it, I got the feeling "but that's not all." I do get the feeling that whatever it is you are involved in or thinking of doing is something that you have some specialist knowledge of.

Neither Kathy nor Lisa knew one another, nor did they realize I had gotten a reading from them both. The striking similarity between

171

the two readings was the reference to doing something on a large scale for the betterment of humanity. I wanted to do something helpful with my newfound understanding of life and the afterlife. Since I had been journaling my experiences and development, I thought that a book might be an appropriate avenue for sharing what I was being taught. What I didn't fully understand would be the thrust of the message: God and spirit(s) are around us for assistance. All we have to do is ask and they will work with us. It was certainly a good message, but it didn't seem to be enough to fill a book.

Nonetheless, through these valuable readings I received confirmation that "The Moms" were now in the background but still assisting when necessary. It seemed that the primary Divine objective was complete, and it was time for a higher authority to take over. And what a great adventure my mother and I had already been on! The synopsis might look like this:

A young mother endured a childhood filled with emotional and physical trauma that remained trapped and festering inside her. The emotional pain resurfaces with the power of a tempest, at the loss of yet another father figure. The intense sadness and grief was sudden and overwhelming. In a moment of confused judgment, the misery is ended. A bewildered family, now grieving a double loss, unsuccessfully attempts to understand and recover.

Upon entering the world of spirit, she must confront her great error. She is sternly reprimanded for her miscalculated act. Learning about eternal life, she now fully realizes there is no escape from the truth. Grief turns into deep sorrow. She wants to right the wrong, erase time and eliminate overpowering emotions, but the unforgiving nature of time has no choice but to repeat the verdict, "guilty as charged."

Destiny Revealed?

She desperately wants to care for her son, regardless of cost. But what can she do? Through her own mistake, she has learned invaluable truths that she wants others to learn. She calls out to God for another chance; a chance, not for her salvation, but for the salvation of others. She pleads with God, "I would not have committed suicide if I had only known the truth about life and the afterlife." She wonders why more people can't discover the truth, and begs God to allow her to work with her abandoned son to help him discover the truth and spread the word, so that others don't make the same mistake she did. And they might choose more loving, caring, sharing, compassionate and forgiving lives as a result. Since God loves us so much, He agrees and offers her support to achieve her goal because, more than anything, He loves a good story.

Can she beat the odds of a predominately negative world and get a message through to a godless man? What will it take? How long will it take? The timing will demand perfection. The signs and clues must contain deeper meaning and defy probability to convince this Scrooge. But will he even see the signs? Can he find the clues? And, if he does, will he acknowledge them or dismiss them as meaningless coincidences?

She struggles to keep him safe through his younger years because he is hardheaded and focused on the material world. Luckily, it's not time for his awakening. He needs to experience life by enrolling in the school of hard knocks. But the universe's appointment with him is fast approaching, as the mother continues preparation. Along the way, she teams up with another friend who has returned home to assist. Together they recruit other departed family, friends, saints, avatars and enlightened masters, and these forces combine to rally around this hardened, lost soul. Bridging the canyon between eternity and time, and awakening a devout non-believer will be challenging, but the incredible power of Heaven silently waits, undetected, prepared and willing, should it be needed.

And nothing happened by coincidence.

Writer's Cramp

Personal experiences with God and Company continued while I studied, and I felt the urge to compile what I was learning into book form. I couldn't come up with a reasonable explanation for why all of these things were happening, except to enlighten me and, perhaps, for the purpose of sharing these experiences and lessons with others. I accepted this and figured that the effort I was pouring into understanding God, spirit and the afterlife was probably being driven by God and Company anyway. I reckoned that most folks didn't have the time to invest in such a quest, so I could do it for them, and hopefully condense it all into something understandable.

I asked God and Company if I was meant to write a book, and the signs said "Yes." I asked if I needed to be in a hurry to complete it, and the signs said "No." Since I still had some doubt about my answers, I decided to try a type of "book divination." I would hold a closed bible, ask a question and, without looking, just open to a page, place my finger somewhere on that page and read the passage. I would let my intuition guide me. I had a lot of faith in my intuition.

We had a little book called *God's Promises,* in our bathroom. One day, I asked, "Should I write a book about my experiences?" I closed my eyes and flipped the book all around in my hands so that I didn't know which end was up, then let my intuition guide me. I opened to a page that said "Change the World." *Wow!* I bubbled up. *That's exactly what I'd like to do, and that's what Lisa and Kathy had alluded to, but what's the punch line of the book? What's the moral of the story?* The story certainly was incredible, but what was the climax of the plot? At what point could I say, "And they lived happily ever after"?

Destiny Revealed?

Since I didn't have the answer to this rather fundamental question, I knew the contents of the book were still evolving.

The desire to capture what I had learned was definitely strong, and I had gotten several signs, but I continued to look for more confirmation. A few days later, I was talking with a friend about an unrelated topic, giving him some lessons I'd learned from my experience, and "out of the blue" he said, "You need to write a book." Was this another sign?

By now, I had received enough signs to begin consuming kilobytes at the keyboard, capturing my introduction to the spirit world and the afterlife, but I wasn't convinced the material would be interesting enough to read. A few minutes later, the phone rang; it was my neighbor, telling me that she had told the bumper-sticker story to her church group. She was excited to say they had gotten a big kick out of it. Right then, I knew God was trying to tell me not to worry. He would make it interesting if I just pulled over and switched seats with Him. He wanted to drive. I simply needed to buckle up for an exciting ride.

That evening, Janice brought home Chinese food for dinner. While we were eating, I mentioned that I had been receiving signs to write the book. I told Janice that the absolute final word would be if one of those fortune cookies provided a clue to write the book. When we finished we opened our fortune cookies, mine communicated a concept I would understand later:

☺ Treat your life as an extended process of creation ☺

It seemed important and unique enough that I decided to keep it. It captured my interest, even though I didn't fully understand it at the time.

Meanwhile, Janice was reading the one I gave her. She said "You're not going to believe this. You're gonna die when you read this one." Here's what it said:

☺ Record your history so others may benefit from it ☺

That was it, the absolute final word I needed! Too many signs had come for this to be coincidence. All of these signs in such short order had to defy statistical probability. I knew I needed to write a book.

I placed both "fortunes" under the transparent blotter on my desk as reminder and inspiration.

The Maytag Repair Men

During another fall and winter season, I sequestered myself in the house for many weeks while trying to re-write a draft manuscript that I had been putting together for a couple years. I had it reviewed by a professional writer, who said it was in sad shape and needed to be re-written. It needed "slash and burn," as she called it. After getting my ego out of the "Intensive Care Unit" I reviewed the manuscript more objectively, I had to agree with her assessment; it would require a lot of time to repair. I knew it would take a tremendous effort, so it hibernated until I could again devote the necessary time.

As I discovered, writing a book takes an incredible amount of research and dedication, and I was quickly gaining a profound respect for authors. I was beginning to struggle with the format and content of the book: what needed to stay and what didn't. I was still being taught new things, which changed some of what was already captured in text. Some of the things I had previously read and heard had been forgotten, so I knew I needed to re-read and re-review all of

Destiny Revealed?

it…which I knew would consume much of my spare time. Sitting at the computer for fourteen hours a day was tough.

A considerable amount of time had transpired since the previous signs and fortune cookies provided the impetus to write. My initial draft read more like a journal and required significant changes to put the pieces together logically. I wondered if I was still on the right track with the change in format. In my daily encounters, I felt compelled to help anyone who might need an encouraging word about life-after-death or God. The conversations sometimes were overheard, and inevitably an atheist, skeptic, cynic or religious person would feel compelled to contribute their own beliefs or contradictions. But I made sure the discussions remained just that. I'm not out to launch an attack on the various religions or the bible, because they teach good and holy things. I would much rather be "for" something than "against" something. Everyone's perspective could be offered but no movement from either camp could be recognized. It seemed futile to even engage in some discussions.

I always try to back up my beliefs with the experiences I've had, to provide evidence of the truth. But it didn't matter how many stories I shared; none seemed to convince anyone of the direct presence of God or spirit's desire to communicate with us. To them, these were all just cute little coincidences. It's easier to deny something than it is to research its validity. Closed minds and pompous egos prevented any consideration of the subject. Some folks don't want to discover, through research, that they might be wrong, and I knew this was part of the problem. In either case, I kept hitting brick walls, and it was frustrating. I knew people would ultimately find the truth in their own time and way. Maybe I wasn't supposed to intervene, after all. Perhaps my awakening was for my benefit and for my benefit alone.

"Imagine That"   A Spiritual Awakening

So I wasn't sure whether to continue with the book or give up. I asked God and Company for guidance.

Out of my second-story office window (at home), I can clearly see the road that passes in front and notice most of the vehicles that go by. The community is small, with only about twenty houses past mine, so traffic is very light. While typing away at the keyboard one winter's day, I saw a blue and white van go by, and simply noticed that it was bright white with a bright medium-blue company emblem on the side. The colors appeared very bright, as if the van was new, just washed, and perhaps even waxed. A little later, another van went by; it was white and blue, also, but not from the same company. Moments later, another white and blue van went by. This time, it was the Maytag repair van, with pictures of the Maytag repair men on the side in their blue uniforms. I questioned aloud, "What the heck is going on with white and blue?" I wondered if it meant something but, as usual, I didn't know what. I figured I would find out when the time was right. I went back to typing and didn't pay any more attention to it.

The next day, I returned to work. In the Control Room, we don't have our own desk. We relieve the off-going watch-stander and take over the desk until we are relieved, twelve hours later. A short while after taking the watch, I noticed a fortune-cookie "fortune" lying all alone next to the computer terminal. I smirked and chuckled because I sensed what was potentially coming. Was it going to be a message specifically designed for me or was it going to be just a meaningless coincidence? The fortune read:

> You begin to appreciate how important it
> is to share your personal beliefs.

Destiny Revealed?

The significant key was that the fortune was typed in medium blue on white paper. I think it's safe to say that I had been through my share of fortune cookie fortunes, and it was the only one I had seen typed in blue. It's still on my desk today, along with the others, and it's the only one in blue!

I understood the message God and Company had intended, and continued to type the book in medium blue text on my computer. That's right...in medium blue text on my computer. It didn't even dawn on me until I was typing this story. Some time ago, I had chosen to switch to blue text because the black ink cartridge in the printer was low. The type color had been medium blue ever since. And it tied the personal sharing of beliefs to the blue typing of this manuscript.

God and Company, (or the universe, if you prefer), is more than willing to communicate with us.

And They are quite clever, powerful and determined.

Chapter 13

All About Sharing

I originally believed the concept of tithing was started by money-hungry churches trying to gain power, but it's actually an ancient teaching that suggests we should all give 10 percent of what we own so that everyone will have enough. It has been said that if everyone gave 10 percent then everyone would have all that they need to survive. What a wonderful idea.

Since God had educated me on the need to be loving, caring, sharing, compassionate and forgiving, my desire to achieve this was rising dramatically. One bible verse states: "That thine alms may be in secret: and thy Father which seeth in secret Himself shall reward thee openly." (Matthew 6:4 KJV). This gave me the idea to test the system, to see if it really worked as stated.

Jesus told us through more than one Gospel writer that if you give (alms or donations) and share with others, God would reward you. Jesus suggested donating secretly because doing it openly, like the Pharisees did on the street corners for their own recognition, would be the only reward received. But to give in secret would cause the Father to reward thee openly.

Joey

A woman co-worker had a physically handicapped child named Joey. Joey was confined to a wheelchair and had only been able to speak about ten words, his entire life of twelve years. Regardless of his afflictions, Joey was an energetic, happy and high-spirited child who loved to tell jokes using his laptop keyboard, which was connected to a computer monitor for others to see.

One day, Joey choked on a hot dog during lunch at school. The lunchroom attendants tried frantically to dislodge the hot dog but were having difficulty. Finally, after much pushing and squeezing on his abdomen, the hot dog was dislodged, but Joey had been without oxygen for too long, causing some motor-function damage to two very important things: his arms. This would require rehabilitation, but first he had to recover from a case of pneumonia that was caused when he aspirated while choking.

Joey's mother needed to care for him at home. This was going to deplete all of her vacation and family sick leave. Personnel Services sent out an e-mail to all employees, asking if anyone would be willing to donate vacation time to Joey's mother so that she wouldn't jeopardize her employment while caring for him. I was saddened to hear about Joey and wanted to do something to help him and his family, so I decided to donate eight hours of vacation time to his mother. This was a first for me. I had always exhausted all of my annual vacation time, and occasionally tapped into "time-off without pay" to support fishing trips and tournaments. I had to optimize my use of vacation time to ensure there was enough to support all of the trips and tournaments.

All About Sharing

I remember how hard it was to click the "send" button on that e-mail to Personnel Services. This was my precious vacation time…but I hadn't had a whole lot of time in the past year to use it anyway. After I clicked the "send" button, a sense of satisfaction, peace and calm ran through me. I liked the way it made me feel.

The next day, while checking e-mail, I discovered that I received one from my supervisor awarding me eight hours of compensatory time. The comp time was awarded for some overtime that I had recently worked. This really surprised me because we always had to submit a request for the comp time and it had to be calculated. It required a week-by-week review of the employee's unpaid overtime, followed by a laborious math exercise that effectively reduced the potential comp time to near nothing. Supervisors would usually award the comp time only after the employee had performed the calculation and submitted a request. Rarely was the comp time calculated by the supervisor of his own accord. And I hadn't planned on submitting for the comp time myself. "Wow! It would seem that this reward stuff really does work."

This story illustrates how one person's life can significantly impact another's, even when the two have never met.

By the way, Joey did fully recover. I plan to share a few jokes with him and thank him personally for the lesson.

Thanks again, Joey!

Jumping Rope

My heart continued to open rapidly to this idea of sharing and being charitable, after my experiences with Christina (the missionary) and Joey. I began to give money to charities quite frequently. I made a deal with God that if extra money came our way I would give 10 percent of it away. Shortly after the deal, some unexpected money did come our way!

I was still trying to find worthy organizations for our contributions when an envelope came in the mail from a charity looking for a donation. This wasn't unusual, but the charity wasn't one I recognized. I was cautious because some charities use the money more efficiently than others do, so I didn't feel comfortable sending this particular charity a donation. As I stood there, opening the mail, I asked God to send a charity that I could donate to comfortably. "Like the *American Heart Association*," I said aloud.

I had just walked upstairs to change out of my work clothes when the doorbell rang. Standing in my doorway were two kids collecting pledges for their fundraiser. They told me they were jumping rope for the *American Heart Association*! I grinned from ear to ear, shook my head, laughed and got the checkbook.

Give Until It Hurts

"Give until it hurts," as Mother Theresa said. A $10 donation from a millionaire isn't impressive, but a $1 donation from one poor family to another is very impressive. But how do you know when you've given until it hurts? I'm sure there are many ways to know but I recently had Mother's statement distinctly revealed to me. We had just finished the Holiday Season and had spent a good deal of money on furniture, gifts, decorations, and an office party. I usually pay for everything using our credit card and then pay it off each month, keeping its balance at zero, but we had spent a considerable amount over the holidays primarily to host a festive office party. This included new furniture that we desperately needed to replace our sagging twenty-year-old family room seating. When the credit card statement arrived I began calculating how long it was going to take to pay it off. With other expected bills and expenses coming, I figured it would take several months to achieve a zero balance. I told Janice that we needed to seriously curtail our spending or it

All About Sharing

would take many months to recover. It seems that once the purse strings have loosened it's hard to tighten them back up! We needed determination and a simple straightforward method to regulate our use of the credit card.

We agreed to ask ourselves one very important question before swiping the credit card to purchase something, "Do I need this in order to survive?" If the answer was "No." then we needed to put it back! We knew we needed to practice this level of control until we regained my definition of credit card control, which equated to a zero balance. Temporarily slamming our wallets shut for everything, including fishing licenses and Friday night pizza, would be a little painful.

Since it was the end of the year I began preparing for our income tax return by calculating how much we had donated to charity throughout the year. It came as no surprise when I determined that the money we had donated would have been just enough to pay our credit card down to a zero balance. Even though we had inflicted our own pain by spending a lot over the holidays we would not have felt it had we not donated so much to charities over the year.

We had experienced "give until it hurts."
Thanks Mother Theresa for a fine story and a good lesson.

Chapter 14

Did You See That?

Deepak Chopra recorded an excellent audio program called *SynchroDestiny,* which is dedicated to explaining the nature of coincidence in our life and all its aspects. I highly recommend listening to it. Chopra explains, the more you work with the conscious energy field (or God, or the universe, if you prefer), the more it works with you. By having this "intention" combined with the necessary "attention", you will begin to witness more and more synchronistic events or meaningful coincidences in your life. Through personal experiences, I was witnessing meaningful coincidences at rather fast-paced rates at times. This was (and still is) definitely exciting. My intentions (or goals) and attention to the answers and signs were focused. My pact with God that "Thy will be done" also seemed to draw us closer together and perhaps magnify the results.

Several times during the course of my studies, I had come across the concept that we create our own realities with the power of our thoughts or intention, as Chopra describes. One of my bosses recognized my belief in the power of positive thinking and gave me a book entitled *The Power of Your Subconscious Mind* by Joseph Murphy, Ph.D., which expanded and further anchored my conviction. This is another excellent work that I highly recommend, which describes the power of our minds to affect our world.

Unfortunately, many folks believe that it is only by the sweat of their brow that they gain any reward in this life. I was finding out that sweat and hard work were definitely components of success, but by adding intention, attention and increased confidence in God and Company, I exceeded my own expectations for the manifestation of my desires. This took place on two levels; some intentions were specific, while others were general. In other words, some of my desires were to accomplish a specific goal, while others were more generalized and left up to God to manage the outcome.

May The Force Be With You

I had landed the job I wanted, after a company downsizing. Many employees went through a very emotionally painful and stressful time of re-applying for employment at a company where they had already worked for many years. It was a humiliating process that I would prefer not to experience again.

After about a year, I was just settling into this new position when I was blindsided by my boss; he came into my office one Monday morning to tell me I was going back to shift work in the Control Room. The reason: another supervisor had been displaced from his organization and needed somewhere to go. Our organization opted to take the supervisor back, since he had worked with us for many years. It was a caring and compassionate decision that I fully supported. The unfortunate fallout was that the best position (or fit) for this supervisor was my position.

I had just left the Control Room three years earlier and didn't think I would ever return—not because I didn't want to go back but because I had left the organization and didn't think my career path would lead back. Because I liked my current job, I was a little angry and confused at first, but I decided to get over the anger. Even though I didn't understand why I was going back to shift work, I sincerely felt that I was being cared for by a greater power and had no need to worry, but I did worry a little anyway. I could only conclude that it was in my best interest.

Many people said I should have been angry because I was a "victim" of circumstance. I decided to look at the bright side and take a very positive approach. Whenever anyone asked how I felt, I emphatically told them that going back on shift meant "more money and more time off!" What could be wrong with that! I had to have faith that everything would work out. And work out it did...in a big way!

Shortly after returning to shift work, several company policies changed which allowed salaried employees, such as myself, to be paid for overtime. This equated to a large sum of money by year's end. The shift crew to which I was assigned had excellent talent and personality, which greatly reduced the stresses of twelve-hour shift work.

My old fishing buddy, and the man responsible for introducing Janice to me, was now my boss. Although we hadn't fished together in many years, at least we had something in common. We both grew up together, so to speak, working for an electrical utility and bass fishing. I wasn't sure how this would work out, because Dave knew the plant extremely well and was a stickler for detail. A discussion (or argument) on nearly any plant subject or system found him accurate, in most cases. Unfortunately, his tenacity, aggressive style and condescending method of proving himself right often irritated others. As soon as the opponent conceded, Dave would lighten up and console the defeated worker by offering words of encouragement and understanding of the subordinates thought process. He had become affectionately known as "The Grinch."

Having learned how to deal with Dave's personality, when we were co-workers many years before, allowed me to employ that skill while respecting his knowledge and leadership role. I also recognized that God places people in various roles for a reason, and that Dave's role was to successfully lead a shift crew in the production of electricity during a time when the electrical-generation industry was becoming more competitive. The industry was experiencing budget and workforce reductions similar to what the airline industry had experienced when it deregulated. Strong leadership was a must, to hold the line on safety.

Being the Number Two guy on shift, as in past shift positions, I always tried to support the Shift Manager as best I could, to reduce his burden. Our relationship worked very well. I was happy to be back on shift.

Another benefit of being back on shift was having some weekdays off, which allowed quiet, uninterrupted time to research and compile my lessons and experiences into words. It was obvious, once again, that God and Company had looked out for me.

This story illustrates how God can take care of us if we let Him. In this case, I had a generalized intention of being happy and successful at work. On the outside of my shower glass is a list of affirmations that I created in order to focus my desires and goals. While showering, I can wipe the condensation off the glass and read these affirmations whenever I like. One of these affirmations is "I am happy and successful at my work." On the one hand, frequently reading this desire aligns my consciousness to choose happiness and be successful at my work; on the other hand, it makes my desire known to God and Company (and the universe). Because the affirmation is general, (and not specific) it allows the universe the flexibility to decide what is best.

Note also that the affirmation does not say "I *will be* happy…" or "I *want to be* happy…" Rather it says "I *am* happy…" And note the connection to the great "I Am." This alone has power. I was careful not to phrase the desire to indicate a future achievement but rather phrased it to decree a current and continuous condition. Decree is a form of prayer or intention that is much more powerful than simply asking for something. The combination of my intentions backed by God's support, along with my surrender to "Thy will be done," creates a tremendous power. An alignment of thought and purpose can occur where we become an instrument for God, allowing God's will to live through us.

After completing the above paragraph, I re-read it and reflected on how incredibly important this concept had become in my life. I also found it very interesting how many separate teachers I had read or heard that contributed to the fine-tuning of an accurate understanding and application of such a seemingly simple concept: developing and achieving a goal.

Although affirmations and goal-setting is certainly not a new practice, I had not considered word-processing them onto a sheet of paper for display. From time to time, in the past, Janice and I had penned out our goals for the upcoming year; then we would put the list away and *not* look at it again, unless we accidentally happened across it later. When we did happen across our list we would find it interesting to see how many goals we had achieved and how many had been changed by events.

The idea to post my goals came from William W. Hewitt's book, *Psychic Development for Beginners*. Hewitt outlined a "Goal Bowl," which was a circle drawn on a piece of paper, divided into slices like a pizza. Each slice had a desire or goal written on it. Because I couldn't figure out how to get the computer to develop a circle cut into slices, I simply made a list. At the top of the list, I also incorporated my rendition of Hewitt's foundational statement, which reads "From the Divine with Harm to No One." This is important, to ensure that your achievements don't come at someone else's expense.

From Ron Roth's audio program, *Reclaiming Your Spiritual Power,* I learned about the power of prayer in the form of decree. Decree is more like a command or demand for a specific desire, such as in the *Lord's Prayer* that Jesus taught during his Sermon on the Mount. "Thy kingdom come, Thy will be done in Earth as it is in Heaven." (Matt 6:10 KJV) This isn't an asking or wanting, this is a powerful statement or demand. To reinforce this concept was the explanation by God in Book One of *Conversations with God,* where God explained the importance of eliminating the word "want" from our goals. When we say "I want to be successful," the universe recognizes a "wanting" and will deliver just that…a wanting to be successful. By decreeing "I am successful," the universe will help make it happen.

The process of bringing our desires to fruition or achieving our goals can be accomplished using a systematic process that builds upon itself. I'll explain the components individually.

1. The basic component required is the desire or intention to achieve something. This desire alone triggers a response in the universe to assist, but it can be weak at this stage. Hopefully the goal is something admirable and pleasing to God and the universe.

2. The second component required is the ambition to follow through on the necessary physical actions necessary to

achieve the goal, such as going to school. You can't be a doctor if you don't go to school. You won't complete the marathon if you don't train properly. The saying "God helps those who help themselves," applies here.

3. Repeating your goal like a mantra in the present tense, as if you have already achieved it, will intensify the universal energy contributed to it. "I am happy, and all things lead to my success."

4. Believing with certainty that your goal is achievable is another huge factor in its manifestation. Doubt only serves to block the positive results the universe is trying to deliver, because doubt is also a thought and therefore has its own power. Negative self-talk such as "With my luck, no matter what I do, this won't work out," is sure to impact complete success or delay it. It might even eliminate the chance of achieving the goal altogether.

5. Eliminate any thoughts of unworthiness. At times, many of us feel unworthy of having good things happen to us, but this simply isn't true. I often end my affirmations with "I am worthy of all these things." There have been enough martyrs throughout history. No need for another.

6. Visualizing the fulfillment of our desire also increases the potential for achieving it. For example, if you are working on a college degree, you might visualize yourself receiving your diploma. You might visualize crossing the finish line in a marathon. I used visualization techniques to help me win tournaments.

7. Ask your unseen helpers to assist. Request assistance from angels, ascended masters, saints, spirit guides and departed loved ones. They'll be glad to help. Our spiritual evolution

continues while we are on the other side and, to a greater degree, this includes assisting others. One of the primary purposes of angels is to help us. Ascended masters and saints have always been unselfish and willing to help others. Our spirit guides judge their own performance by how much they have helped us. They are always there for us.

8. Look for the signs and heed their message. God and the universe will place the resources in your path to achieve our goals, but we must recognize and utilize them. We must pay attention in order to see those important messages when they're delivered. The universe will also guide us and help us make decisions that can affect the outcome. If you're on the brink of a big decision that has multiple choices, you might ask for a sign to help you decide. This is where synchronicity turns into *SynchroDestiny*.

9. A huge factor affecting the success of a goal is whether it is aligned with the will of God. In other words, is the goal self-serving or will it help others in some fashion? Ego-based goals that are self-serving will require more personnel commitment, dedication and sweat to accomplish. Sometimes it can be both. For example, the goal might be to establish your own small business that serves others, such as auto repair, for example. The business serves the owner with a source of income, and serves others as a place of employment. It also serves the customer who can get his car fixed. The more unselfish the motivations, the more likely the business will prosper. If the auto-repair-shop owner charges greedy prices or takes advantage of unsuspecting customers by replacing unnecessary parts, the business may very well fail.

10. Always remember to express your gratitude. Much has been written about the power and purpose of gratitude. I always say thanks, usually repeatedly.
11. If others have the same goal or intention, you can use the power of multiple or collective intention to amplify your chances of success. This can work when trying to achieve a common goal that a group of individuals might have, such as a team of employees trying to successfully complete a project on schedule and under budget. The power of collective intention seems to be multiplied rather than additive, so it's important to be focused and precise on the goal.

The more components that you can incorporate, of the eleven listed, the faster and stronger the results will be. The icing on the cake is that your worries will diminish and your confidence will soar. You'll begin to see meaningful coincidences more frequently. These coincidences might be the universe instructing your next move. And if the instruction is another step towards achieving your goal, then the universe is probably also trying to tell you that you can, in fact, achieve it. So go after it with confidence, eliminating any doubt and negative self-talk, thus making it that much more powerful. Be careful not to get cocky, thinking your goal will just be handed to you, allowing you to stop effort toward it. It might be handed to you but, if I were you, I wouldn't chance it by not applying myself.

The first list of affirmations that I hung on the shower glass consisted of about eight goals. I was amazed at how many, and how quickly, I achieved them. Before long, I removed the first list and replaced it with a new list of goals. I also kept some of the original goals, such as "I am happy and successful at my work" and "I take charge of my future and live to my full potential," because they are continuously applicable goals.

The importance of visualization can be underestimated. After I had learned of its power and importance, I happened upon a television program where the home life of a superstar basketball player was showcased, so I decided to watch a little. The basketball player stood in his kitchen, describing the daily activities around his house. He mentioned that there were usually many folks in the house, doing various things, which kept the house abuzz. But after lunch everyone knew they needed to leave or remain quiet because he used this time to conduct his visualizations. He explained that he would go to his special room and visualize his upcoming game and the moves he would put on his opponents in order to score. Then he looked directly at the camera and insistently claimed that we would be surprised at just how many times it happened just the way he had visualized it.

On a later program, I watched a superstar professional bass angler make similar claims about the power of visualization. Coupled with my own experiences, this made it clear to me that there is power in this practice.

Power of Prayer

No matter what the subject, there are always two or more viewpoints. There rarely is complete alignment of thought, and when it does occur it is usually on a small scale such as a team, group or community. If there were complete alignment, then that belief would manifest itself, provided it was something possible. In some rare cases, large groups of people have aligned their thinking to manifest incredible outcomes.

On the one-year anniversary (9/11/02) of the terrorist attacks on the World Trade Center, the three-digit lottery number in New York for that day was 911. This wasn't mere coincidence or a "fixed" lottery; it was the fact that everyone was focused on the number 911. It was on everyone's mind. The power of our collective subconscious minds worked a miracle. Other results like this have occurred, especially when prayer was involved. Prayer, being the alignment of thought and intention of a group, can work miracles. The Governor of Alabama appeared on television some years ago to ask the people of Alabama to pray for rain, since their state was suffering a severe drought. No rain was in sight and yet, after a few million people prayed for rain, they received five inches the next day.

The power of prayer has been scientifically proven. One of the more noted studies occurred in the early '80s. Nearly four hundred heart patients admitted to the San Francisco General Hospital's Coronary Care Unit participated in a study to assess the affects of prayer. The study was conducted, using what is referred to as the "double blind" method. This means that neither the patients nor their doctors knew who were being prayed for, or who weren't. The "In Charge" experiment coordinator, Randolph C. Byrd, M.D., selected people from around the U.S. who were religiously active with a strong belief in prayer to conduct the praying. A computer was used to randomly select patients who would receive prayer. This eliminated the possibility that any of the participants could influence the results. Because it is a tamper-free process, the double blind method is considered the gold standard of research.

The researchers were aware that some patients in the control group would likely be prayed for by family and friends, but so would some of the patients in the test group. Ultimately, this would balance out in each group and was not considered a factor that could alter results.

The results were "statistically significant," showing that the patients who had received prayer were healthier than those who had not. They required less anesthesia, less recovery time, less need of cardiopulmonary resuscitation (CPR) and less need of mec' ventilators. Recovery drugs such as antibiotics and pain reducers were in less demand, also.

The power of our consciousness, especially our collective consciousness, is phenomenal, and yet many of us don't know we possess this incredible power. Once we become aware of this power, we will want to monitor our thoughts more closely, rejecting the thoughts that don't represent our true desires and feelings.

Signs, Signs, Everywhere Signs

I have been talking a lot about recognizing and following the signs I had been given. Signs come in many forms and many different ways. Signs may help you achieve your goals or they may simply be communications to let you know something is coming that you might want to be on the lookout for. It is important to look for those meaningful signs, but it's also important not to blow things out of proportion every time you see your favorite number, for example. Once you start to focus on a number or an object, you will have a tendency to attract those things to you. That's the power of your subconscious mind to create your own reality. As a brother-in-law once told me, "When you have a hammer, you have a tendency to find nails." So if you're looking for the number 13 to give you the green light of approval before proceeding, you will probably not have to look very far, since we are literally surrounded by numbers. Finding the number 13 would be more compelling if it came to you in a surprising way while you weren't directly looking for it.

God and Company wants us to have a safe and happy life here on Earth, so They're willing to guide us if we let Them. God and Company do not coerce, however, so you must request Their assistance. You'll be thankful you did. I've witnessed enough strings being pulled for me that it greatly reduces my worries. I'm usually quite confident that everything will turn out alright.

Did You See That?

I developed a method of communication that They could easily use and I could easily understand. These communications center a great deal around numbers. Here are some examples.

If I'm in the right place at the right time, I might see 7's, 13's, 21's or 41's, or combinations of them. If my day (or night) will be very busy or something is about to break, I usually see 5's together and frequently. If there is going to be minor difficulty, I might see 8's, meaning I'm behind the 8-ball again. It's important to do a "gut check" to validate a warning, to ensure that you don't overreact and manifest trouble just because you've convinced yourself it's destined to happen. Just because I see 5:55 a.m. once doesn't necessarily mean it's going to be a bad day. But when my lunch (at work) cost me $5.55 I took notice because it hadn't ever cost me that in the past, and I usually get meals that cost five or six dollars. I immediately jerked my head around to catch a glimpse of the register's display to ensure I had heard the cashier correctly. When I confirmed the number I thought, *Oh no, something is coming.* And my gut check confirmed my suspicion. After lunch "an event" (as we call it) occurred that I was associated with. Nothing was damaged and no one was hurt, but we made a decision to continue a job that we should have stopped for further evaluation. My warning was clear but I quickly forgot it when I got busy.

Other people, who can be influenced by God and Company, might provide an answer to us "out of the blue" and not even know it. They may say a word or phrase, tell a story, or strike up a conversation about canning vegetables or buying stock just when you're trying to figure these things out. And many times these answers are provided without any initial prompting. I've witnessed this many times, but the most memorable occurrence was the time the "The Moms" convinced my stepmother to purchase the fireplace as a Christmas gift for us.

199

"Imagine That" A Spiritual Awakening

On one occasion, my shift crew was preparing for a unit start-up. We simulate the entire process and prepare for potential equipment problems. Later, while reviewing procedures, my mind drifted off and began to wonder about likely problems with the main turbine. A new turbine had recently been installed, with extremely tight metal tolerances between the rotating and stationary surfaces within the turbine. This equated to potential "rubbing," as the metals heated up at different rates during start-up. While I was contemplating and visualizing the correct crew response to mitigate turbine damage, a co-worker came over to me and "out of the blue" said, "The turbine won't rub. It'll be fine." I knew this was a message to help calm my concerns. The turbine was returned to service smoothly and without a hitch.

God and Company know what we need and want to make our life easier if They can. All we have to do is watch and listen...and then do our part.

When we realize that life doesn't have to be an endless, miserable struggle, and that we are worthy of help, which includes miracles, they will come. But we must have faith and believe we are worthy. If we deny ourselves happiness, God and Company have a difficult time delivering it through the wall of fear we have built.

The Flood

There once was a man of great faith who became caught in a flood. As the water began to rise, a large four-wheel-drive truck came to his house to take the man to safety but the man refused assistance, saying, "I'll be alright. God will save me." As the water rose into the first floor of his home, the man retreated to the second story. When a boat idled up and offered to take him to safety, the man refused once again, saying, "I'll be alright. God will save me." The water continued to rise into the second story of his home, so he climbed

Did You See That?

onto the roof. A helicopter then arrived and hovered above his home. The pilot spoke over the loud speaker, saying that they were there to rescue him, but the man waved them off, saying, "I'll be alright. God will save me." Soon thereafter, the house succumbed to the pressures of the flood waters and was swept away, drowning the man.

The man then found himself face to face with Saint Peter at the Pearly Gates of Heaven. Somewhat angered and confused, he said, "I am a man of great faith. Why didn't God save me?" To which Saint Peter replied, "We sent a truck, a boat and a helicopter...what more do you want?"

Our saviors and the answers to our prayers aren't usually provided by a supernatural being or occurrence, such as a burning bush that speaks. Saviors and answers come from everyday people through whom God is working.

A Major Change

For about nine months, I kept seeing the number sequence 556. At first, it started as 5:56 a.m. or p.m. Some days, I would see it in the morning and then again in the evening. While I was driving to work, assessing its meaning, a car drove by with 556 on the tag. Since I wasn't looking for another 556, and because it came as a surprise just when I was examining its meaning, I was convinced that the number had significance, but I didn't have a clue as to what it meant.

I continued to see the number, and knew that eventually the meaning would be revealed. Then I got an e-mail from a friend (Sandy) who had located a book that discussed the process of publishing books. Sandy just happened to run across this information while researching something for herself, and she knew I was looking for this information. She sent the web address for the author, Doreen Virtue, PhD. While I was checking out the website, I noticed that another of Virtue's books contained a chapter entitled "Number

Sequences from the Angels." I figured this would explain the number, and immediately ordered the book.

When I got the book, the first thing I checked was the meaning of the 556. The book, *Healing With The Angels*, said "Your material life is changing significantly, such as a new home, or car, or other possession." We had a relatively new home, so that seemed out of the question, but our cars were getting old, with a lot of mileage on each.

My senses told me that we were getting a car. The problem was, I wasn't planning on buying one in the near future. So how could that be true, unless one of our cars blew up beyond repair or was wrecked? But I didn't get that feeling, either. We had planned to purchase Janice's father's car in about a year, when he planned to buy a new one. The number seemed far too insistent to refer to something we planned on doing in a year. So, were we getting a different car sooner?

A few weeks later, Janice's father passed away unexpectedly. Now I knew where the car was coming from. Janice's father had promised her the car, and it was settled as part of the estate.

The message of the number combination 556 was accurate. It took a while for God and Company to get through but, once they did, I was able to learn another form of communication, using number sequences as prescribed in Virtue's book.

Bingo Joe

Janice's entire family was in town for her Dad's funeral. The day after the funeral, I needed to get back to work, to catch up on things. The family was running around, taking care of business, and everyone was tired and stressed out. Through the hand geometry reader, I got a 13 and it was Friday. I sensed something good was going to happen, either on Friday or sometime over the weekend.

Did You See That?

When I arrived at my desk, I had a voicemail from Janice's sister, asking me to play Bingo at the local Bingo hall in honor of her father, who annually took his daughters to play the game. Since all of the family was in town, this would be a good opportunity for everyone to partake. I was tired and had a lot of work to catch up on at the office, and Janice needed to run Alex all over town for other evening activities. I thought it was too much traveling for one night. Even if we decided to play Bingo, we would probably be late for the start because of the other activities. I was doing a good job of talking myself out of it when I remembered that I had gotten a 13 on my way in. Despite my fatigue and our busy schedule, I told Janice that I agreed to go, only because I knew I was going to win something. And win I did.

I won a $250 game (split 2 ways), which was enough to cover the evening's expenses plus a few bucks extra. Bingo wasn't as cheap to play as I thought. Winning the first time I played, especially after being told I would, was satisfying. Since I had goofed up a couple of other communications, it was rewarding to get one right.

The Tournament Struggle

I had just completed a fishing tournament on my home body of water, the Potomac River, where I should have had a home-field advantage. I finished "three ounces out of the money," as we say. One fish, only three ounces heavier, and I would have taken home a small paycheck for my efforts. Since it had been a hot July day, that paycheck would have eased my pain, at least a little.

I did finish fourteenth overall, which bumped me up a few positions in the points race, so I tried to focus on the positive aspects and shrug off the loss, simply letting it go. The next day, on the drive home from work, I started to think about the tournament and all of the preparation time I had put into it, not to mention the money for tackle and gas. I got frustrated.

I had spent eight days out of the last eleven, prior to the tournament, on the river attempting to locate quality (large) fish in the hot summer sun. I did manage to locate good fish during this practice, but on tournament day the larger fish evaporated and I had to settle for smaller fish, which meant a lighter "sack" of fish for the weigh-in. Rarely did I have that much practice time available, preceding a tournament. The sacrifices anglers make to chase these little green fish are enormous, and perhaps self-centered and crazy. We skip weddings, funerals, parties, family gatherings, painting the house, repairing the toilet and cutting the grass to ensure we're on the water enough to do our best on tournament day. I concluded, if there was ever a tournament that I had a chance to win, based on sacrifice and preparation, that was the one. And it didn't materialize.

So, as I continued the drive home, I began speaking openly to God and Company asking for guidance. "Maybe you don't want me fishing," I theorized. "Maybe I'm supposed to continue on my spiritual development and leave fishing behind. I don't know. You need to tell me and I'll do it. I put my best foot forward in this last tournament and I still didn't win. I've been fishing this circuit for over ten years and I still haven't won a tournament. What do I need to do to win one?"

I quietly continued on my way and decided to blindly grab a tape out of the cassette holder. The cassettes were a randomly mixed collection of our tapes, so I didn't know which one I would ultimately grab. I plugged the cassette in and listened for the first song, to see if God and Company had a message for me.

The first song to play was *Make It Happen* by Mariah Carey. The lyrics of this song spoke volumes to me. The words said to never give up, be strong, hold on to your faith and pray to the Lord and He'll make it happen. It stated that we can make it happen if we just keep our heads up and keep trying. My eyes began to well up with tears as my mixed emotions surfaced. On one hand, the frustration and disappointment was building, while on the other, I was grateful that God and Company cared enough about me and my silly game to encourage me. The inspiration was incredible.

One of my shower-stall affirmations was "I am a consistent tournament fisherman winner," but I had not yet accomplished this goal. Being a form of prayer, I continued to focus and repeat this goal, and believe that it was possible. From time to time, I had visualized myself standing at the weigh-in stage, holding the first-place plaque and check. I even visualized the shirt I was going to be wearing when it finally happened.

My tournament performance over the years had been admirable, but the winners circle had eluded me at larger-scale tournaments. My trophy wall was full of second and third-place plaques—so many, in fact, that I began to doubt my ability to break through the fictitious second-place barrier that I had mentally created. The adage "always a bride's maid and never a bride" was haunting me. I began to believe a first-place finish simply wasn't meant to be. I recognized that this doubting self-talk was stifling my performance and that I needed to change my mind. I had to believe in myself.

A couple of months later, our next stop on the tournament trail was changed, due to the destruction caused by Hurricane Isabel. Just days before the tournament, the location had to be changed to the Choptank River because the boat-launch ramp at Dundee Creek Marina, on the Upper Bay, was damaged from the strong easterly winds. This didn't give the competitors much practice time. I only had about twelve hours of practice, and didn't feel that the fish I had located were enough to do all that well. I asked for a sign, prior to the tournament, to reveal how I was going to do. I received a very positive sign in the form of the number 13. I knew I was going to do well and suspected I might even win but my practice performance didn't support that conclusion. I had to have faith and believe in miracles.

Tournament morning started with me hooking a three-pound bass on my second cast. Surprised and caught off-guard by the early strike, my hook set was weak. My partner and the net were also unprepared, and yet I managed to get the fish in. The day seemed magical, with a cooperating partner and cooperating bass. It seemed as though I could do no wrong with my spinnerbait as I cast it to everything in sight, catching bass frequently and culling to a heavier sack of fish for the weigh-in.

I won the tournament, just as I had been told…and yes, I was wearing the red, white and blue pit crew tournament shirt I had visualized for the victory.

Brians' Rule

For the first time, we rented a house right on the water at Deep Creek Lake and were staying the week. The tournament was on Friday, so we had plenty of time to figure out where and how to catch the bass. This kept the stress level low, at least until it got closer to tournament day, when I still didn't have a solid game plan established. We had been catching fish but they were small and sporadic. The day before the tournament, I stood on the bow of the boat, faced forward so Janice and Alex couldn't hear me, and asked God and Company to give me a clue. I had exhausted my bag of tricks and needed help.

That night, after dinner, Janice and I went to the local tackle shop to get some lures (although they are artificial we call them "baits") that I theorized might catch more fish. Upon returning, I laid them on the kitchen table, and one of the other anglers (Brian) started to laugh at what I bought. The baits were small because I thought the bass were being finicky; this was a standard tactic for that situation. But Brian just laughed at how small they were and said that I didn't need to downsize that much. I asked him to give me a clue since my observations seemed to support my conclusions to downsize.

Brian, a very skilled and competent angler, said that he had experienced success using the color I selected but was able to catch the bass on the larger version of the same bait. He went on to explain that the bass were on the ends of the docks until about 10 a.m.; then the bite quit. Brian's rule was exactly the opposite of how I was fishing the docks. I concentrated on fishing the shallow water early, while the sun was still low, and then switched to the deep water ends of the docks later in the day, when the sun was high. His strategy was completely opposite and was counterintuitive to the way many anglers approached early-morning fishing. This explained why I hadn't tried it. I figured that reversing my strategy was worth a try.

A little later, while sitting on the deck, another angler (another Brian) who had overheard my request for a clue told me what he had learned the year before. He had caught all of his fish on the dock poles or near a dock's ladder. Most docks on Deep Creek Lake are floating docks, held secure by two-inch pipes driven into the bottom. I didn't consider the pipes large enough to be a powerful attractant for bass to use as an ambush point; however, based on his account, I was obviously wrong. I invested a significant effort in fishing the docks but didn't focus my casts specifically close to the poles.

Brian went on to inform me of a technique his father used when he tournament fished. When his father woke up, the first fishing location that came to his mind would be the first place that he would stop, even if he hadn't caught fish there during practice. Right then,

I knew that God and Company was definitely working through this Brian to provide another clue. Being familiar with the altered states of consciousness, and knowing that one of our most susceptible times for spirit to deliver a message is right after awakening, I figured they would help if I just listened.

Tournament morning came quickly and the first location that came to mind was a cove where we had located some fish in the farthest reaches (or back) of the cove. Included in the vision were several docks near the entrance of the cove. These docks, however, were some distance away from where we had caught bass. We'd even tried them during practice and had blanked. Since we had only caught several bass in this cove during practice, it hadn't become my primary location. Consequently, I wasn't sure whether my analytical mind was making this up or if the thought really was inspired by spirit.

Unsure, I decided to stick to my original game plan and start at a different spot, where I had previously had decent success. But the spot was a flop, not even a bite for a half an hour of flogging the shoreline. The image of those docks and the cove continued to haunt me, so I vowed to get to them as soon as possible. I made several quick stops along the way and managed to catch one bass in deeper water off the end of a dock, just as Brian had suggested. "Brians' Rules" were materializing before my eyes as requested.

Before long, I arrived at the cove of my visions and immediately began catching fish. I hooked five bass in the cove and lost a couple of nice ones off the docks that I had visualized upon awakening. One of the fish I lost would have given me enough additional weight to win the tournament. I came in fourth place and was only one pound behind the winner.

Did You See That?

It is normal for bass to leap out of the water in an attempt to throw the hook, and they are experts at it. The fish that got away did just that. After sharply setting the hook, the large bass felt the sting of the cold steel in his jaw. This triggered his innate response to race for the surface, where he could exit his dense, watery world and enter the thinner world of air. Once in the thinner air, his muscles could violently shake his head back and forth, like a dog wrestling a towel. This rapid headshake is incredibly effective at throwing hooks. I saw him rocketing for the surface in the, nearly crystal clear, lake water, but I failed to perform the evasive maneuver that might have prevented him from throwing the hook. I should have held my rod tip down into the water and cranked the reel hard, as soon as the bass breached the surface, in an attempt to sharply turn his head back down and into the water, thus defusing his explosive launch. I stood there, shocked, as I watched the four-pound bass pause, regain his composure while I lost mine, and then swim freely back into the depths. The irony was debilitating as I fell to my knees and dropped my head in disbelief and despair.

Yet I am still very grateful, because this minor tragedy was a valuable lesson I needed to learn. God and Company can lead us to the prize but many times we will have to make the right decisions and do our part, to earn the prize that awaits. God will open the door but we have to get through it without stumbling. In bass tournament jargon, this is called "execution." We must exhibit nearly flawless execution to reap the rewards of life. God and Company can only do so much and then it's up to us to execute flawlessly. Sure, the game-winning "Hail Mary" might be thrown to us, but we'll have to securely tuck it into our chest once it touches our fingers, because several testosterone-crazed defenders, who would like nothing better than to kill us, are trying to steal our glory. It takes many hours of practice to learn to maintain your concentration in that environment. Since many of these goals and opportunities are ego-based in nature, the support we receive from God might be in short supply. God will offer "Hail Marys," but we have to be practiced and prepared in order to flawlessly execute our free will and make the catch. Every now and then, we might receive a miracle, but this world is ruled by physical laws that maintain some control over us. For example, many folks work hard to further their careers or their athletic ability, and after all of your hard work, God may present you with an opportunity to receive a promotion. While at a party that you didn't plan to attend, a friend of a friend mentions a job opening at their company. It may be the job you've been waiting for. But you'll need to write an excellent résumé and flawlessly execute the job interview. The miracle was the party, your final decision to attend, the meeting with a friend of a friend, and the eventual conversation. The rest depends on your free will to execute flawlessly.

That evening, back at the rental house, I reflected on the good day. Suddenly I realized the final clue in this lesson. The cove where I caught and lost the majority of the day's fish is called "Holy Cross Cove." How fitting that God and Company would arrange a little PR for themselves.

If Cookies Could Talk

In a hallway between classrooms, at work, are bookcases loaded with many of the procedures we use to operate the plant. During training week, I entered the hallway in pursuit of a specific document to review. As I walked past a storage cabinet, I noticed a lonely fortune cookie resting by itself on the cabinet top. There was nothing else on the cabinet but *that* cookie. I chuckled but continued to retrieve the procedure I was looking for, while deciding whether or

Did You See That?

not to open the cookie. I was cautious because I didn't want to go overboard about what every fortune cookie had to say.

I considered the circumstances for a moment. Most of these fortune cookies and/or their messages weren't because I was going to Chinese restaurants and grabbing a handful to see what they said. The cookies were finding their way to *me* in unique ways. I muttered, "You know I've got to know what it says. What are you trying to tell me now? I'll open it and see if it makes sense. If it doesn't, I'll just attribute it to meaningless coincidence and keep going."

The fortune said that I "would soon be honored with a great award." A group of my co-workers were in the nearby classroom and had previously heard some of my "meaningful coincidence" stories and knew that I attributed them to communications from the universe. I showed them the fortune and said "Well, we'll just have to watch and see if something really *is* coming." Later, I relayed the story to another co-worker, who was an atheist but also knew some of my story. I thought it might be interesting for him to witness this. Perhaps God was interested in providing a shred of evidence that my co-worker could ponder.

I had recently completed a rather large and important site-wide project that could potentially net an award, but I wasn't sure. Now that I had received this fortune, I was fairly certain the award was coming.

Several weeks later, I received an e-mail, informing me that I had been selected to receive an award for the project at an awards luncheon. I wasn't able to attend the luncheon due to schedule conflicts and expected the award certificate, or other related material, to be sent to me by mail, but it never came. *Oh well, some award.* I thought.

During our next training week, our entire shift crew was told to gather in one of the classrooms at noon. We didn't have any training scheduled for that time period and I wondered what was going on. I figured a plant issue had occurred and we needed to be updated.

One-by-one, upper level management walked into the classroom: the Manager of our department, the Plant General Manager, and then the Vice President of our site. I thought, *This must really be something big, with all this top brass!* Then our Manager got up to speak, starting off by saying they were gathered to honor someone who was not able to attend the recent award luncheon. That's when I knew what was going on. He continued by reading a speech he had put together, detailing the project and its accomplishments. I was surprised, flattered and appreciative of their willingness to take time out of their busy schedules to present the award in person.

And what better way for God to show those I had shared my fortune with that it had, in fact, come true.

Aligning the Stars

My experiences revealed that I had received communications in a wide variety of ways: from blinking lights to complex synchronistic events requiring the proper alignment of many players and factors to ultimately deliver the message. I certainly appreciated all of the help I was receiving but I also realized that not all spirits, on all levels of Heaven, possessed complete knowledge and understanding of the universe. So how would I know if the message was from the highest source? How could I be sure that I wasn't being set up by some mischievous spirits or demons, out to have some fun at my expense?

From the start I prayed for protection and right discernment, and I used visualization techniques to call forth and surround myself with the Divine Love and Protection of God. The more I worked with God and Company, the more frequently communications came along with good results. I felt surrounded and protected, so I wasn't overly concerned about a corrupted message and I began to marvel at some of the more complex synchronicities. How were these being arranged?

Speculation has it that not all spirits are privy to the future, especially those on the lower levels of Heaven (or Hell). And fortunately their powers seem to be diminished concerning their affects on a person's thoughts (not decisions), electronics, poltergeists, Ouija Boards and the like.

The complex synchronicities seem to be the product of a much more powerful force. Too many stars had to align for these messages to be received. That offered a significant level of comfort. Satan doesn't exist as is traditionally portrayed, so I knew it couldn't be some fictitious power that he possessed. And if the underworld possessed this type of power, wouldn't they be sabotaging everything? Traffic lights would be a constant deathtrap. Air travel would be a nightmare. Since that wasn't the case, it appeared that the amount of power possessed coincided with the level of Heaven. The higher, the more powerful.

I knew I could trust the guidance I had received, but if I ever had a question, I could apply this logic to help evaluate the purity of the source.

With harm to no one.

Chapter 15

What Goes Around Comes Around

The Storyteller

As my awakening transpired, I kept thinking what a wonderful story was unfolding. No sooner had I completed one story, complete with its lessons, then another one presented itself. I kept finding myself saying, "Wow, what a great story." And some of the best parts of the books I'd read, during my research, were the stories that illustrated a point. At the end of his audio program *SynchroDestiny*, Deepak Chopra suggested a different way of thinking about God (or the conscious energy field). He suggested that God was an incredibly ingenious storyteller Who was telling His stories through each of us. When I heard this, I smiled wide, shook my head emphatically, and said, "That He is." I was like the old cavemen who finally invented the wheel; the clues had been all around me for a long time, but this incredibly simple and obvious revelation to assemble the pieces hadn't occurred to me.

My experiences have taught me that God loves a good laugh and a good story. It even appears that He enjoys it when someone passes the story along, as I'm trying to do here, because He continues to provide me with material worth writing about.

Goin' Round in Circles

From time to time throughout my adult life, a situation would arise where I would hear someone declare a warning, using the phrase "what goes around comes around." I considered it nothing more than a clever cliché, with no basis in reality. Fortunately, in most cases, the warnings weren't directed toward me.

During my spiritual awakening and subsequent research, I encountered this "full circle" concept a number of times, lending credence to its legitimacy as a universal law. This dashed my theory of it being merely a clever cliché and placed me on guard regarding my actions and behaviors. Kabbalah teaches that the universal effect (reward or retribution) of our actions, or the "comes around" component, is delayed in our world of linear time. And herein lies the problem; the universal effect is delayed until the appropriate time. Unfortunately, this disconnects the universal effect from the cause, potentially concealing the reward or retribution of our actions. Universal effect shouldn't be confused with physical effect. In other words, we typically experience the physical effect of our actions in short order. Example, the physical effect of giving five dollars to a homeless person is obvious; the person is thankful and can afford a meal. Finding ten dollars, three months later, might be the universal effect and yet not be recognized as such, due to the time lapse.

An Eye for an Eye

Alex was playing outside with his step-brother and step-sister. His step-sister was teasing, taunting and otherwise irritating him. Alex asked her to stop but she continued until she pushed him over the edge. In a moment of rage, he picked up a rock and threw it at her. The rock struck her just above her eye and caused a rather long laceration. Alex received a severe verbal scolding and was sent to his room for the evening.

That same evening, Alex's father called Janice to report on his behavior and gave Janice an opportunity to speak with Alex, to ensure that he learned his lesson. I was surprised when I heard Janice tell Alex that she felt sorry for him because he would become the recipient of an equivalent act, from a universal perspective.

About a month later, Alex was again playing outside, this time with a friend down the street. Going from game to game, Alex decided to hit a soccer ball with a plastic baseball bat. He tossed the soccer ball up in the air and tried to smash a home run with the plastic bat, which caused the bat to bounce back with a vengeance. Instead of a home run, what he got was a sacrifice eye (fly) as the bat struck him above his eye, causing a rather long laceration.

While still in tears, Alex called his mother to tell her of his accident. No sooner had he recounted his story than his mother said, "What goes around comes around." Janice reminded Alex of what he had done to his step-sister, a month earlier. And how fitting for the injury to substantiate the biblical phrase "an eye for an eye."

Statistically speaking, boys injure themselves frequently, but what's the probability that he would injure his eye in much the same way as he had injured another's; and in a relatively short period of time after the initial infraction—short enough, indeed, for the memory and the scolding lecture to be fresh in everyone's mind.

A Shocking Experience

When I was a teenager, I liked to build muscle cars. I didn't have much money, but the money I had was put into making my Hot Rod more powerful, even before other parts were repaired or replaced. I had recently purchased a 1967 Dodge Dart GT and was in the process of restoring it. Some extra horsepower was installed under the hood, but I hadn't done much else to the tired old car.

One night, while cruising with friends, I caught up to a car on a single-lane road. The car was going slower than my high-performance testosterone level could tolerate. I attempted to pass, but an oncoming car prevented safe passage. When I stomped the gas pedal, I noticed the front end of the car lurched upward sharply. When I let off the gas, the front of the car abruptly did a nose dive, bottoming out on the Dart's frame. The shocks were shot, but I saw an opportunity to have some fun.

I began alternating between full throttle and no throttle, to see how high I could get the front end of the car to jump while doing about fifty miles per hour. We thought the old Dart was going to leap off the pavement, as the headlights violently heaved up and down, shining through the back window and over the roof of the car in front of us. Assuredly, the driver had no idea what the heck was going on behind him, so he pulled over and let us by. The crazily bobbing headlights probably caused the driver no small amount of apprehension, if not fear, causing him to yield to our silliness.

Many years later, while driving to work one afternoon, a teenager pulled up behind me on a single-lane road. He pulled in very close and began to tailgate; so close I could see him clearly in my rear view mirror. Soon he began to bounce his car the same way I had done, over twenty years earlier. For some reason, I became incredibly irritated and glared at him in my rear view mirror and pointed my finger at him to stop. Instead, he flipped me off.

It wasn't until my awakening that I recognized what cycle was completing here. I theorize that the universe doesn't always repay with a similar situation, but this was one of those times where it could. Now that I am aware of this universal law, I keep an uncut open eye on the lookout for their occurrence.

Lawful Twisting

God truly has a sense of humor, and sometimes I think I'm His crash-test dummy. It's apparent (painfully so) that He wants me learn certain aspects of life so that I get the message, and perhaps share that message with others. Over time, I have "hooked into" a couple of twists or different spins to the law of "what goes around comes around." Hopefully, these stories will "clear the air" as to their lessons.

Off the Hook

Janice, Alex and I were on another fishing vacation at Deep Creek Lake, which included preparing for the tournament at the end of the week. Fishing was slow, and once again I was stressing and struggling for a reliable fish-catching method. The day before the tournament was hot, adding to the level of difficulty and my short-temperedness. Smallmouth bass can be finicky, so I wanted to tie on a different bait to see if they would eat it rather than just come up and inspect it. It's unnerving and very frustrating to clearly see a fish charge your bait like a torpedo, only to stop on a dime and just look at it, and then leave. So I was on a mission to determine what bait or color would "get their goat." Alex, being hyperactive, was up to his usual antsy movement all over the boat. I was sitting in the bottom of the boat, trying to quickly tie on another bait, complete with dual treble hooks, when Alex leapt past me, snagging the line with his foot. The line snatched the lure from my hand and sent it flying. I immediately saw red as I read Alex the Riot Act. I told him that, if he had hooked me, I would have kicked his butt all over the boat.

Tournament day delivered a severe cold front, complete with wind, rain and much cooler temperatures. My partner and I went to the same place where I had yelled at Alex the day before. Again, I wanted to quickly tie on a different-color lure that included brand new treble hooks, before the wind blew us off course, so I got down into the bottom of the boat. With the fresh knot tied securely to the lure in my right hand, I hastily reached for my rod with my left hand, while standing up. Unfortunately, the line clung to my wet left hand, which attempted to yank the lure from my right hand without success. No, my right hand wanted that bait badly enough to bury one of those six hooks into a fingertip...right in the densest area of nerve endings, so that I could experience maximum enjoyment.

I prick myself rather frequently with sharp hooks, as most anglers do, but in all my years of fishing I had only buried one other hook past the barb, making the timing, location, and overall circumstances of this "hooking" more than coincidental. As soon as it happened, I recognized there was some meaning to this event. I could hear the universe say, in a loving yet laughing tone, "So, whose butt are you going to kick now?"

When hooks are buried past the barbs, they are incredibly difficult to extract, because flesh and skin are very tough, especially the skin on our hands, which is thicker and tougher. Pulling a hook out against the barb, rather than pushing it through, increases the force required to dislodge the hook. I had to have my partner put his thumb on the tip of my finger and hold it on the floor while I sharply snatched the hook with a pair of pliers. With the onboard surgery complete, I went back to fishing, slightly distracted by my bleeding, throbbing finger and quest for meaning.

What I took away from this event was that we all make mistakes, and some are completely unintended. Finding a scapegoat because we're having a bad day is not the solution, and can only bring negative results back upon us. When Alex accidentally snagged the line and almost hooked me, I should have been more thankful that he hadn't, and simply cautioned him about his movements in the boat. Yelling wasn't a necessary ingredient for the lesson. Another way of looking at this might be: don't punish the child as if he shattered a glass on the floor, if it didn't break. This isn't to say that a more severe scolding isn't in order if you find your child walking around with a loaded gun, ready to play "Cowboys and Indians." But scolding is usually better served if it is commensurate with the infraction.

Nonetheless, as this lesson faded back into the spiritual realm, my physical side emerged enough to allow yet another lesson to be learned.

Ooh, Ooh, That Smell

On another fishing trip, I let Alex drive the boat a good bit to get him accustomed to the properties of boats and water. He loves operating the boat and would frequently ask to drive if I forget to offer. The morning of our departure, we cooked all the remaining eggs and bacon, making breakfast sandwiches for everyone. Alex came up from the dock and got his sandwich, wrapped in plastic wrap. He asked if he could drive the boat all the way back to the ramp, and I told him he could. Euphoric, he ran back down to the boat to prepare it for take-off. He now had motivation to hurry and stow gear while warming up the engine.

After loading the truck, I met Alex at the dock and let him live his dream of driving back to the ramp, where we loaded up and headed home. About a week later, I was searching for something in the boat when I stumbled across Alex's breakfast sandwich, neatly stowed in the compartment behind the driver's seat. In his excitement, his perpetual drive to eat temporarily shifted gears to his drive for driving the boat. The boy is driven! I was glad I found it before it rotted too badly and caused a major stinking mess. Regardless, I planned to give him an appropriate ribbing about his forgotten sandwich. I was a little irritated at his forgetfulness, but not angry, since I found the sandwich before it became a problem. The next time I saw him, in an effort to see if he would remember what he had done, I planned to ask questions like, "Hey, do you remember that breakfast sandwich we made you on our last fishing trip? How did it taste?"

Some days later, I got into Janice's car to take her somewhere and noticed that it had a faint foul odor in it. I asked her if she could smell it, but she said she couldn't. I assured her that I smelled something bad but couldn't figure out what it was. Immediately, I blamed Alex for probably leaving something in her car, as he had done in the boat.

Several days later, after her car had baked in the sun at work on a ninety degree day, Janice returned to find that it wreaked of a stench so strong that it almost made her sick. She opened the doors and rolled down the windows, then searched everywhere until she finally found the source in the trunk. About two pounds of stewing beef, that she recently purchased at the grocery store, was rotting on top of a storage box in the trunk. And who could have done something so stupid...? Yep, it was me.

Janice had come home with a trunk load of groceries, and I unloaded them, while she put the groceries away. I usually check the nooks and crannies of the trunk and back seat of the car, to ensure nothing is left behind, but this time I missed something. But why couldn't I have missed a can of peas instead of the worst possible thing to leave in a trunk? Because there was a message?

I make mistakes and have done some incredibly dumb things. Sometimes I consider myself lucky to be alive, considering the many times I have electrically shocked myself, either intentionally or by accident. This was the universe's way of telling me not to place myself higher than someone else by pointing out their mistakes or shortcomings, because clearly I wasn't perfect and above mistakes, myself.

The next time I saw Alex, I told him I had a funny story for him. I shared with him my intention to give him a hard time about his abandoned breakfast sandwich left to become a science project, and how, when I did the exact same thing, I decided that it was better to admit that I make mistakes, too.

> We recognized our errors, laughed, and then
> went to get something good to eat.

Chapter 16

Visiting Hours

A "visit" is a very vivid visual encounter in which a loved one or friend pays us a visit during sleep. This seeming dream actually feels real, and that's probably because it is! Many ADCs (After Death Communications) are in the form of visits. When our mind is quiet, spirits can cut through the mental noise to deliver a message or just say hello. I rarely remember any dreams but I remembered these visits, which is another testimony to their validity. Throughout my spiritual awakening, I received several visits from departed loved ones and friends. Perhaps they knew they wouldn't frighten me because I had grown to accept the presence of spirit.

Patience is a Virtue

The first visit was from my mother. I don't remember ever dreaming about her in the thirty-six years prior to my awakening, so I knew it was her paying the visit. The image was vivid but the room she was in seemed rather dismal and confined. She seemed happy as we briefly talked about flowers. She said something to the effect that they didn't grow fast enough. I replied that she was impatient like me and now I understood where I got it from. With that, she said, "That's right," then disappeared.

The message, although very brief, was to be patient and all things would work out. I was disappointed that she didn't have any more to say than that, but figured there was probably a good reason. As I stated earlier the universe seems to safeguard some of its information to protect free will. Perhaps this was one of those situations.

Male Bonding

In another dream I was walking past a set of stairs, and at the top of the steps there was a door that was cracked open partially. I walked up the stairs and opened the door to find Uncle Dutch, Uncle Carl, Pop-Pop and Uncle Frank sitting around in a room, grinning from ear to ear.

They said something to me but, upon awakening, I couldn't remember what it was. I was probably too stunned from seeing them.

They knew I would have difficulty remembering the visit since I struggle to remember any dreams, so they left me some signs to help. At the time, I was trying to breach the thin veil (or door) that exists between the physical world and the spirit world. The partially cracked open door at the top of the stairway symbolized that the connection was opening slightly but it wasn't wide open.

These guys were happy and relaxed-looking, which helped bring comfort to me regarding what to expect on the other side.

I wasn't positive that Uncle Frank was one the guys in the room because I didn't remember what he looked like. A few months later at a wedding, one of my cousins, who I grew up with on the farm, came up to me and asked if I remembered Uncle Frank. I told him that I didn't, so he proceeded to tell me as much as he could about him. He mentioned that my mother and he got along really well and joked

Visiting Hours

around a lot together. This was my clue that the relative of whose identity I was unsure was probably Uncle Frank. I hadn't prompted the conversation, and Uncle Frank was probably the farthest thing from anyone's mind.

At this same wedding, I found an opening that allowed me to deliver good news to Aunt Anna, the aunt who had stood beside me, crying in the driveway as my mother was rushed to the ambulance on a stretcher. She supported me then and many times throughout my life, and now I had an opportunity to support her.

Somehow, a conversation I was having with her and other relatives shifted to our departed loved ones or something very similar in nature. I don't recall exactly, but I may have mentioned something about Christmas. Aunt Anna then proceeded to tell me that Uncle Carl had died on Christmas Day, a fact I had long since forgotten. Ever since then, she has had a huge hole in her heart, and Christmas had become the antitheses of joy for her. All it served to bring was bad memories and sadness over the loss of a man she dearly loved. I was very fond of him, too. He used to pull coins out of my ears, teach me card tricks, and bring me trinket gifts that I thought were the greatest. To a youngster, Uncle Carl was "cool."

I asked Aunt Anna if she had ever received any signs or dream visits from him. She said she had not, and wasn't aware that these things could happen. That's when I told her that I had seen Uncle Carl in a dream, and that he was doing fine with the other relatives. She began to cry with what appeared to be tears of cautious joy, to find out her beloved Carl was fine and patiently waiting for her. I can only hope the news was cherished and not subsequently denied.

So perhaps Uncle Carl's visit had more purpose than to just say hello to me. He knew the opportunity would present itself for me to say hello for him to his beloved Anna.

Dick's Debut

I had been wondering if my mother had been reprimanded or, worse yet, punished because she committed suicide. A co-worker named Dick had also committed suicide several years earlier. We didn't know the reasons or the details and didn't need to know. We were more concerned about the family and our loss of a good friend and co-worker. The books *Hello From Heaven* and *One Last Time* suggested that different fates for suicide victims were possible, depending on circumstances. Neither book painted a picture of eternal damnation but they did suggest that the individual would have to deal with their mistake through spiritual rehabilitation, and perhaps another life here on Earth under similar conditions. Some spirits communicated feeling great sorrow and remorse for committing suicide, while those who were terminally ill expressed joy at their freedom from suffering. It appeared there was not a standard "sentence" for this offense. I no longer believed that my mother was condemned to an eternal Hell, but I didn't know what fate had befallen her.

One night, Dick paid a visit to answer my question. There he was, standing in the bright sunshine of a cloudless day, dressed in dark dress pants and a polo-style shirt. The place seemed beautiful. We were outdoors, with land all around us. My attention focused on him as I said, "Dick, is that you?" and he nodded his head *yes*. His face was mildly serious, which was unusual for Dick. He was always cutting up about something. Perhaps he was serious because of the message he was about to deliver.

The next question I asked, as if I was being guided not to be too specific, was "Did you get into trouble for what you did?" and he replied, "Yes, I got into trouble." But I couldn't really hear what he was saying. It was as if the communication came telepathically. In addition, his telepathic voice was weak, which added to the difficulty of understanding. His lips moved when he spoke but his voice was not externally audible. Then I asked him if my mother got into trouble, and he replied, "Yes, she got into a lot of trouble."

I don't know why my mother may have gotten into more trouble than Dick, but that's the way he seemed to characterize the situation. He didn't elaborate at all, and then he was gone. The extent of that trouble didn't seem to be all that bad if Dick was in such a great-looking place. So perhaps the books were right; he and my mother had to work on their spiritual development a little more rigorously than most.

Once again, I sensed that the universe was safeguarding information.

The Homecoming

Several days before Janice's father passed away, I received a second visit from Dick. This time he brought my old friend, Chip, with him.

Janice and I were walking through a hotel hallway at the beach. I could see sand and sunshine outside a doorway. We were on the ground level. When walking past a doorway that was closed, Janice told me the name of the woman in the room and said that she was a sweetheart. I quickly forgot the woman's name but I did remember it to be a common last name. We walked further down the hall and then I turned left through another door, into a room, while Janice continued on.

I crawled onto a tabletop, wrapped myself in a blanket and fell asleep. A moment later, I woke up and the room was surreal. Dick and Chip were in the room. The interesting thing about some visits is that you really *are* somewhere else and you are fully *aware* that you're someplace else. Somehow, the spirits take you with them. I was no longer asleep in my bed. I knew I was fully awake and I knew I was somewhere else.

Dick and Chip were behind what appeared to be a breakfast bar, seated on tall chairs. Dick's appearance seemed a little different, so it took me a moment to recognize him. His facial features were more chiseled and squared. Dick may have opted to alter his appearance because I hadn't seen Chip in so long that he wanted me to take a long hard look to figure out who they both were. Once I figured out who they were, I asked them to confirm their identity, and they nodded *yes*.

I turned to Dick and asked him how he was doing. He replied that he was all right, but once again I couldn't hear him very well and resorted to reading his lips. I asked Chip how he was doing, and got the same reply.

Next to Chip was an empty seat with a uniform in it. The uniform was sitting in the chair straight up, as if it had a body in it with no head. When I first saw it, I was a little frightened and tensed up. Then I realized it had what appeared to be a hanger or wire framing holding it firm in place, so I relaxed a little. It wasn't a headless horseman, after all.

Then they vanished and I heard angel music for a few minutes. Some people claim to be able to hear angel music coming through from the other dimension. I had been wondering what angel music sounded like, and now I was hearing it, courtesy of Dick and Chip.

Several days later, Janice's father passed away. A neighbor, Mrs. Curtis, had noticed that Dad hadn't picked up his newspapers off the front step in a couple of days, and his car was still in the driveway. Dad always got his paper if he was home, so she suspected something was wrong and called the family to see if he was with them. Since Dad wasn't with the family, or away on a trip, and didn't answer his phone, they went to check on him and found him deceased in the house. Janice told me about Mrs. Curtis and mentioned that she had been an excellent neighbor and was a sweet woman. She may have described her as a sweetheart, as in the dream, but in all the emotion I couldn't remember for certain. But I do believe the woman behind the door in the dream was Mrs. Curtis. I surmised that being behind the door was symbolic of being on Earth. The hallway represented the middle ground, veil or divide between the dimensions. It wasn't until I passed through another door on the opposite side of the hallway that I entered the next dimension. Perhaps falling asleep on the tabletop represented entering another altered state of consciousness accessible by spirit.

Janice's dad had been a Marine. I think Dick and Chip were trying to communicate that the uniform was for him and that he would be coming home soon. Perhaps they were part of the welcoming committee. And perhaps they had a freshly cleaned and pressed uniform waiting for him. I could only hope this was the meaning behind their visit, but I wasn't positive.

Dad was a Catholic who attended church every Sunday, but the depth of his faith wasn't easy to read. Several of his daughters felt his faith was strong, or at least adequate, but Janice had a different opinion. She hadn't heard some of her sister's stories supporting the faith that Dad, in fact, had. She had never seen a bible in the house while growing up, and Dad never discussed God, religion or faith openly. He probably felt that he didn't need to, since he was sending all seven of the children to Catholic schools. From time to time, as an adult, Janice would ask his thoughts about God, Jesus and the afterlife. He would typically avoid the conversation or not provide a meaningful answer, convincing Janice that his faith was weak. She wondered if he would safely find his way home in the afterlife. We both wanted to know that he was okay, so we asked for a sign.

After spending all day at the funeral home and the florist, making arrangements, the family was tired and hungry, but mostly hungry. It was decided that the family should go out to dinner together. The area had many restaurants to choose from, so I figured we would quickly get a bite at one of the closest, and then make our long trip home. Instead, the lead vehicle kept going and going for what seemed like an eternity for a hungry clan. *Why so far?* I quietly brooded. Finally, we pulled into the parking lot of a restaurant named *Rip's*. Immediately I got the connection: *Rest in Peace*. Dad was just fine.

Silence is Golden

It had been quite some time since any of my departed friends had paid me a visit. I was wondering if my lack of meditation sessions, along with my immersion into physical life, including work activities and the completion of this manuscript, had weakened my intuition and connection to the other side, thus blocking fine-tuned "gut feelings" and spirit's ability to get through to me.

But now my manuscript was complete and in the capable hands of my editor, Judith of EditAvenue, an online internet service. While waiting for her comments and corrections, I now had time on *my* hands to devote to my spiritual health. I meditated on several consecutive mornings and evenings, prayed more frequently and performed several chakra-clearing meditations to improve my connections and to remove any blockages that may have existed. My intentions were more geared toward improving spiritual health than a tune-up to prepare for a visit.

But during this time of strengthening my spiritual condition, I had a dream just before awakening that included an old friend, named Danny. I had worked with Danny for many years at the power plant, before he accepted a job elsewhere and moved on. Danny, a Viet Nam War veteran who was shot during a skirmish, said very little about his fighting days. Co-workers and I knew the subject was taboo and didn't bring it up. What we did know was that Danny had a big heart filled with courage, integrity, and a degree of combat-generated toughness that yielded to no one.

More than a year prior to this writing, Danny was found in his truck, dead from a heart attack. He managed to pull his truck to the side of the road, thus preventing injury to anything or anyone else. That's the way Danny would have wanted it.

As usual, the dream was brief. I found myself in the Control Room at the plant with a number of operators in the audience, but I didn't attempt to identify them because I immediately noticed Danny and Dick at the center of attention. Danny was young and vibrant-looking, with a thousand watt smile on his face. I couldn't hold back my enthusiasm for seeing him and his contagious smile, so I walked up close to him, got his attention, grinned excitedly and said something witty like, "What are you doing in the Control Room? You're not really here. You can't fool me." Immediately, we were whisked away to a beautiful small field lined with trees. The open area contained green grass with multi-colored flowers mixed in, and a large shade tree in the center.

Danny walked diagonally in front of me, from left to right, while he spoke. His distance from me was far enough that I couldn't read his lips and it may not have helped because he was looking around and gesturing as he spoke. It didn't matter because I could hear him in my mind relatively well. Danny told me that visiting the Earth plane was easy to learn and easy to do and they could visit whenever they wanted. He went on to tell me that a problem the spirits encounter while here is tolerating the noise (I vaguely remember him referring to a high-pitched, shrill sound), as he placed his hands over his ears. He mentioned that he couldn't get too close because he couldn't tolerate the noise that some people generate.

As soon as he was done with this unusual and short explanation, he was gone. When I awoke, I actually forgot all about having the dream, until sometime later that morning when something triggered the memory. I tried to recall what I remembered but was baffled by the meaning of his conversation, and I questioned what I thought I'd heard. Telling me about noise didn't make sense, so I began to think it was just a dream that my subconscious mind created.

That evening, I decided to pick out a book that I'd read before and randomly select chapters that captured my interest. I selected James Van Praagh's *Talking to Heaven* and began reading. Van Praagh is very spiritually connected with highly developed hearing, or clairaudience. Before long, I had read two stories where Van Praagh mentioned the high-pitched sound generated by earthly things. The first case involved his hearing houseplants that hadn't been watered and were wilting. They generated a high-pitched squeal as if they were screaming for water. The second case involved a client he was trying to perform a reading for. The woman was so emotional that her energy created an interference in the form of loud static that blocked his ability to connect until she was calmed.

So that's what Danny was trying to tell me! And he knew the future well enough to know that I would stumble across that information in the near future. This confirmed that the dream was in fact a visit, and prompted me to recall the details so that I could accurately relay the story.

I also wonder if Danny was trying to tell me that my own spirit had become noisy and needed quieting. In any case, I'd like to thank Danny for a beautiful tour and an intriguing message.

And I can't leave out Dick, who seems to be in most of my visits, even if it's just for a cameo.

Thanks, Buddy!

Chapter 17

Inspiration, Intention and Interpretation

As autumn progressed, it was time to head back to the bookstore to get a fall and winter supply of reading material so that I could continue to learn and develop.

My sights were still focused on learning more about God and Jesus, so I looked for books to satisfy that desire. When I first began researching, I noticed a book title that intrigued me but I chose not to buy it. The book was entitled *Conversations with God*. I thought how interesting that sounded, but figured it was just a catchy title, because no one could really have a conversation with God. But for the next year, the title of the book kept coming to mind, as if to nudge me into buying it the next time I purchased a load of books. So even before I entered the bookstore, this book was on my list.

I discovered that the author, Neale Donald Walsch, had written a trilogy and several other books related to the *Conversations with God* series. When I picked up Book One of the trilogy and glossed over a few pages to check the context, I found it interesting enough to buy Books One and Three. A copy of Book Two wasn't available.

It didn't take me long to conclude that Walsch was actually having a conversation with God. Since Jesus had communicated with me, I no longer considered it impossible for someone to talk to God. But I was naturally on guard for the dreaded "false teacher," so I read with optimistic caution. I remained convinced that God was, in fact, talking with Walsch.

God spoke very lovingly and from a highly intellectual level, with concepts beyond the comprehension of our finite minds. He explained many mysteries. He was patient and systematic in His approach to slowly bring Walsch, and ultimately the reader, to understand. I gained new insights and was able to tie together some of the loose ends I still had.

God explained concepts such as:
- His desire for experience and why we are here
- Knowledge verses experience
- Life after death
- Our relationship to Him
- Punishment verses rehabilitation
- "Wrong;" what it isn't
- Hell; what it isn't

I finished Book One within a couple of days by reading at every chance I got. I felt on top of the world because God had confirmed several of my own conclusions. When I completed the book, I set it down and quietly sat, misty-eyed in the afterglow, absorbing the peace and love of God. After a bit, I walked on sunshine upstairs to get something. When I passed my computer, I noticed the screen was black because the screen saver had turned off the screen, as designed. But this time it had one of those irritating "pop-up ads" in the middle of it. I was agitated over how determined those damned pop-up ads were and that they actually would override the screen saver. But this one was probably there for a special reason: it read "YOU ARE A WINNER." I knew that was my cue from God that I was on the right track, and that the *Conversations with God* books were a "must read."

I dove into Book Three and purchased many of the other books written by Walsch. I wanted to hear all that God had to say, and He wanted me to hear Him, too. Some of God's words seemed to have been spoken and written just for me to hear and read. I was touched to the essence of my being as I began to understand the universe with increasing clarity.

I now understood why I hadn't purchased these books a year earlier. It was designed that, through my own personal experiences and studies, I would be able to more easily comprehend the more complex and controversial subjects that God discussed. A year earlier I didn't have the fundamental knowledge and understanding needed to grasp these new teachings.

I considered (and still do) *Conversations with God* to be a very important series of books that I read to understand who and what we really are. The concepts might have been tough to grasp if they had been my first stop on the path to awakening. Many of the concepts conflicted with the more customary beliefs instilled in me since childhood.

Even after reading the *Conversations with God* series, I had a few lingering questions and was further led to other books and tapes to help confirm my intuitive feelings. Another author, Dr. Doreen Virtue, has excellent insight because of her strong connection to the other side. I highly recommend Virtue's books such as:

The Lightworker's Way
Healing With The Angels
Archangels & Ascended Masters

I learned a tremendous amount from Virtue's books. Many pieces of the puzzle now fit neatly and logically into place.

Pure Intentions

Through my research, I chanced upon many books and documents, some of them quite by accident, or perhaps Divinely orchestrated. In either case, I found a myriad of different authors and writers from different eras who recorded information containing striking similarities and yet contained a few unfortunate contradictions. Being able to corroborate evidence helped to establish the credibility of a specific concept, while contradiction served to undermine it. I had to come to grips with it. Should I reject a witness's entire testimony because one account didn't completely agree with another's, or might the witness have had a different vantage point? I had to reconcile the data. Much of this information pertained to Heaven, Hell and God. I'm going to take some time and attempt to explain and condense these writings, as well as build a case for their validity. I'll start with the bible.

The bible claims to be the absolute word of God, and states that no man should alter God's word for fear of severe punishment. But the bible itself contains a number of contradictions that only serve to fuel skeptics and cynics who can use this as a burning platform to attack its veracity. That doesn't mean we should take the entire bible, discount it, and throw it into the fire. The bible contains a tremendous amount of truth and wisdom, if we can just separate the wheat from the chaff. If we can just try to understand the complexity of God and His universe and the primitive nature of life in those ancient times, we might better understand why there is much confusion. And is there a reasonable explanation as to why this has happened? I think there is.

Inspiration, Intention and Interpretation

Probably the most understandable and obvious reason for biblical contradictions, disconnects and misunderstandings is in its translation. In ancient times, paper (papyrus) was not readily available, so the word of God had to be memorized and passed down from one generation to the next. Many villages had their own translation of sacred scripture, which was called the *Targum* or "Torah on the lips." Selected individuals called "meturgeman" paraphrased and memorized scripture. It seems reasonable that all of this handling of the same information over many years could change the original meaning and intent, at least to a lesser degree.

Most of us have seen the demonstration where a short bit of information is communicated to one person at the end of a line and then the information is whispered down the line of people, one at a time, like a baton in a relay race. The person at the end of the line then shares the information with the audience. The results are usually hilarious because the original information has been significantly changed to where it may not even resemble its origin. Add in a few hundred years, cultural influences, personal beliefs and ego driven motives and you might find a significant change in the teachings of any tradition.

The Old Testament was written almost entirely in Hebrew. A small portion was written in Aramaic. The New Testament was written in Greek because that language was widely understood in the region. When sacred scripture *was* written, it was written without the use of vowels. The writers relied upon the readers to know which vowels to insert to form the word. To complicate things even further, there are no spaces between the words, so it is difficult for translators to determine the beginning of one word and the end of another. Another factor affecting translation is the changing dialect and meaning of words. We see this in our own language, with words such as "awful" and "awesome." Fifty years ago, "awful" meant "full of awe," much like awesome means "something phenomenal or great." Somewhere, somehow, awful changed to characterize something terrible. Another word more recently changed is the word "gay." Its primary definition used to mean "happy," but now it is more frequently used to label homosexuals.

The back of some bibles provides a more detailed explanation of the origin of sacred scripture, the difficulty of translation, and the rigor used to translate responsibly. Even with this huge potential for errors, I don't think this is the largest contributor to misguided doctrine or the presence of contradiction.

Kings, queens, rulers, and dictators have forever been trying to control the peasants. It seems that they have determined that a powerful mechanism for doing so is through religion and sacred scripture. All that was necessary was to write or translate it into a form of fear-based control, turning God into a jealous, angry and vengeful patriarch. Control could be achieved by eliciting fear within the masses—fear of the wrath of God.

At the Council of Nicea, in 325 C.E., Roman Emperor Constantine called together roughly three hundred bishops and priests from the surrounding churches. Christianity was rapidly splitting into two factions because of the fast-spreading teachings of a priest named Arius, who claimed that Jesus was a created being and did not co-exist with God from the beginning. Constantine hoped his kingdom would begin to settle after his defeat of Emperor Licinius in 323 C.E. Lucinius had been horrifically persecuting the Christians of Constantine's empire. Nevertheless, this new controversy was intense and threatened to divide the church, which meant disunity and unrest within the kingdom, so Constantine called the council to settle the dispute, once and for all. Church leaders had recently endured great suffering for their beliefs and weren't about to easily yield to another priest who was attempting to alter their fundamental belief. The arguments were enraged enough to promulgate an agreement between the clergymen, called the *Nicene Creed,* to eliminate further debate and to unify doctrine. Many weeks of debate and discussion followed on various other topics that needed clarification.

Constantine, not being a Christian, was primarily interested in the control of his people and simply wanted a unified religion to prevent internal conflict and persecution. From my research, it is not clear how much influence Constantine wielded on the council. There are many insights asserted about this historical meeting. Some maintain that Constantine directly ordered the inclusion or exclusion of certain doctrine and scripture in biblical texts, while others maintain that the council performed its duties unencumbered.

During this period, it was not unusual for Roman Emperors to involve themselves in the workings of the church and utilize their power of office to control decisions. Arius found this out first-hand when Constantine publicly declared his teachings evil and ordered all of his books burned, "to eliminate any trace of his existence." But how much of the bible was accurately maintained and how much was changed or altered? And what might have been eliminated because an Emperor wanted control of his people? I don't know for certain, but this council presented Constantine with an opportunity for significant change using an incredibly powerful channel: religious beliefs and sacred scripture. Clearly he had motive and intent.

Throughout history, men have claimed to be divinely inspired. Where did this divine inspiration come from that commanded these biblical figures to pen doctrine and perform tasks for God, and how did the recipient know God was actually providing the direction? It would be very convincing for a leader to stand on a mountainside and claim that God commanded a certain action.

How would Abraham, Moses, Job, Noah and any of the many other bible figures know for certain that God was talking to them? Had any of them actually seen God? John 1:18 (KJV) says "No man hath seen God at any time." Similar statements are contained in Exodus 33:20, Timothy 6:16, John 6:46 and 1 John 4:12, while Genesis 32:30 says "for I have seen God face to face." Other supporting verses claiming the sighting of God are contained in Exodus 33:11 and 23, Isaiah 6:1 and Job 42:5.

The vast majority of the communications from God to earthly beings was done through hearing. Job 42:5 says "I have heard of Thee by the hearing of the ear: but now mine eye seeth Thee." In the bible, there are countless numbers of communications purportedly from God. If the communications weren't from God, then who were they from, and why? And if God commanded actions, such as the various attacks He allegedly ordered in the Old Testament, then doesn't this violate the universal law of free will and also violate one of the Ten Commandments? "And the Lord sent thee on a journey, and said, go and utterly destroy the sinners the Amalekites, and fight against them until they be consumed." (I Sam 15:18 KJV) The Amalekites experience genocide at the swords of the Israelite Saul and his army. Justifiable homicide? I don't believe God really commanded this atrocity, or many of the other attacks on human life as told in the Old Testament. Thousands upon thousands of men, women and children were murdered at the command of God? I refuse to accept this.

And did God only communicate with people in biblical times? My own personal experiences had convinced me that God was getting messages across. Perhaps these messages were delivered by His emissaries and not coming directly from Him. I couldn't tell for sure,

Inspiration, Intention and Interpretation

but I was certain that communications were coming. And were there other people in more recent times that claimed to be receiving divine inspiration and communications? It seemed discriminating that God would only talk to folks from ancient times. Why wouldn't He talk to us? Had we become too evil? That didn't seem reasonable; the bible contains many stories of evil, abuse, slayings and perversions. Biblical times were uncivilized, to say the least. Our society still has acts of evil, but overall we are more civilized and there are many spiritual people among us. It was easy to conclude that communication from God in modern times was very possible.

A couple of these books are *A Course in Miracles* and *Conversations with God.* While searching for something totally unrelated, I happened across another web site that sparked my interest. The web site claimed that Jesus had channeled information through a man named James Padgett.

A rudimentary explanation of channeling is a process by which a spirit mentally aligns with a susceptible human and transmits information by directly speaking with, talking through or writing through the individual. Both Helen Schucman, author of *A Course in Miracles,* and Neale Donald Walsch, author of *Conversations with God,* stated that their communication was a form of dictation where they could hear the voice inside their head. Basically, they took dictation from the voice as it spoke. This form of communication may more accurately be labeled as clairaudient (or "clear hearing") in the psychic community. In Schucman's case, the voice claimed to be Jesus; in Walsch's case, the voice claimed to be God's.

One of the most noted channels of the twentieth century was Edgar Cayce, who would lie on a couch and seemingly go to sleep while spirits used his body and vocal cords to speak through him, thus delivering messages. His voice would change and he would take on the personality of the spirit. When the session was over, Cayce would never remember a thing about the episode, and refused to believe some of the things that had been channeled through him, even though they were recorded.

James Padgett was an attorney in Washington D. C. during the early 1900s when various spirits began to channel through him, using "automatic writing." These spirits included such noteworthy figures as some of the Apostles and Jesus. Automatic writing occurs when one grabs a pen and paper, sits quietly and allows a spirit to take control of the muscle movement of the hand, thus penning a message.

After reading the books and documents that these individuals had channeled, it was obvious that knowledgeable and evolved spirits were in fact trying to deliver truth to us about God, Heaven, Hell and the nature of the universe and its laws. Many of the laws, concepts and descriptions were remarkably similar, which allowed me to corroborate the information and deem the information presented as plausible. The only snag I encountered was that some of the information was contradictory.

The subject of reincarnation is often a heated topic in this dimension, and it seems to be no different in the other. In *Conversations with God,* God openly talks about the many lives we all live here on Earth in the process of perfecting our souls, while in *A Course in Miracles* Jesus reluctantly admits that reincarnation is possible and acceptable to discuss if it is utilized for the proper reason. He explains that reincarnation is impossible in the sense that there is no past or future. He seems to treat it as if believing in reincarnation is fine, while not believing in it is fine, also. In the Padgett Papers, Jesus vehemently denounces the possibility of reincarnation and takes the time to technically explain how "utterly impossible" it is.

Inspiration, Intention and Interpretation

Will the real Jesus please stand up? God, will you please get your people straight on these issues? I thought with great frustration. After spending many hours deciphering page after page of the old style English, and trying to understand concepts that are foreign to us, I hit the wall. All of these documents are challenging to comprehend. The Padgett Paper's description of reincarnation and the technical explanation trying to prove why it was impossible wasn't very convincing. This called into question the entire series of papers written by Padgett. Literally hundreds of pages of excellent answers, explanations and descriptions were potentially foiled by a few pages of obvious inaccuracies. I set the papers aside and didn't look at them for over two years.

With a great sense of urgency, I still sought the truth about all of these topics. The more I researched, the more I uncovered minor conflicts and contradictions between these documents and others, all of which claim to be divinely inspired. Then, finally, rather luckily once again, I collided with a reasonable explanation.

While searching a different, unrelated topic, I happened across yet another collection of papers allegedly channeled through from Judas Iscariot. Judas, who betrayed Jesus, had served his sentence, so to speak, and is now spiritually rehabilitated. Judas has channeled many messages through on many, many topics similar to the Padgett Papers. (Search the internet using *Conversations with Judas* for interesting reading.) As with many inhabitants of the spirit world, his mission, purpose or passion has become trying to communicate useful information to help us make the right choices while on Earth. He claimed that many spirits would try to get messages through to us whenever they could. Padgett received a similar message from the Apostle John. Just like our spirit guides and departed loved ones, they're around us, trying to ensure we remain on the righteous path to Heaven. And since we cannot usually see them, it is easy for them to deliver a message by using a more powerful and meaningful alias, such as Jesus, to really get our attention. It might seem like a rather deceitful activity, but it is out of love for us and mankind that they are trying so hard to keep us straight.

An analogy: a young child burned her hand a few days ago on the stove. As the tears rolled down her cheeks, you applied an ice-filled cloth to the palm of her hand, to cool and sooth the injury while compassionately pointing out that the stove was "Hot!" After several iterations of "Stove, hot, burn," you check for understanding, and the child slowly nods her head up and down, while saying, "Hot, burn me." Several days later, you witness the same inquisitive child reaching for a sharp knife on the countertop. You lunge toward the child but there's no time to spare, so you instinctively yell, "No! Hot!"

I think the spirit world is sometimes in this same predicament. They're trying desperately to provide us with a good set of rules to live by, even if it means falsifying information to ultimately protect us from our own destructive devices. In other words, it's not important whether or not reincarnation is true; we don't need to concern ourselves with a concept that has no bearing on developing impeccable characteristics in this life. We need to concentrate on living our current life in a more saintly way, and not believe we can transfer that responsibility to our next incarnation. And if we need to be "scared straight" every now and then, that's okay because, in the end, just like children sternly taught for their own good, we will benefit from it.

We do need to be cautious about the dreaded "false teacher." "Beloved, believe not every spirit, but try the spirits whether they are of God: because many false prophets are gone out into the world." (1

Inspiration, Intention and Interpretation

John 4:1 KJV) An evaluation of the message or doctrine would be appropriate in this case. Simple questions such as "Can anyone be harmed by this teaching and does it contain pure intentions?" would help pass judgment on a message's merit.

By having first-hand experience with spirit communications, combined with tons of research on all aspects of the spirit world, I was ready to develop a theory and draw a conclusion regarding spirit communications.

The Old Testament cites many instances where God supposedly commanded death, destruction and even genocide. He also declared Himself as an angry, jealous and vengeful god who even created evil. Could this have been unhappy or evil spirits with an axe to grind? I believe it's possible. Or did God really create these things to maximize His experience through us? I don't think so, but I can't completely rule out the possibility. Our egos are evil enough to create these things on their own, without God's influence, so I'd like to believe that we have done these things to ourselves, and that God wants nothing but pure and holy things for us.

The lowest astral levels or lowest levels of Heaven are the ones closest to the Earth plane. Spirits on these levels are closest in vibration/frequency with ours, and therefore possess the greatest chance of getting a message through to us. And perhaps, in these primitive times, when there wasn't an overabundance of highly evolved spiritual beings, some less-than-godlike guidance was provided and captured in Targum and text. Some of which might also have carried over into the New Testament, as well?

Had biblical accounts created an angry, jealous and vengeful god from spirits communicating from the lower astral levels who were trying to "scare us straight"? And perhaps these spirits believed they understood God's laws but really didn't, and had the best of intentions to help us.

> Was the confusion intentional, to prolong
> this dimension of experience?

Chapter 18

Some Assembly Required

I now had devoted much of the past four years of my life to discovering and awakening my spiritual side, along with learning about God, Heaven, Hell and anything related. As if the Catholic tradition of Lent was in season, I gave up many of the things I loved to do, in order to walk this path. Following the lead of God and Company, I was guided to research a tremendous amount of material, most of which had at least one "golden nugget" or "silver bullet" to make the pieces of the puzzle fit. The answers came slowly, at times, but in my mind my dogged determination to find the truth paid off. On many confusing and frustrating occasions, I looked toward Heaven with my hands outstretched, pleading, "I just want the truth!" And many times I temporarily revolted against the answers I was given; my mental model fiercely defended its childhood programming. The saying "all great truths start as blasphemy" applied to much of what I was about to learn. Ultimately, however, a large contribution to understanding God and the universe derived from my personal experiences. There's simply no substitute for experience.

"Imagine That" A Spiritual Awakening

It was time to put it all together.

As I began to assemble the pieces of the puzzle, I found them to fit rather comfortably in a logical explanation. I was sure I wasn't the first person to ever figure these things out, but perhaps I could explain them from an "average Joe's" perspective.

Embracing the cliché "fact is stranger than fiction" might help us understand some of these concepts. For example, it is difficult to imagine the ends of the universe because, if it has an end, what's on the other side? If there is a wall on the edge of the universe, what's on the other side of the wall? If there is nothing on the other side of the wall, how far can you travel in the "nothing" before you reach the end of nothing? There is "nothing" between the planets in outer space; it's a void. If this "nothingness" extends beyond the edge of the planets, wouldn't this be part of the universe, too? So there is no end to the universe. But how can that be? These concepts are mind-boggling and easily prove the limitations of our finite minds to understand the complexities of God's universe. We can only begin to understand the universe, and we sometimes require simple analogies to make things clear. It was time to give it a try.

Home Alone

In the beginning, God was everything. He was all there was. There was nothing outside of God because God was all of it. He was pure knowledge and love, emotion and intellect. He surmised He was a superior intelligence and thought He was magnificent (not in an arrogant way), but had no way to experience how magnificent He was. In other words, He didn't have a mirror to see if His tie was on straight because He *was* everything. There was nothing external. He was all dressed up with no place to go and no one to admire Him, so to speak. An eternity of knowledge with no experience, like Webster's Dictionary He had all the definitions but no context.

A similar experience might occur if we first became aware of our existence in a state of suspension, in the dark, without a physical body, perhaps like closing our eyes and losing the awareness of our body; no physical or external sensations. We can't see a thing externally because it's too dark. We can't go anywhere because we don't have a body. And we don't know where "anywhere" is, *anyway*, because we can't see *any-thing*. It appears that all that exists is you and what's inside of you. All there is, is thought, knowledge and hopefully love and a desire to share.

God didn't know how smart He was because He had no one to compare Himself to, but He could think wonderful thoughts which gave Him a desire to create and come to know Himself. According to *Conversations with God*, God also had a desire to experience various relationships that He could not experience in His state of suspension. God wanted to experience up from down, hot from cold, left from right and other similar experiences. Since God had eternity to contemplate this, and since He was mostly thought, He was tremendously good at dreaming wonderful things, so He began to create a plan—a plan to create.

God recognized that, in order to achieve His goal, He had to create something that He could love, something that could reciprocate that love and appreciate His magnificence. Not being selfish, He wanted to share His magnificence, so He decided to create something like Himself: a separated being (in appearance only) had to be created to experience life for God. He created us, His children, in His image and likeness. As the saying goes, "there is no substitute for experience," and God wanted to know Himself through us and through these experiences. It has also been said that God knows our every thought even before we think them; we're connected (or invisibly wired) to God (or the Godhead) so that He can experience what we experience, through us. A motive, method and vehicle was now established to begin the journey.

At this point in eternity, we might have been tiny beings of light in the exact image and likeness of God. We were very aware of God, and our connection to Him was strong. Mere sparks of the Divine, we possessed all of the powers of God to a lesser degree. Images reported from Near Death Experiences (NDE's), visits and mediums reveal some entities as human-looking, while spirits from higher realms (as determined by their increased pure and loving "feel") appear more as bright light, with perhaps a human image within the light. Highly evolved spirits are beings of light but reveal themselves to us as human because that doesn't frighten us. One of the most frequently used phrases in the bible is "fear not," and it was typically spoken when angels appeared before humans. Human form fits our mental model and reduces the fear factor. Some NDE's simply report a bright, loving light that emanates an incredible calm, peace and joy. Based on these accounts, I believe that God is a being of light (and/or energy) similar to (but obviously much greater than) more advanced spirits. He is probably the highest frequency of intensely bright and beautiful white light, beyond our comprehension, which also equates to the highest spiritual vibration/frequency.

Once created, the symbolic Garden of Eden came into existence, because this is where God placed us, external to Himself. The concept of the Garden of Eden simply symbolizes a beautiful place that was perhaps our first residence, rather than an actual place on Planet Earth. Genesis goes into quite some detail, describing what God gave us in the Garden of Eden, but I'm not convinced we had physical bodies at that initial time. The biblical rendition tells the story in human terms so that we can more easily understand the parable of the "fall of man." We simply didn't need physical bodies, as beings of light. Nor did we have our total individuality at this point, because it wasn't until the "fall" that we wanted to experience complete separation. We were probably happy to share the "oneness" of the uni-verse (one verse or one song), together with the other sparks and God, at least until we grew tired of perfection and wanted more (or less, as it might be more accurately stated). The belief that everything in the universe is connected is not new and not just a Zen thing.

Kabbalah explains that God gave us everything we needed here. We needed nothing and couldn't give anything because everyone had everything they needed. After an eternity of constantly receiving, we experienced what the Kabbalah refers to as "Bread of Shame." We were made in the image and likeness of God and needed to love and share, just like God, in order to respect ourselves. Finally, we asked God to "Stop!"

I believe this was a very important point in our creation and evolution. As many believe, life is circular, like the four seasons; birth, newness, growth, ripening, maturity, harvest, preparation, reflection, weakening, giving back, passing along. Then birth or re-birth begins the cycle again. When God first created us and placed us in the Garden of Eden, it gave Him an opportunity to see and experience Himself in His highest, most loving and pure form. It also gave us a data point, or reference point, of our own highest form. This monumental quest would become our aspiration and inspiration to re-climb this mountain to re-achieve and reclaim our highest purity and holiness: our target, our goal, our nemesis, to rediscover who and what we really are, and what we should strive to be. Perhaps in the end we'll arrive at the beginning...with experience under our belts.

The Separation and Fall

There we were, happy as pigs in mud, in our "oneness" when, as Kabbalah explains, someone (or group) had this thought: "Is this all there is? I wonder if there could be something else." Since we were all connected as "one," we all heard the thought. The remainder of us pondered the idea immediately, and some of us thought, "Yeah, let's try something else!" Yet others thought, "No thanks, I like things just the way they are." And yet a third group thought, "Well, it does sound interesting." At that exact moment, the terms "left wing," "right wing" and "undecided" were born. Then God immediately answered our question and desire by separating us into three groups of souls. The "dark" souls (absence of the Light of God) that definitely wanted to experience "something else" were created. This "something else" was the opposite of the perfection that we were experiencing in Heaven. Another group was the "white" souls (containing the Light of God) who were *not* interested in "something else" but out of love for one another agreed to participate if necessary. The third group was the "gray" souls, or those souls in the middle, who simply thought it might be interesting to experience. Instantly, God also invented the first cliché: "Be careful what you wish for; you might just get it."

Did God Himself have anything to do with this desire to separate? I believe He did. Wanting to know Himself experientially, this was the next logical step. Because we are in God and He is in us, the desire for experience probably came from both. This is a major point: God's will and our will were aligned because we were one in the same.

By wanting "something else," we were basically requesting experience which had to be gained through a dramatic play, an act, a tragedy, a stage, a simulator…a third dimension. We knew that experience was the best teacher. We wanted to experience it all. We were in Heaven with God, where everything was perfect, so we didn't know hot from cold, for example. We didn't know "opposites" and we wanted to experience them. We wanted to experience relationships of all kinds, to truly know and appreciate God and ourselves. And God wanted to experience these things through us. To fully appreciate and enjoy a good meal, you need to be hungry. And the hungrier you are, the better it tastes. To fully appreciate and enjoy a vacation, you need to work hard. And the longer and harder you work, right before the vacation, the more rewarding and deserved it feels.

This is where the meaning of the story of Adam and Eve becomes clear. It always seemed strange to me that God would kick Adam and Eve out of Heaven for eating of the "tree of knowledge," which was symbolic of their desire for more knowledge. I could never understand why the quest for more knowledge was a bad thing. I figured, if it was a bad thing, then why do we send our kids to school and college?

God didn't kick us out of Heaven; we had to leave in order to experience our desires. We had no choice if We (God and us) wanted to experience the relationships We sought. It was time to bite the bullet, or "forbidden fruit" as was the case. It was time to leave home…at least temporarily.

God is everything that is pure, holy and wholesome, and cannot be contaminated by evil thoughts or character traits unique to humans, such as anger, vengeance, jealousy and hatred. So we couldn't gain the experience we sought within the confines of the Pearly Gates of Heaven. Something else had to be done. Something else had to be created, because God's purity and the purity of Heaven could not be corrupted.

God loves us so much that He was willing to let us have absolute freedom to do as we pleased. Love is total freedom, as stated in *Conversations with God*. Therefore, He gave us the free will to do whatever we pleased, including the impossible, even if it seemingly hurt others or ourselves. This also seems logical because, in order for God to fulfill His desire to experience everything, He had to let us have absolute freedom.

So the separation and fall was about to begin. Our connection to God would weaken (from our perspective) and we would "fall" to a lower frequency (vibrational level) to assume residence in this slower-vibrating dimension of density and matter.

Empty Nest

Soon it would be time for us to leave the comforts of Heaven to experience that "something else," but we needed a place to fulfill our desires. We wanted to experience time and space, up on a mountain and down in a valley, far from home and close to a lover, cold winter nights and hot summer days. We wanted to have a "relationship" with various things, since all of life is about our relationship to *every-thing*, whether it is good or bad. And perhaps we even wanted to experience pain, suffering, sickness, anger, hatred and all of those other negative human traits we created. And here is where we, as little gods, made this world of death, destruction, ruin, rust and rot for our experience.

God gave us permission to be creators like Him, so we created a plan, another plan to create. We borrowed a little energy from God and caused this thing called "The Big Bang" to keep scientists gainfully employed and at odds with religions. *A Course In Miracles* says that nothing God creates is destructible. Everything in Heaven is beautiful, perfect and eternal. Theoretically then, God may not have created many (or any) of the things of this world that deteriorate, which is nearly everything. Some assert that this world is nothing more than a projection of our egos and is completely a dream.

Perhaps we, as little gods, created the less-than-perfect things. We probably asked God to help us with the truly beautiful things, like sunrises, sunsets, snowflakes, oceans and mountain ranges.

Conversations with God suggests that God created the universe with our help. Considering that God is in us and that we are in God makes it difficult, if not impossible, to determine who actually desired the creation of the universe. It seems reasonable that the desire was mutual, but because we see ourselves as separated beings, it becomes easier to describe this process as if the thoughts were separate, as well.

In an effort to reconcile religion and science, it is safe to say they are both right. God did create the Garden of Eden or first universe, where life was Heavenly. After that, with God's prompting, permission and help, we decided to make another dimension, where we could experience things opposite of Heaven for God and us, a dimension where evolution would occur, giving rise to the survival of the fittest and most adaptable. What a wonderful and remarkable story to create.

But it isn't real; it's just a vision, an illusion that we "made," and therefore it's only temporary and yet is incredibly magnificent. As the bible states, we were created for the glory of God. One way we glorify God is by experiencing physical life for Him.

Anything God "creates" is indestructible and eternal. Consequently, we had to disguise this dimension's creation so completely that it would be the source of tremendous debate for eons. We accomplished this quite well.

We had to ingeniously disguise our origin, to make it difficult to uncover the truth about ourselves. To discover the truth about ourselves too early would eliminate thousands of years of meaningful experience, creativity and fun because, as soon as we all recognized the truth and became aware of our godlike characteristics and powers, we could collectively decide to solve all worldly problems. All the impoverished would be fed, clothed and sheltered. Charities wouldn't be needed any longer. Wars would have no purpose, and neither would weapon-builders. Sickness wouldn't exist, and the need for doctors, nurses and HMOs wouldn't exist, either. Our "specialness," or occupation, wouldn't be required. Feeling like we "make a difference" motivates many humans, and this would assuredly diminish. Pain, suffering, sickness, death, destruction, theft, war, power struggles, litigation and all of the rest of the misery would vanish, thus bringing Heaven to Earth. This dimension would no longer be needed. Its purpose would be fulfilled and complete. The drama of it all—the search, the hope, the quest, the failure, the discovery, the success, the cure, the triumph, and re-discovering God—would no longer be necessary. All of these experiences would cease because we would rise above them all and reconnect with God and maybe even find ourselves back in the Garden of Eden. It would appear that at least some of the world doesn't want that; we love the drama of life! Perhaps we should choose to celebrate it.

Once everything was in place, we began to inhabit the Earth, but there was another ingenious catch: we couldn't incarnate with the godlike knowledge and abilities that we possessed from our time in Heaven. We had to disguise our true identities.

Gods, Devils and Man

Being sparks of the Divine (souls), we were part of God and therefore knew everything that God knew, and possessed His ability to create. In other words, we were all gods, with a little "g." I really struggled with this concept when I first happened upon it. But I remembered the phrase "all great truths start as blasphemy," and kept an open mind. Jesus was murdered for his claim of being the essence of God. When the Jews asked Jesus if he was God, he answered by quoting scripture, which Jesus often did when he answered questions. He quoted Psalm 82:6: "Is it not written in your law, I said, Ye are gods?" (John 10:34 KJV). To the Jews, this was blasphemy so they decided to stone him…but somehow he got away.

And Jesus also said, "If ye have faith as a grain of mustard seed, ye shall say unto this mountain, remove hence to yonder place; and it shall remove; and nothing shall be impossible unto you." (Mat. 17:20 KJV) He was trying to tell his disciples we were all made in the image and likeness of God and could use God's powers through us to accomplish anything. All power comes from the Divine, explaining why Jesus also said, "Verily, verily, I say unto you, the Son can do nothing of himself." (John 5:19 KJV) Jesus was saying he had the ability to reconnect with God and become a channel for God's power, which is available to anyone. His purity and "right-mindedness" refused to acknowledge our earthly illusions, thus allowing him to reconnect with his Higher Self and God. Our Higher Self, which is much closer to God and more strongly connected, made Jesus a stronger conductor of the power of God, which allowed Jesus to manifest miracles. Ego-based thoughts and actions that are selfish and self-serving are largely disconnected from the power of God.

When Jesus told his disciples they could move mountains if they only had the faith of a mustard seed, his meaning was far deeper than some of the explanations I've heard religions provide. On the surface, it may seem that all we need is a tiny amount of faith to move mountains. On the contrary, the mustard seed is the tiniest seed but yields the largest tree, suggesting the seed has a tremendous amount of faith in its ability. The true meaning of what Jesus said was that one needs to have a tremendous amount of faith in one's ability to connect with God and become a conduit for His powers. Most of us don't even believe that God listens to us or is communicating back to us, much less the belief that He would manifest miracles through us. If we have enough faith or belief, which means a complete lack of doubt, we could work miracles as Jesus did. And many churches, faiths, individuals and organizations do perform miracles quite frequently through practices such as "laying on of hands" healings.

An analogy: if God is an ocean, then we are drops of water that are disconnected from it. The farther inland we are the more disconnected we become from the power of the ocean and the many things it offers. The chemical composition of our drop of water may be vastly different from the ocean, but in essence our drop is still the same basic component and can combine with the ocean water and attain all of its attributes.

The entire life-cycle of water serves as a great metaphor for life itself. We begin as precipitation from the heavens. We can incarnate in the visible form of a thirst quenching rain, a quiet and beautiful snow, or a destructive tempest. Our lives may be long and gentle, where we journey through brooks, streams and rivers, ending in the sea. Or we may become a category five white-water rapid during a flood, experiencing a rough and challenging lifetime course. Eventually, we physically die and transform (evaporate) into an invisible mist rising back into the heavens until it is time to return, once again, as precipitation.

I believe we *are* gods but have lost touch with our godlike qualities and abilities because we wanted to experience something different. In this dimension, we gave up this stronger connection with God so that we could experience our "separateness." God is experiencing this separateness through us. Our mission then; rediscover God and reconnect with Him. Like "kryptonite" to Superman, our beliefs in the physical laws of this world pose limits on our abilities. If this world is limited to its laws of physics, then why do miracles happen? Miracles defy the laws of physics. People *are* miraculously healed. Many of us have witnessed miracles. If you choose to research miracles, many stories to support their existence will be found. Jesus was trying to reverse the incorrect thinking that humans have limitations, by showing and teaching us who and what we really are.

If we had been born aware that we were little gods, complete with the power of God, then we would have arrived acting like perfect little gods. Everything would have been just as perfect as it was in Heaven. That would defeat the whole purpose of this dimension of opposites and challenges.

Many of us don't believe that we existed until we were born in this physical body. The bible contains evidence, in the story of Job from the Old Testament, to support the theory that we were all created prior to our physical birth. This doesn't mean that we have to accept the concept of reincarnation; it is merely suggesting that our soul was created and resided with God from the very beginning.

Job was a righteous "God-fearing" man of great wealth. At God's request, so the story goes, Satan was empowered to destroy Job's wealth to test his faith. Job remained strong in faith for a while but eventually began to complain of his misfortune and wonder why God had cursed him. Finally, God spoke to Job and began referring to the many steps of the creation of the universe, and then confirmed everyone's existence when He said, "When the morning stars sang together and all of the sons of God shouted for joy." (Job 38:7 NKJV). All of us sang at the same moment.

Like Job, we were born into this world disconnected, to a greater degree, from our higher (true) selves or souls. We go through a process which causes temporary amnesia of any of our previous lives, to allow for a pure, unbiased (blind) experience with a fresh start. In Greek Mythology this is called *The River of Forgetfulness*. In the Greek afterlife resides the *River Lethe*. Before "the dead" reincarnate, they are required to drink from the *River Lethe*, which means forgetfulness or oblivion. With these excellent disguises, there came an inherent problem: what if we became totally lost and never could find our way back home to Heaven?

God knew this journey was going to be tough for us, and He knew we might lose our way because of our separation from His love and direct guidance. So He devised a plan to ensure our return to Heaven. This plan included much patience and many spiritual masters, saints, avatars and enlightened beings to lead us to the truth. It also includes many wake-up calls or hardships to re-kindle our spiritual connection, for it seems that we look to God for guidance when we are at our weakest. The bible references forty days and nights, or forty years, during several stories to represent a time of transformation caused by a challenging time or "dark night of the soul." Noah and his family spent forty days in his Ark during the *Great Flood,* and the Israelites wandered in the desert for forty years after their escape from the Egyptians, while Jesus spent forty days in the desert before his ministry. When everything is going just peachy, when we've got money in our pockets, a nice place to live, a nice car and a nice lover, we tend to forget about God, it seems.

The biblical story of "The Prodigal Son" sums up God's perspective and promise. God didn't want His son to leave but He knew His son wanted to see the world, which meant he was going to be away from home for a while, perhaps a long while. He sensed he might even get into trouble along his way, but God knew that wouldn't matter because He loved His son dearly. Someday he would return home to His open and welcoming arms. And when the son finally returned home, that is exactly what the biblical father of "The Prodigal Son" did. God made sure that this story found its way into the bible. It illustrates the truth behind the relationship between God and us. No matter what we do, we are all going home someday.

Fortunately, those "white" souls were smart enough to leave a trail of breadcrumbs, to lead those determined seekers to the truth and ultimately back home into God's welcoming light.

Illusion and Confusion

Some believe that the world we live in doesn't really exist. It's just an illusion, just a dream or perhaps even a nightmare. But is that true? Are there any clues or evidence to support such a claim?

Everything in our universe is created out of atoms, which are composed of electrons, neutrons, protons and other smaller subatomic particles. The protons and neutrons are tightly packed together in the nucleus (center) of the atom, while the electrons spin around the nucleus in the electron shell or cloud. The space between the electrons and nucleus is quite large, compared to the size of the particles themselves—large enough, in fact, that the over-all empty space that contains nothing is greater than 99.99 percent of the atom. In addition to this is the fact that each atom is rapidly moving, caused by both the electrons zinging around the nucleus and the natural vibration of the entire atom. Each element has its own vibrational frequency, similar to a variable-speed massager. My point here is that everything that we perceive to be solid and at rest is actually moving quite rapidly and is greater than 99.99 percent free space, or nothing. Saying it differently, everything we see is optical illusion! We think it is not moving and yet it is. We perceive it as solid and yet it isn't. It is mostly a vibrating empty space, or… nothing at all.

Yet all of this is an incredibly difficult illusion to see through. We had to make an almost foolproof disguise to extend the life of this dimension, to allow us to complete all the great things we wanted to create and accomplish. We were quite successful.

The values, beliefs, judgments and perceptions that we develop while we're on Earth create our ego which is separate, and opposite, of our Higher Selves. We become more and more removed from our Higher Selves the more we stay immersed in a predominately negative world, being subjected to negative human characteristics. That explains why Jesus said, "I am in this world but not of this world." He was in this world but insulated himself from the backwards thinking that we had established here. We believe that wood is solid and yet it's mostly made of nothing. We believe that a brick isn't moving and yet it is vibrating all the time. We believe in disease and yet it can be miraculously cured in a heartbeat, suggesting it wasn't real in the first place. We believe in death, and yet there is only life. And the list continues.

Jesus was one of the few people to remember who and what we really are: children of God, made in His image (not human, but spirit) and likeness (godlike creators capable of miracles). He spent his ministry trying to get this message across. I understand the tremendous challenge he faced, struggling to get people to understand the meanings contained within his messages. In some cases, what Jesus was really trying to communicate was radically different from what our ancestors have interpreted his words to mean. Modern-day science actually assists some explanations. Jesus didn't have this luxury and had to use very primitive analogies and explanations, resulting in the many parables he told. He often began his description of Heaven by saying, "the kingdom of Heaven is like…", and he often tried to explain that Heaven was "in our midst" and not within the stars. Obviously, he couldn't compare Heaven to radio frequencies because they hadn't been discovered. Speaking today, perhaps Jesus would say, "The kingdom of Heaven is like the radio frequencies that surround us. They are everywhere, and yet the unaided or untrained human is not capable of seeing or hearing them. We must use devices such as radios, TVs and phones to access this

Some Assembly Required

higher frequency dimension that exists on many levels. Heaven is similar in that it exists at a higher frequency and, like radio signals, is within our midst and surrounds us. And, like the radio, we are capable of receiving and converting the great resources of Heaven into good and holy things if we learn to tune in."

The difficulty Jesus faced explains, in part, why his discipleship waxed and waned during his ministry. People were drawn to his miracles and magnetic personality but couldn't grasp his teachings. They probably stayed with him until they realized they could no longer grasp his words or understand his unusual concepts, no matter how hard they tried. I can't help but wonder if many simply "used" Jesus for his healing ability, then returned home.

Initially, Jesus tried to take his message to the Jewish people but continually ran into trouble. Multitudes witnessed miracles and yet they didn't repent or change their ways, as Jesus instructed. Despite the miracles, the Sadducees and Pharisees accused Jesus of being a drunkard and using Satan to perform exorcisms. They even requested an additional "sign," suggesting his miracles weren't enough proof or evidence to support his teachings. Jesus told them that the only sign they would be given would be the sign of Jonah, who spent three days and nights in the belly of a whale and emerged alive. He explained that he would spend three days and nights in the "heart of the Earth." (Matt. 12:40) From this passage, it is understood that he meant that he, too, would emerge alive.

Jesus recognized that his miracles had limited impact on the greater population in some cities; therefore he condemned them. Jesus said, "Woe unto thee, Chorazin! Woe unto thee, Bethsaida! For if the mighty works, which were done in you, had been done in Tyre and Sidon, they would have repented long ago in sackcloth and ashes." (Matt. 11:21) He preached and performed many miracles in

Chorazin and Bethsaida, but had not done so in Tyre or Sidon, and believed they would have listened to him had he done so. The ego was a powerful enemy, blinding the people to the truth. The ego refuses to be wrong, and cleaves to what it has been taught, especially what we were taught in our childhood years by respected authority figures such as parents, priests and teachers. Once programmed, the ego will risk physical death before admitting it is wrong, in many cases. To suggest that humans are stubborn about their beliefs is a gross understatement.

Jesus soon realized his teachings would be better received by the so-called sinners of the times. Among this group were tax collectors, prostitutes, social outcasts, poor, diseased and crazy people, folks with very low self-esteem and therefore an underdeveloped ego. These were the people that Jesus could attempt to program correctly. And because of some of these people, his teachings live on today. Unfortunately, many tried to interpret his words to suit their ego-based mental model and/or to gain control of the masses. If this weren't true, there would only be one version of the bible; instead, there are around twenty-six.

This isn't to say that the ego can't be broken or humbled; it simply recognizes the difficulty involved. To borrow and modify a phrase that Jesus used, it would be easier for a camel to fit through the eye of a needle than it is for a man to destroy his own ego and become born-again to his Higher Self and Holy Spirit. Once again, it's not impossible, but it sure is difficult.

On many levels, our mature egos prevent us from seeing through the illusion and confusion to the truth. Our egos demand unquestionable proof that can be experienced through our five senses, and even then we will sometimes simply say, "I still don't believe it." The programmed or mature ego won't attribute much credibility to

Some Assembly Required

the unseen or spiritual, either. Interestingly enough, the immature ego will believe and accept at face value the religious teachings it was exposed to when it was young, impressionable and programmable. Once programmed, it might literally take an act of God to alter. An excellent example of this can be witnessed in the classic story, *A Christmas Carol,* where Ebenezer Scrooge isn't convinced until no fewer than three ghosts pay him a visit.

So here we are:

- In this make-believe world that seems so incredibly real to our ego
- With no memories (not easily accessible memories) of life in Heaven
- Physically separated from one another, solidifying the belief that our spirits can't be joined, either
- With strongly opposing beliefs from science and religion confusing potential spiritual conviction
- With strongly opposing beliefs from one religion to another confusing potential spiritual conviction
- Believing in a bible (Old Testament) that depicts God as angry, jealous, vengeful and judgmental
- Believing in a God that had ordered the death of thousands in the Old Testament and yet we also believe in His commandment that "Thou shall not murder"
- Translating a bible many different ways, which only serves to increase the division between us and our religions

The continued existence of this world depends on conflict causing confusion. It's not surprising that we're so confused. We intentionally did this to ourselves for the fun, the drama and the glory of God. If everyone saw beyond the illusions and discovered "who" (spirit) and "what" (gods, because we are God's children) we really are, and practiced a life of love, caring, sharing, compassion and forgiveness, with harm to no one, then the thin veil would melt away and Heaven would appear before us.

To rediscover who and what we really are would threaten the existence of this dimension. This would threaten our "specialness" as individuals and eliminate the need for "relationships" of every kind.

In the meantime, our egos and the negative force of this world (satan) are fighting for their very survival. They don't want us to know the truth. Their fun would be over.

A Dichotomy

God, along with us, created a world of opposites, a place where we could choose various experiences. A place where we could choose to experience Heaven or Hell while we're here. A place where we are subjected to at least a little of both, all of the time.

Hell on Earth is where:
- There is sickness, injury, pain, suffering and death
- There is hatred, jealousy, envy and lust
- There are traffic jams and airport delays that keep us from important appointments, such as vacation or getting back home
- There is anger, fighting, destruction and loss
- Our neighbor doesn't take care of his yard, and his weeds constantly invade our manicured lawn
- There is poverty, even though there is more than enough for everyone
- Natural phenomena such as tornadoes or hurricanes can wipe out everything we have, in the blink of an eye
- The thousands of dollars of insurance premiums we pay for do not cover the damage that just occurred

Some Assembly Required

- There is separation from God
- Sadness is frequent and joy is scarce
- Our boss is a jerk and our co-workers are incompetent, and yet we still can't get promoted
- The best years of our lives are spent working for a living or going to school
- People drive slow in the fast lane
- Everything we own eventually rusts, rots, falls apart or breaks
- We sit for hours in an emergency room, waiting to be cared for
- Bad things happen to good people
- Good things happen to bad people

Yes, in a sense, we are in a form of Hell! But our life doesn't have to be a living hell if we remember who and what we really are. And we can choose *not* to make someone else's life a living hell. We can bring a piece of Heaven to Earth by what we believe and how we act.

Beliefs or affirmations like:
- All things lead to my success
- Nothing ever goes wrong in my world
- I am happy with the simple things in life
- I am happy, healthy, wealthy and wise

Actions like:
- If we want more love, then make others feel loved
- If we want more happiness, then make others happy
- If we want more money, then give money away (to charity, for example)
- If we want more respect, then respect others

Universal law dictates this cause-and-effect response. We can choose to spread peace and joy, thus bringing a more Heavenly experience to our own lives.

Even though the world has many hellish qualities, we can still have a pleasant and even Heavenly life, as many folks do. We have the power to bring a little piece of Heaven to Earth, if we try. Pieces of Heaven are already here; we just need to recognize them, enjoy them, and share them with others.

Heaven on Earth is where:

- We can travel to see any of God's (and humanity's) wondrous and beautiful creations
- Beautiful yellow and orange sunrises and red and purple sunsets touch our soul and remind us of the magnificence of God and the serenity and beauty that awaits us
- The bold and bright colors of spring flowers fill us with awe and invite us to plant our own, so that we might share the beauty with others
- We can plant, grow and nurture trees, shrubs, flowers and plants of all kinds, bringing us great satisfaction in return for our care and attention.
- Fragrances surround and ignite our senses, such as those of a fresh spring shower, a freshly cut lawn, the salty breeze of the ocean, or the delicious smell of an apple pie, hot out of the oven, while we feast at a dinner of peppercorn-marinated steak and baked potatoes with lots of sour cream and butter
- The smell of bacon sizzling on the stove after returning home from Sunday-morning Church service; breakfast with the family
- Rainbows attempt to overload our eyes with beauty and metaphor

- The purity, innocence, preciousness and miracle of babies touch us all
- Puppies and kittens tug at our heartstrings with their playfulness. Then they become our loyal pets, who love us unconditionally
- Waterfalls attract us to see and feel the cool mist
- We can witness Divine beauty in many forms, such as a quiet, snow-covered landscape or mountaintops
- We can lick the bowl after the chocolate batter is in the baking pan
- We can create whatever we like
- We can watch as majestic birds soar effortlessly on warm breezes
- We can walk into a forest, watch and admire nature of all kinds, even if it's just watching squirrels practicing suicide leaps from tree to tree
- We take the time to roast marshmallows or weenies over an outdoor fire with family and friends
- We can play Santa Claus and change a child's life, or an adult's life
- We can create or admire and appreciate humankind's greatest creations, such as art, architecture, music, literary works, statues and sculptures
- We can go snorkeling and see the amazing color that lives below the sea's surface
- We can perform tremendous feats. The tricks our young people can do with bicycles, motorcycles, skateboards and snowboards, to name just a few, are incredible. We continue to push the limits of the human body and creativity, and we continue to reach new heights. It's as if there really is

no limit. Perhaps the god that is within us can perform the impossible when we believe that we can, without doubt.

Humans (and egos) absolutely love the drama of physical life. We come back time and time again to have another go at it. We all want to be special in some way or another. We want to be doctors, teachers and firefighters, rich, poor, famous and maybe even infamous. Somebody has to do it! Somebody has to be the bad guy! And through all of this drama mixed with happiness, adversity and even the terror we must endure, we ultimately "experience" our way back home to God. Even after all the misery and terror we might endure, we can ultimately cross over to a beautiful Heaven where everything is made new, fresh, happy and alive.

We are loosely connected to our Higher Selves, the part of us that is loving and kind. But as we develop our earthly egos and take on these nasty negative human traits, we weaken the connection to our "natural" loving Higher Selves. Our mission, then, is not just to reconnect with our Higher Selves, as some of us try to do during meditation, but to become a walking example of our Higher Selves, much the same way Jesus did.

Our Higher Selves cannot be killed or destroyed. When we think someone's life was cut short, we usually find ourselves saying, "He had so much life left to live," or "She had so much going for her." We need to realize that these folks are probably in a better place. They may have actually planned an early departure, in which case someone else was probably meant to grow from the loss of the loved one. On the other hand, in this world of free will, accidents do occur and people are killed accidentally and/or needlessly. In this case, they might return home frustrated that they were not allowed to achieve the success and accomplishments they were meant to accomplish.

Our lives are pre-planned, to a certain degree, to ensure that they fit properly into the cosmic play, song or dance, if you will. It's the age-old concept of "destiny." We come here with a roughly predetermined destiny. We may be in a support role or a lead role. Our lives will still have many forks in the road where a critical decision will be required and a specific path will be chosen. Those decisions will set the course for future decisions, successes or failures. We'll still meet the necessary people to guide and influence our destiny, no matter how large or small our part in the cosmic dance.

And so the drama continues, perfectly as planned. This is what we wanted for God, and what He wanted for us. Oh, the drama of it all!

The Rainbow Connection

As discussed, every object has its own vibrational frequency. This applies to humans, as well. We typically refer to our vibrational frequency in the context of "up" or "down" or a lightness or heaviness.

- "Are you up to it?" or "I'm feelin' kinda down today"
- "I feel lighter than air" or "That's weighin' heavy on my mind"
- "I'm walkin' on sunshine" or "I'm down in the dumps"

These "frame-of-mind" feelings aren't by chance. Our overall personality, which includes such things as our spiritual development, happiness and beliefs, can dictate the level of Heaven we achieve when we exit this world.

The notion that various levels of Heaven exist is supported by the phrase. "I'm in seventh Heaven." There are various levels, suited for our level of development. Most of these levels are probably very nice indeed. From my own experiences on the other side, as well as those reported by others, I believe the other side is very similar to this world (if not a mirror image), except that it has no need for transportation, sleep, food or rest. So beautiful, in fact, that we may not want to come back here to do this again, but may have to, in order to advance our spirituality or help others. The higher we go, the better it gets. This dimension is one of the best ways to advance our spiritual development and return home to God, because a life on Earth represents a true "trial by fire." If one can find God and remain loyal to Him through all of this hell, then that person is truly successful and deserving of Heaven.

Author Doreen Virtue reports that, while conducting therapy for her patients, she sometimes finds the spirits of relatives or friends clinging close to their loved ones who are still here on Earth. They usually cling to the Earth plane because they did something to the individual that they were ashamed of, and are trying to make amends for their wrongdoing by helping the victim through life. The victim (still here on Earth) may still feel resentment or even hatred towards the departed. Once Virtue convinces the victim to forgive the departed, angels appear and the spirit is then escorted to a higher (or different) plane of existence in the Heavens. Virtue believes this because the background color changes as the spirit of the departed moves on.

The background color-change is associated with the chakra system, which also corresponds to the colors of the rainbow. The word "chakra" is Sanskrit, meaning "wheel of light." There are seven chakras that comprise the major energy centers of the body. These energy centers are vortices that penetrate the energy field (or body double, spirit) that encases our physical body. By allowing energy and information to flow, they connect us to God and the universe, which explains phrases such as "gut feeling." Most of us have had gut feelings about things, either good or bad, and have used this instinct

Some Assembly Required

to make a decision. The third chakra, called the Solar Plexus chakra, is responsible for this feeling. From bottom to top, the colors are red, orange, yellow, green, medium blue, indigo and purple (violet). It is believed that, the more spiritually advanced a person is, the higher the chakra from which that person will predominantly operate. These seven colors may also represent the seven levels of Heaven, or at least the lower levels of the Heavens assigned to Mother Earth. Virtue has noticed that the background color changes in this order when spirits are being escorted to a presumably higher level, thus supporting this concept.

It is interesting to note that white light, when passed through a prism, will split into the seven colors of the chakra system. And, when passed through another prism, will combine back into white light. Red is the lowest frequency of the seven colors and violet is the highest. I think this clue is both an analogy and a metaphor for the progression of life. We were created from the highest spiritual vibration (the Divine White Light of God). Through our desire to experience opposites, perhaps we were split and categorized into these various light frequencies as our starting point in our soul's evolution back to rejoining the white light.

The complete opposite of white light, however, is darkness. There are several "negative" ADC stories contained in the book *Hello From Heaven* in which the spirits of the departed visited family members, revealing their dismal situation. Several of these negative ADCs were associated with suicide victims. Some asked their family for prayer and forgiveness to release them from their misery. The pleading spirits managed to appear in various ways, including dream visits, which allowed the family member to see into their world or temporarily be transported into it. These lower levels of the Heavens were dark and desolate, as if a form of solitary confinement, although some of these locations did contain more than one lost soul. Some of these unfortunate souls recognized they weren't confined to eternal damnation; rather, they realized there was a way out through prayer, repentance and forgiveness. Some seemed lost and didn't know what to do to get themselves out of their predicament, other than to ask the family to pray for them.

In none of these cases was there an eternal "lake of fire" consuming their flesh, while a red devil tortured them endlessly. These lower levels of Heaven were a temporary holding place of spiritual rehabilitation. Nonetheless, I wouldn't want to find myself in one of these lower levels. They didn't sound pleasant in the least.

It is important to understand the afterlife, at least on a basic level, so that we might be aware of what our options are, once we cross over, especially if we find ourselves in a dismal predicament. Joan Borysenko related a story she heard at one of the workshops she conducted:

A woman that Borysenko called Janice recounted her NDE. At age ten, Janice had drown in a pond. It took quite some time for her to be resuscitated. During this time, she conducted a full-life review, and then one of her guides took her on a tour. He took her to a room filled with confused and unhappy people. Janice asked why they were so unhappy. The guide told her that these people didn't believe that their souls were immortal and consequently were victims of the limitations of their minds. There were many compassionate beings around the room who wanted to help, but who couldn't assist until they were called upon by the confused people. To assist without being asked would violate the law of free will. At least this room wasn't a dismal abyss. Evidently the earthly lives these spirits had lived didn't warrant a severely hellish existence to work through. The room might resemble the Catholic version of Limbo or Purgatory.

The Hells

Hell is not the eternal "lake of fire" that the bible describes. Men, in an effort to "scare people straight," probably injected these words into the bible in an attempt to gain control of the "heathens." This doesn't mean that there isn't an undesirable experience that we may have to endure for our negative earthly actions. In *Conversations with God*, God seemed to somewhat downplay the existence of Hell. At first, I had a very difficult time swallowing the notion that eternal Hell didn't exist, because I felt that some infamous characters from world history definitely belonged there. Walsch, the author, also struggled with this revelation and continued to question God until he gained a better understanding. The resultant description explained that a life-review would be conducted by each person upon returning to the other side. This would prompt a time of reflection and a self-inflicted judgment and reckoning. This punishment still seemed far too mild for some of our more notorious villains.

I had been around the block enough times to believe there might be more to this subject, so I was on the lookout for further clues or information. When an entire world makes reference to a concept, there is usually some shred of truth in it, even if it has been exaggerated. Even Jesus spoke of Hell frequently, providing another data point that it existed to at least some degree. I couldn't be sure how much the bible writers, religious leaders, emperors and translators may have intensified the afterlife punishment that Jesus spoke of, but I considered it highly probable that he did speak of some negative experience awaiting evil-doers.

Since we are all connected as one spirit, we can draw the conclusion that whatever we do to someone else, we are really doing to ourselves. Hence, it would stand to reason that if we can't experience what we did to someone else in this dimension, then we might be required to experience it in the next. Here we can learn from our mistakes and hopefully decide not to ever do these awful things again. And we can't escape this. We are all required to do a full-life review. Even if we initially avoid the light when we cross over, we will sooner or later have to experience this.

Now that would be pure hell: everything that we have ever done to anyone re-lived by us through *their* eyes or perspective. Hitler probably had to endure tremendous suffering to re-live each of the millions of deaths he was responsible for.

Knowing this, why would we want to hurt anything?

I watched a television program where a young man had been sucked up by a tornado for several seconds before the winds slammed him back down to Earth under a pile of mud and debris. The young man recounted his ordeal in the tornado and claimed that he had visions while in the whirlwind. He reported seeing everyone he had ever met in his life flash before his eyes, and then saw himself in a casket at his own funeral. He told God he didn't want to die, and was returned to Earth to tell about it. There are two very interesting pieces to this:

The young man didn't have visions of places he had been or things he had done; these things didn't seem important to whoever was running the projector for that condensed period of time. What was important was all the people he had ever met or encountered. It's not unusual to hear folks say, "I saw my life flash before my eyes," either seriously or humorously after scary or life-threatening situations.

The other interesting point: what was probably many hours worth of a "video" to review took place in just seconds, confirming again that time is not linear the way we perceive it in this dimension.

So there are many levels, or planes of existence, in the afterlife, of which the top levels of Heaven are probably the most beautiful and pleasant. I sincerely hope that what we experience will be the more pleasant things. I did come across other descriptions of Hell that were far more frightening. It's not by chance that the farther we are from God, the darker and more dismal the environment is.

The hells are the lowest astral levels assigned to the Earth plane. The following is a description taken from the channeled Padgett Papers from a spirit who spent time there:

> *"In this Hell of mine, and there are many like it, instead of beautiful homes, as the other spirits described, we have dirty, rotten hovels, all crooked and decayed, with all the foul smells of a charnel house ten times intensified, and instead of beautiful lawns and green meadows and leafy woods filled with musical birds making the echoes ring with their songs, we have barren wastes, and holes of darkness and gloom and the cries and cursings of spirits of damnation without hope; and instead of living, silvery waters, we have stagnant pools filled with all kinds of repulsive reptiles and vermin, and smells of inexpressible, nauseating stinks.*
>
> *I tell you that these are all real, and not creatures of the imagination or the outflowing of bitter recollections. And as for love, it has never shown its humanizing face in all the years that I have been here - only cursings and hatred and bitter scathings and imprecations, and grinning spirits with their witchlike cacklings. No rest, no hope, no kind words or ministering hand to wipe away the scalding tears*

"Imagine That"   A Spiritual Awakening

>which so often flow in mighty volumes. No, Hell is real and Hell is here.
>
>We do not have any fire and brimstone, or grinning devils with pitch forks and hoofs and horns as the churches teach; but what is the need or necessity for such accompaniments? They would not add to the horrors or to our torments. I tell you my friend that I have faintly described our homes in these infernal regions and I cannot picture them as they are.
>
>But the horror and pity of it all is that hope does not come to us with one faint smile to encourage us that there may at some time be an ending to all these torments, and in our hopeless despair we realize that our doom is fixed for all eternity.
>
>As the rich man in Hell said, if I could only send Lazarus to tell my poor, erring brothers on Earth of what awaits them, how gladly I would do so and save their souls from the eternal torment."

A terrible place indeed, but it's temporary, lasting only until you seek help. As with the poor spirit above, it is assumed that the damnation is eternal. The torment and despair are so overwhelming there that the spirit soon becomes hopeless and resigned to believing he is doomed to eternal punishment. He gives up. Friends and other helpers arrive from time to time to instruct the hopeless spirit on the process of getting out of his Hell, but the depression is so strong that the resident can't comprehend his reformation and forgets or discards the instructions.

The following is from the channeled messages of Judas Iscariot through the medium or channel identified as H.R. Here he discusses his entry into Hell. Note that this Hell is a little less frightening,

Some Assembly Required

dangerous and disgusting, as compared to the first description provided:

> *"As you will remember, last time I told you how the spirit who accompanied me informed me that the time had come for leaving this entrance place into the spirit world. I had come to understand perfectly well that I lived no longer on Earth; I had even arrived at the knowledge that my "physical" state, that is, the condition of my spiritual body, was horrible. It was ugly, and I felt very bad.*
>
> *The spirit took me by my hand and led me to a very different place, at the same speed as he had taken me from the place of my death to the spirit world. Now I want you to describe what you are seeing."*
>
> *[H.R.: It seemed as if I was standing at the top of a mountain or hill. Below I could see a pretty valley, with forests, meadows, springs and streams. I heard birds singing; it was like a beautiful summer day. Suddenly, everything began to dry off. The green colors turned brown, the leaves fell off the trees, and after a short time, I saw a disastrous landscape. Everything was dry, the earth cracked, a few trunks like skeletons without life, the streams had disappeared, leaving behind only their stony beds. There was no sunshine anymore, everything seemed dark, like a winter dawn in the northern regions, but without snow, and the silence of death reigned.]*
>
> *"What a contrast! Well, this is how the place looked like, where the spirit took me. There he left me, saying that I could find an abandoned house,*

and that there I would have to live, until I had the capacity to leave that place.

You think that it was horrible, but I tell you frankly, I didn't find this so bad in the beginning. I met with many spirits in my own condition, I got used to the little light and the barren landscape, but eventually I almost despaired. The negativity, so much negativity in those spirits! I had always been a cheerful person, I liked to joke, to sing, to dance, but at this place, in this Hell, there was no singing or dancing, neither laughter nor a single word of comfort. Everybody took care of his own business, there was not much communication, there was not much to do, nothing to read, nothing to write, only thinking. And there were no children.

And my memories came, good and bad memories, but mainly the recollection of my betrayal of the Master and of my suicide. I don't know which one was worse.

One day, one of my taciturn neighbors broke his silence and told me that Jesus had visited this place some short time ago. He had told them that there was hope for them, that they could leave this place, and that further on a better world was waiting for them. But very few paid attention to him.

When I heard this, I really broke down. Maybe there was hope, yes, but not for me. I had caused Jesus' death, of that luminous spirit, as the neighbor described him to me. What could I do? Nothing, but to be resigned.

I also found out that there were better places which I could visit, and I did so. I found places very similar to Earth, with more light, much more light than where I lived, and the spirits were better, that is to say, they looked better, they treated me well in spite of my ugliness, but I simply didn't belong there, I had to return.

As I visited these brighter places, we were visited by spirits from the lowest hells, but what a horror! They were disgusting! And with that I not only refer to their appearance, but to their way of being, with so much negativity; they were furious, wild, and we rejected them. They did not stay with us, but returned to their place, where they belonged.

Some of my neighbors told me that they had lived in these deeper hells before, and that the place where we lived now almost seemed like paradise to them, compared with that place. They described the constant aggressions, physical, verbal and mental, which these spirits suffered and inflicted, and that their world was even darker than ours, and that they often, almost like some kind of sport, tried to influence mortals, looking for people with certain inclinations and inciting them to commit atrocities.

When they had incited some poor fellow, whom they had chosen, to violate a girl, they hollered at him: "Finish her off! She will denounce you!" And when the violator had murdered his victim, they went away screaming and screeching with pleasure. They also tried to satisfy their addictions, clinging to the mind

> *of an alcoholic, of a sexual abuser, of any person with these inclinations, but the satisfaction that they took out of living this "second hand" remake of what the mortal experienced, was not true satisfaction. They pushed the mortal deeper and deeper into his vice, but they themselves, in turn, obtained little pleasure.*
>
> *It was a hideous image they painted, and although our small Hell vibrated from negativity, it was even worse there, it was like a swamp of perversions. We were lucky being able to live here, they explained to me."*

I get chills when I read this. And to think this kind of afterlife might await us because of our earthly lives of mental, verbal and physical abuses, along with perversions, addictions, hatred and probably just about any other negative trait. Quite sobering indeed. I'd rather choose love, caring, sharing, compassion and forgiveness.

Evil Spirits, Demons and Satan

Kabbalah teaches the meaning of the word "satan," (without a capitol s), as used in ancient texts, simply means "chaos," or that force that opposes all things, including us. Many of us experience satan frequently, referring to it as Murphy's Law; if it *can* go wrong, it *will* go wrong, and at the worst possible moment. We wanted to experience the opposite of Heaven, so there had to be a force to challenge and oppose us, a powerful, antagonistic, unsympathetic and almost hostile force created to test our spirit and, perhaps, destroy the egos we were destined to create. The biblical story of Job provides evidence of the use of this force, when God gave Satan permission to test Job's loyalty and love for God. Satan stole or destroyed all of Job's livestock, and then Job was afflicted with disease and great suffering. It would be easy to argue either side of this debate—Satan the devil

Some Assembly Required

verses satan the negative force—because the story of Job gives Satan a voice as he talks with God. In either case, it is not necessary for Satan to be a ruler of the darkness. The negative force that opposes all things is powerful enough to bring any man to his knees; a "Prince of Darkness" isn't required. Therefore, I conclude that satan is not a red devil with a pitch fork, it's just the negative force that challenges us and makes everything fall apart, rust and rot. Hell is not an eternal lake of fire with Satan, the "Prince of Darkness," residing over it constantly, forcing its ill-fated inhabitants to shovel coal to keep the inferno smelting red-hot. It's also interesting to note that, throughout history, the image of Satan and the characteristics of Hell have been changed many times by authors, painters and religions. Satan has taken on many images, ranging from a multi-headed carnivore devouring its inhabitants limb by limb to a humanlike red devil in a fiery barren underworld and, more recently, a blue devil inhabiting a cold, dark, dismal underworld.

I do subscribe to the notion that Hell is a broken, rotted, ruined, dark, dismal, foul smelling and disgusting place, as described in the Padgett Papers and by Judas Iscariot. To believe a ruler resides over this place suggests it has some semblance of order or government, meaning it is controlled. To truly be a living hell, it would have no control or regulations for its inhabitants, just total anarchy, corruption, harassment, perversions and more, which is all the more reason to support the notion that Hell has no ruler.

In the New Testament alone, Jesus eradicated (exorcised) approximately 3300 evil spirits or demons from possessed people. The most memorable may have been the seven demons he exorcised from his friend, Mary Magdalene. So how did these spirits get here? How did they manage to stay on the Earth plane? And why weren't they in some level of Hell, working on their spiritual rehabilitation?

Since we all have free will, we can choose to avoid the light when we die and cross over into the afterworld. In the *Gospel of John,* Jesus says "For every one that doeth evil hateth the light, neither cometh to the light, lest his deeds should be reproved (examined)." (3:20 KJV) If we make this choice, we might become what is called an "earthbound soul." The deceased may fear the purported "wrath of God" for a life of evildoing, or simply not believe in life after death, and become confused by the light, deciding to avoid it out of fear. The light may not even be presented to non-believers, or the death may have happened suddenly and the spirit may not realize he has passed on. These spirits get caught in the middle and become the spectacle in many haunted houses and dwellings. These restless spirits are lost and somewhat confused, caught in a dimension that seems to lock them in their moment until, somehow, they are saved from themselves. Many of these souls are simply lost and harmless, in search of answers. When will these earthbound spirits continue on their spiritual path? I don't know, but a start may come when they seek help.

For other evil spirits, the party may be just beginning as they roam around, looking for someone to torment. These evil spirits might find that their primary residence is on one of the lower astral levels (or Hell). They learn that they can temporarily leave to wreak havoc here on the Earth plane, since it is very close to the vibrational level of Hell (unfortunately). This also helps to explain why our world is so negative. Our dimension is vibrating very closely to the levels of Hell, thus allowing Hell's negative influential energy to bleed into our world. Since we are an energy field that can be influenced by other energy fields, these dark spirits travel until they find weak-minded humans who might be susceptible to their suggestions, someone they can possess and loosely control. Once they find a likely subject, they might try to influence that person's decisions. They may attempt to make the host aggressive and violent, in an attempt to satisfy their own sick pleasures, all of this in an effort to continue the trail of misery and destruction they were so fond of when they were in physical form.

To think that Satan has employed these spirits for his treachery seems unreasonable. If Hell really existed, as described by religions, then it would be a place of eternal damnation, not of temporary evil pleasures orchestrated by Satan. God wouldn't allow these evil spirits out on "work release" to have a little fun for Satan. This wouldn't be the historical punishment we were taught at all.

Once again, I find no reason for Satan to exist as a single ruler of the underworld; rather, I've discovered that there are probably millions of little Satans (demons or evil spirits) that have departed from physical life and yet continue their evildoing here in the physical world. The stories air on the 6 o'clock news frequently, when a parent murders their spouse and children and then commits suicide, or a lone gunman slays innocent victims at a mall or in a high school before turning the gun on himself. It is easy to see why much of the world believes in the notion of Satan, with evil spirit activity as rampant as it is. But evil spirits and/or Murphy's Law are not Satan, "The Prince of Darkness," acting against us. Evil spirits and demons act on their own wicked and sinister impulses and Murphy's Law is simply the faceless negative force that challenges us in our everyday life. It might be the check that the mail service loses, forcing us to waste time resolving the issue with the payee, or the flight that's two hours late, making us miss our connecting flight, or the car that breaks down a month after the warrantee expires. And does Murphy work through other people to irritate and challenge us? How about the technical support representative who can't seem to understand our computer problem, the waitress who is slow and forgetful, the guy who cuts in line, or the slow poke we can't get around? We face these trying situations all the time, in an effort to test our virtues.

Are some spirits destined to be dark entities over and over again, to test and challenge us? There may be some truth to this, but knowing that egos can become so twisted and damaged leads to the possibility that any one of us might play the antagonist from time to time. Someone has to be the bad guy so that others can experience and learn the things they need in order to find their way home again. But do they have to be evil, damaging, disrespectful, demonic, destructive and cold-blooded to the degree of a Hitler to motivate us? I don't believe so. I don't think evil acts of this caliber are part of the universal plan. Our egos have allowed us to stray far off course and create incredibly diabolical opposites that exceed the necessary requirements for us to experience the relationships that we desire. The challenges Murphy is designed to deliver are probably far less destructive than the more malicious objective of evil spirits and bad ego.

Heaven

After living an honorable earthly life, we should find ourselves back home in Heaven, where we will rejoin family members once our life-review has been completed. Then we will take up residence on a Heavenly level that is equivalent to our spiritual development. More than likely, our friends and family members will host a large party to celebrate our return. We will then enjoy the "good life," away from the trials and tribulations of this world. But unless we have achieved a higher level of Heaven, we might plan another life and return here to complete the perfection of our souls. As *A Course in Miracles* states, "it is in 'time' that we achieve salvation." The sole purpose of "time" is to work our way back home to God.

We might choose other methods of developing our spirituality, if we are too afraid to attempt another life here on Earth. Even in Heaven we still have a free will to choose our actions and beliefs. Included in our free will is the choice to accept God and return to His Divine Love or to deny His existence forever, which can only be until the end of time.

We take up residence in Heaven at various levels but this is not the "final" or highest level of Heaven. Jesus, along with other ascended masters, resides at an upper level of the Heavens (or astral planes) assigned to this dimension. They are patiently waiting for all of us to reach some upper level so that we can all return home through the real Pearly Gates of Heaven at the same time, an event frequently referred to as the final judgment. This supports the words of Jesus when he said: "Heaven and Earth shall pass away." Once we pass through the true gates of Heaven, (that reside above the levels of heaven assigned to this dimension) this world and its levels of Heaven will have served their purpose and will no longer be needed. Therefore they will cease to exist.

Reproduced here is a version of the seven levels of Heaven produced by the *Centre Christian Spiritualist Church*. It is a very well-written plain-English description of the levels of Heaven, or astral planes.

> *As spiritualists, it is our belief the first astral plane after death is called the first Heaven or the lower astral plane. This is a hell-like realm of purgatory and self-recrimination from which escape is very slow and difficult. It may take hundreds of years of Earth time for its inhabitants to accept their misdeeds, put them right and move upward. Here you would certainly find criminals and materially-*

obsessed individuals. We are told that the demons and poltergeists, which readily interfere with life on Earth, originate here. The "bad" parts of Heaven are the closest to Earth, which explains why religion wrongly equates the occult as a pact with the devil. Messages on Ouija boards, for instance, often come from troubled souls in these near-Earth realms.

The next astral plane is called the second Heaven. Most people who die initially find themselves in the second Heaven or intermediate astral planes. Viewed as a sort of resting point on the way from Earth to the more rarified upper dimensions, it is a thought-created universe that closely resembles an idealized Earth. Its inhabitants seem to live in physical bodies, wear clothes and so forth – but of an etheric kind that would be invisible to those living on Earth. Most attempts to communicate from Heaven stem from here; but because the inhabitants of Earth are as yet unfamiliar with the afterlife, these communications can be confusing or wrong.

The next astral plane is called by many names, such as the third Heaven, Summerland, or Marduk. This plane is the closest thing to the Christian concept of paradise. The most inspired and pure souls from Earth pass directly here after death; most people, however, must strive to reach it after a sojourn in the second Heaven, where they assess their life on Earth and try to understand what they did wrong. It is from the third Heaven that rebirth back on Earth supposedly occurs – although the decision to go back and try again is allegedly an individual one, and some may opt to forsake material life altogether and move into the higher spiritual dimensions. Some of the most accurate and most inspirational messages received via mediums are said to originate here.

The fourth Heaven is the mental and causal plane. Here, most of the trappings of materialism have gone. It is here that selfless individuals work together to bring spiritual enlightenment to the lower dimensions and Earth. Supposedly all great inventions, religious and moral progressions, spiritual leadership and so on come from here, inspired by beings who were once on Earth but have had the opportunity to increase their talents in the afterlife. A few rebirths to Earth do take place from this higher place: great teachers are sent back for special reasons. Spirit guides who talk through mediums are often in this dimension, as well, bringing their enhanced knowledge to Earth.

The fifth Heaven is the next astral plane. Reaching this dimension is difficult, for it is devoid of a physical state and aspired to by great religious figures, from Jesus to Buddha. Even those in lower dimensions view it as most of us still on Earth imagine Heaven – a distant, magical, unknown place.

The sixth Heaven is the next astral plane. This dimension is cosmic consciousness, where the unity of souls is perfected and a kind of universal being exists. This may be close to what we think of as God, but it is even less understood by those in the lower dimensions.

> *The seventh Heaven is the next astral plane. To reach the seventh Heaven, one has to step not only beyond material and physical reality but beyond mental and individual reality as well. It is simply not possible to define what this ultimate level may be, but it is supposedly the goal of all individual souls. Everything we do, on Earth and in the higher dimensions, is directed toward that final transformation, for there is evolution of the soul in just the same way as there is evolution of the body, or indeed of all life, back on Earth.*

The above description also explains why Jesus said "I am the way, the truth, and the life: no man cometh unto the Father, but by me." (John 14:6 KJV) If Jesus resides on the fifth level, then we must pass by him to achieve the higher levels of Heaven and ultimately return home to God. But what exactly does it take to get there?

The bible claims, "For by grace are ye saved through faith; and that not of yourselves: it is the gift of God: Not of works, lest any man should boast." (Eph 2:8-9 KJV) I have heard this many times, obviously suggesting that you can't get to Heaven through your good works alone. This always bothered me because it didn't make sense that God would cast me into Hell with murderers and rapists just because I didn't understand him correctly, even though I had been an excellent human. The *Epistle of James* says this: "Ye see then how that by works a man is justified, and not by faith only." (James 2:24 KJV) Two verses later, he drives the point home by saying, "For as the body without the spirit is dead, so faith without works is dead also." (2:26) (supporting verses Rom 3:28, Matt 19:16-21 KJV)

This may seem to be a biblical contradiction, but I believe it was a simple misunderstanding in terminology. The various documents I'd uncovered regarding the levels of Heaven and the criteria for upward mobility stemmed from good works and faith. Our good works would certainly result in a pleasant and pleasing realm in the afterlife, but our progress would be limited by our lack of love or faith in God. In other words, it's a two-part equation: good works + loving faith in God = Heavens upper levels.

The Last Judgment

The final judgment isn't where God judges us but where we judge ourselves against the criteria that is finally revealed to us on "Judgment Day." The criteria with which we now come face to face is simply truth and knowledge. Our old perceptions are replaced with truth, while beliefs and faith are replaced with knowledge and understanding. There will be no questions because everything will be answered. We will have no choice but to accept correction for any errors in our thinking to which we may still have been clinging. Everything will become crystal clear beyond doubt. The final judgment is about judging and correcting our own errors of thought. It's not about eternal punishment for our physical errors while on Earth. Throughout time, we had many opportunities to atone for our earthly errors and rehabilitate ourselves spiritually.

On many occasions, I have wondered what that meeting with God, after the final judgment, might be like. Here is my rendition:

I can see all of us in the audience of a huge, ancient amphitheatre patiently waiting for God to appear. We're not sure what He's going to say and we're all nervously hoping we meet with His approval. We keep ourselves busy in conversation with family members and friends with whom we shared our various lives. There is so much to talk about that we can hardly prevent ourselves from cutting each other off in conversation. Like excited children requesting attention

"Imagine That"   A Spiritual Awakening

("Daddy, watch me!"), we all want our turn to speak, to share our stories.

Suddenly, unlike in most theatres, the lights go up rather than dim, as the light of the great "I Am" draws near. Onto center stage walks the most magnificent being anyone has ever laid eyes upon. The being is shrouded in the most brilliant white light we have ever witnessed, almost blinding and yet easy on our eyes. We can feel the gentle warmth of His intense light as it projects outward, illuminating our beings as if we were lying on a beach in a warm summer sun. We feel the tremendous love emanating through us. A love like we have never known before, a love that mortal words could never define, energizes and fills us. Some begin to weep with joy at the vision, while others are drunk with elation. We want to clap our hands to welcome our host but we're not sure of the appropriateness of clapping for a host with the unique distinction of God. But slowly we begin to clap anyway, one by one, until every hand pounds the other, creating a thunderous roar that rocks the Heavens. Before long, there is a standing ovation, as God stands silent on the stage, smiling gently. After several minutes, the clapping subsides; God begins to speak.

He slowly lifts His arms outstretched, with a huge smile on His face, and says, "Welcome home, my beloved children." Once again, the audience erupts with cheering and applause, while many shed tears of joy. There is a huge sense of relief because He is genuinely happy to see us all together again. After a moment, He lowers His arms, while at the same time motioning for quiet. His dialogue begins.

"What an amazing and wonderful journey we have been on together! There were many good times and a few not-so-good times. You created many magnificent things and solved many difficult

problems. You invented the wheel and discovered the many uses of fire. You discovered electricity and then invented the light bulb and the laser. Creativity was never higher than through this period, when the many uses of energy and light became clearer; the many uses of the essence of God. You developed cures for many diseases and eventually even learned to control the weather. You learned to protect the environment and replenish the ozone layer, and you even stopped global warming. Although it took you thousands of years, you learned that war was senseless and that there was enough of everything to support everyone. You learned the value of family, friends, your community, country and the world. You learned of the many values and relationships that you could only experience on Planet Earth. You took an early environment of constant hard labor, tragic wars, famine, disease and suffering and turned it into an automated society of caring citizens working together, with enough food, shelter and quality time for everyone."

"The most important thing that you finally remembered was that I was here for you, all along. Even through your technological age, instead of growing apart from Me, you grew closer, partly because your science could explain My existence. You began to realize the power of your godlike minds and collectively used them for the benefit of all humankind, until the day came when you indeed brought Heaven to Earth."

"Congratulations and welcome home, My prodigal sons and daughters. Welcome home."

And again the audience explodes with cheering and applause, as God smiles and nods His head slowly in approval of a job well done. Many of us are in tears and in awe of our Host and His kind words. After a standing ovation, we begin to quiet as God turns to walk off stage. He takes several steps toward the opening in the center of the curtain and pulls it aside with His right hand. He pauses for a moment with the curtain apart and then turns to the audience. With His eyebrows raised over wide-eyed excitement and a grin likened to that of a mischievous child, He says,

"Hey...do you want to do it again?"

Chapter 19

Seeing The Light

To neatly bundle and package what I had been taught would look like this:
- We're here because we (and God) wanted to experience opposites such as hot and cold, good and bad. God did not kick us out of Heaven and exile us here. We wanted this for our enjoyment and experience.
- This world is an illusion, a projection of our desire for opposites. It's a method for experiencing various relationships. Things that we can't find or do in Heaven had to be created by God (and us) and therefore aren't real, in the eternal sense.
- Our mission and challenge is to re-discover who and what we really are (godlike beings of light) and find our way back home to God. We're not physical beings with egos, we're spiritual beings temporarily in physical form.
- Eventually we all will be with God, happy in eternity, as the story of the Prodigal Son suggests.

- It may take thousands of lives or years for us to "get it right" and find our way home.
- Heaven has many levels for our enjoyment as we progress, and some "not so nice" levels that we might visit temporarily but would rather avoid.
- When our spirituality, as a world, has graduated beyond this world, this world will no longer need to exist, thus supporting Jesus' words that the "Earth shall pass away." This doesn't mean we must experience Armageddon.
- Hell does not exist as an eternal lake of fire, but there are seriously negative planes of existence that we should strive to avoid.

Formulas for Life:

The universe we live in is guided and controlled by an incredible intelligence known to many as God, Yahweh, Jehovah, Allah or Jesus, just to mention a few of His names. Regardless of what we call this intelligence, it is indisputable that there is order and logic to its operation. Even in this world of apparent random chaos and troubled relationships, there is order and reason to the flow of energy and its composition at its basic levels. With certainty, we know that the Earth will continue to rotate and the sun will continue to shine. Humans will continue to be born and die. Atoms will continue to contain protons, neutrons and electrons. Recognizing a universe of energy, intelligence and order can foster theories, hypotheses, formulas, understanding and conclusions. Perhaps some of this certainty can also apply to the success or destruction of our lives. I thought it might be interesting to attempt simple formulae, combining relationships and attitudes, to illustrate their potential effects on our lives. First, my assumptions:

Separation from God *is* hell. Specifically, what I mean is a denial of God and His love and concern for our happiness. It can also include separation from our Higher Selves which contain the essence of God. The greater the degree of separation from God and spirit and Their virtuous qualities, the greater difficulty we may endure. Our primary source of motivation would therefore originate from ego. Our reward will be proportional to the reputable and ethical ambitions of our egos, or lack thereof. Separation might include the belief that everything that happens is random and uncontrollable. Separation from God, combined with a denial of immortality, can result in an unwanted isolated experience in the afterworld, as was discussed earlier.

A positive attitude is vital for success and happiness. This is based on the fundamental concept that our mind has the power to create the external world we experience. If we believe we are in charge of our destiny and have positive and loving motivations we will be successful. It also includes a loving, caring, sharing, compassionate and forgiving behavior and character.

A negative attitude, such as the belief that we "sinners" are meant to endure suffering and sacrifice, or that "if it weren't for bad luck, I'd have no luck at all," can manifest in a lackluster life filled with troubles. Recognizing that experiencing suffering, sacrifice, loss, grief and anger (and many more negative emotions) is inevitable and normal while it should not be our expectation to endure frequently. It should be regarded as an exception to the rule. Negativity breeds negativity. Pain is inevitable but suffering is an option. What we believe becomes our reality. In the past I believed in the cliché that "bad things happened in threes." When something broke I would look for the two other associated breakdowns and routinely could find three events close enough in time to draw the conclusion that they were related to the cliché, thus giving the cliché life in my world.

Approaching this realistically, if we live the normal life expectancy of about seventy years we will probably have experienced many occasions on which we were angry and, at least a few times, where we grieved over the loss of a loved one. These situations are a normal part of life but shouldn't be something we wake up and expect on a daily basis. While brushing our teeth we shouldn't be thinking, *I wonder who I'll yell at today or who will yell at me?*

A relationship with God, which includes love, gratitude and a belief that we are worthy of happiness, will promote quality of life. A relationship that works with God to carry out His will, utilizing His assistance, will promote a richly fulfilling life. Add to that a heaping helping of love, caring, sharing, compassion and forgiveness toward others, and we will have an incredibly joyous life of service.

Therefore:

1. Separation + Negative Attitude = a living hell, especially if there is no ego-driven motivation to accomplish anything good.
2. Separation + Positive Attitude = a decent, perhaps great, life but with a void, or without full meaning, feeling something is missing. The nobility of ego-based motivations will impact the outcome in the afterlife.
3. Relationship with God + Negative Attitude = a decent, perhaps very good, life believing God does things to us for our own good, maintaining a belief that suffering is a necessary gift from God. Our negative attitude will block many of the gifts God had for us.
4. Relationship with God + Positive Attitude = a wonderful, richly fulfilling life, knowing that God loves us and only

wants the best for us. Bad things might happen but they happen for someone's benefit and are probably part of our plan but not expected as routine.

So Why Do Bad Things Happen to Good People?

We roughly plan our lives with the assistance of our guides, elders and others we will encounter, before we incarnate, so these bad things are built into the plan for our own development or for someone else's benefit. As in "Formulas for Life" (Number Three), some of us believe that bad things are meant to happen to us because we are meant to suffer just for the sake of suffering. One spiritual leader remarked; "Nothing bad can happen to me unless I decide it can." This leader recognized the power of his mind to control his outer world. This isn't to say that the free will of mankind can't accidentally cut a life short, or that suicides are part of the plan; it simply recognizes that many of the encounters of life are pre-determined. How we evaluate and respond to them is up to us.

Kabbalah teaches: life can have many endings. Like a computer game, there are millions of options and paths leading to an end. The ending may not be the successful completion of the game but, rather, the demise of the character. Usually, the gamer endures many failures before unlocking the secrets to all the levels of play. And there may be several options for achieving the same outcome. There are many forks in the road of life, many decisions. In this life you may have chosen a variety of outcomes based on the decisions you will make along the way, or during your game. When we decide that everything is going to be fine and reject negative thinking, we can dramatically change the experiences life presents to us, the game might become easier. We don't have to continually endure failure, rejection, pain, suffering, sacrifice and demise. At any time, we can affect the outcome of the game (our life) by a simple decision to choose a path of spreading love, caring, sharing compassion and forgiveness. The universe will respond by reciprocating. Because it *is* universal law, this will be an improvement, in and of itself. Granted, it can be difficult to spread love and caring when our world seems to be falling apart, but we must begin the cycle somewhere.

This is where ego can be beneficial. Let your ego say, "I'm not going to take it anymore! I'm going to do something positive about it!" Use the ambitious drive, conviction and commitment of your ego to manifest your Higher Self. Now *there's* a good use for the ego. Reach up there and grab your Higher Self by the shoestrings and pull your wonderful butt down here for all of us to enjoy. Realize you are worthy of a wonderful life, and willing to share coming fortunes, and watch your life change.

But when seemingly bad things happen, don't blame anyone or anything; realize we may have planned it for our own growth, or that it may be the result of an incorrect decision that we made. I always evaluate my experiences or hardships after they have occurred, to see what I learned. Usually, I find the lesson worth the trouble it took to learn as you have read in previous chapters.

And Why Do Good Things Happen to Bad People?

Because they believe in themselves or they believe in their cause, no matter how villainous it may be. The power of our thoughts to create reality does not differentiate between our good thoughts and our bad thoughts. They simply create as we desire. Even the bible says, "That ye may be children of your Father which is in Heaven: for He maketh His sun to rise on the evil and on the good, and sendeth rain on the just and on the unjust." (Matt 5:45 KJV) This seems to clarify that God doesn't get directly involved in the fight against evil. That would violate the law of free will. Ego-based intentions are very powerful indeed but usually require extra effort on the part of the thinker to see the desire to fruition. Since God is not supporting the evil thinker, he must arrange everything with careful attention to ensure all the i's are dotted and t's are crossed, because universal law dictates an equal amount of trouble to foil the plan now or at some later time.

When an evil person chooses to do wrong, it's as if there were an assistant helping them carry out their dastardly deeds. They seem to get away with entirely too much and much too easily. The stars seem all too eager to align for their hurtful and destructive desires. But these people don't have guardian angels or spirit guides helping them inflict their ill will. They may, however, have demons and evil spirits tagging along, who recognize an opportunity to continue their wicked ways by assisting the human's path of destruction, combining their negative energies together to form a more powerful alliance of ill will that becomes an incredible force to reckon with.

God did establish the universal laws, and the law of cause and effect will prevail. At some point, cause and effect will catch up to these "bad" people due to a similar universal law, "What goes around comes around." We cannot escape cause and effect. Sooner or later, the hammer drops, and they will get their just reward, if not in this life, then in the afterlife for certain.

I find it interesting how many criminals and law breakers are apprehended during routine traffic violations. I rarely listen to the news because of its predominately negative stories, but when the local radio broadcast covers regional news I find it intriguing the number of drug arrests made during routine traffic stops. More notorious offenders such as Ted Bundy (serial killer) and Timothy McVeigh (Oklahoma City Bombing) were both caught after being identified during routine traffic stops. I truly believe that God and Company are just waiting for the "bad guys" to make a mistake so They can arrange for their wrongdoing to be stopped dead in their tracks. I'm not convinced that God endorses our methods of punishment but I believe he supports stopping the harmful actions, which result when a criminal is caught.

So, keep a watchful and analytical eye open for these kinds of stories and I'm sure you'll find many throughout your life where the unjust meet universal law. You may even notice how seemingly small acts of injustice or abuse are dealt with on a universal level: it's all about cause and effect. And you'll probably draw the same conclusion that many criminals have; "crime doesn't pay."

A Sobering Hypothesis

If reincarnation is true and we continue to incarnate until we find our way back home to God, then we have been doing this for thousands of years and still haven't figured out how to get home. In other words, if we had lived correctly in a previous life, we wouldn't be here today, unless we intentionally chose to start over again, perhaps to help others. We've been clinging to incorrect beliefs and perhaps lived godless lives for centuries. But here, before us right now, is another chance to get it right, another opportunity to do the right thing, because there is still plenty of hope for us. God doesn't care at what age we get life right; He just hopes that at some point we do! But we can't go wrong, since we will all end up with God in the end.

And herein lies the reason why we must protect Mother Earth and the environment. We need "time" in order to achieve salvation for each and every one of us. The amount of time that we need may be thousands of years. If we have to come back here time and time again to work on our spiritual evolution, we most certainly would want a beautiful and friendly atmosphere, complete with all of the conveniences of technology that we have today, perhaps even more fringe benefits, as the future will undoubtedly hold, making life even more pleasurable. We don't want to "nuke" ourselves back to the Stone Age. Mere survival was incredibly tough in those barbaric times. Life can be a lot more pleasant and convenient now, being able to travel around the world at the drop of a hat, or e-mailing a photo to a friend, and sharing good times.

This may very well explain why we have environmental activists. They may be pre-programmed to save Mother Earth from our destructive ways so there is something left for our future use. So hug a "tree hugger;" they might just be saving the Earth so you don't have to complete your spiritual development in a bombed-out dump reminiscent of a World War II battlefield.

Choose a Better Life

Life doesn't have to be a struggle, filled with evil bosses and eighty-hour workweeks…unless we believe that's the way it's supposed to be. Just ask God and Company to make it better, and then trust and believe that you are worthy of a better life, and so it shall be.

Life doesn't have to be filled with suffering…unless we believe that suffering is a part of life that we cannot control. Then it will control us. If we believe that God wants us to suffer for a reason, then we will probably continue to suffer. We create our own reality. I've seen many folks traditionally regarded as "less fortunate" because of physical handicaps who are beaming with happiness and completely comfortable in their condition. Suffering is an option that we impose on ourselves.

Life doesn't have to be constantly about illness and pain…unless we believe it is. We can choose to think healthy and be healthy, to a certain degree. Having physical bodies in a physical world, complete with the stresses of life, can reduce our physical and spiritual immunity to disease. Spending the vast majority of our time in the physical world (and not in the spiritual world), and believing only the physical laws that govern this dimension, can make us more susceptible to illness. Even spiritually attuned enlightened masters, avatars and saints have died from diseases such as cancer, and yet people are miraculously healed every day. *A Course in Miracles* suggests that sickness and diseases are *not* real and can only affect us if we *believe* in the disease, thus giving it the power to affect us. But the concept of sickness and various diseases is so engrained in our minds that suggesting we can easily talk ourselves out of getting sick is hardly practical without a tremendous amount of time secluded on a mountain, meditating on health. And in the end, like the saints and avatars, we'll have to die from some disease, anyway. The key is *not* to take a negative approach toward the affliction, since that will give it the power to harm us in severe or advanced stages of the disease. For example, it *wouldn't* be wise to believe the onset of arthritis would completely incapacitate you within a year. A better approach might be to continue fighting the disease while firmly believing it can be reversed or at least controlled. Lance Armstrong is a great example of the sheer power of will to overcome disease completely. There are many other documented (miraculous) recoveries by strong willed people including athletes like Quarterback Joe Montana. Doctors have told many they will never walk, run or play sports again, only to be proven wrong by the determined spirit who refused to accept the prognosis.

A Simple Agreement

You may not agree with me when I say that Hell does not exist as an eternal place of damnation. You may not believe me when I say that your departed loved may be near you and assisting you through life. You may not believe me when I say that angels, spirits and enlightened masters can communicate with us if we take the time to be quiet and listen. You may go into denial when I say that we are never alone and that there is always someone watching over us. You might vehemently disagree with me when I say that we are all one spirit in one universe. You may even accuse me of blasphemy when I claim that we are all gods, with a little "g." You may not even agree with me when I say that there are various levels of Heaven. All of this is perfectly alright, because I believe there are many rivers to the sea, or paths back home to God.

But I sincerely hope we can all agree that living a loving, caring, sharing, compassionate and forgiving life will benefit all of mankind.

Loving: Make it a part of your day-to-day life to spread love, even in the simplest of ways, such as offering a smile to others. Perhaps it's a cheerful hello or a courteous nod. Just watch the smiles and the love come back to you. Loving people are warm-hearted, happy people, and their love seems to effortlessly flow from them. They always say hello with a smile and want to know how you're doing. They like to engage in friendly conversation and usually take the time to engage in a brief chat. They're good listeners and pay attention. They are never so consumed with their own agenda that they don't have time for someone else. Loving people are also respectful of everyone and don't consider themselves superior to others.

Caring: Genuinely care for others when they need our help or support. When we see someone in need of care, take a minute to express it. Just because we may not know them doesn't mean they won't appreciate it. It will probably be more appreciated from a stranger. Volunteers know the good feeling they get when they help needy folks. And one of those needy folks might be us, someday. Storms, tornados, hurricanes and car accidents are just a few of the ways we can quickly and unexpectedly become victims in need of care. See why someone is crying and see what you can do to help, *because you care*. Visit someone in an old folk's home, *because you care*. Make sure your elderly neighbor is okay when the power goes out, *because you care*. Take the time to communicate and/or visit with your Great Aunt who lives alone in another state, *because you care*.

Sharing: "Give until it hurts," as Mother Theresa said. A $10 donation from a millionaire isn't impressive, but a $1 donation from one poor family to another is extraordinary. Give of everything you own; books to libraries or children, money to charities, clothes to charities (old or new); share your home with friends and family, share your car by taking friends to work when needed, share your time as a volunteer. Even share knowledge, stories, or a lesson you have learned in life. Being a little league coach, mentor, tutor, or instructor as well as simply helping someone that is lost find their way to their destination are forms of sharing. There are a million ways to share our good fortune, and it all comes back to us, in some way, shape or form. Since I have been sharing, I have to keep things moving out of the house in order to keep up with what comes in. People are always giving us stuff, it seems. It's heartwarming to watch God at work.

Compassionate: Be compassionate towards others. Be a good listener and comfort them as best you can. There are no coincidences, so if we find ourselves in a situation where someone needs compassion, and we're in the vicinity, perhaps we are uniquely qualified to assist that individual. We may have had a similar experience and might be just the person to heal the situation. Compassionate people are *not* quick to judge and condemn, but rather offer understanding when others may not. Fortunately, compassion usually leads to sharing and caring, but you may also find that you are not in a situation to directly help. Send prayers to those we cannot help directly, perhaps as we drive by an accident. Try not to be so consumed by your own busy life that you can't help.

Forgiving: Forgiveness is a huge step in our spiritual evolution. It was one of the first things I was prompted to do when the ADCs from my mother began, signaling its tremendous importance. Perhaps my unwillingness to forgive my mother for thirty-six years kept her in bondage on the other side. I don't know for sure, but it was the first thing I felt compelled to do, so it must have been important for both of us. Once I discovered the reasons that led to her suicide, I was able to release that negative energy and forgive her. Holding a grudge can cause that nagging knot in your stomach, and may even deter the spiritual evolution of others, as "thoughts are things" that always reach their intended target. If nothing else, don't let an offender have that power to make you angry or sad. Let it go and relieve yourself of the stress. Your anger does more harm to you than it does to them. As Jesus said, "Forgive them, for they know not what they do."

And if the crime is too much for you to forgive, then turn it over to God and know that God will handle it. "Let go and let God," as the saying goes. Revenge *is* the worst thing we could engage in. Like a boomerang, it will surely come back to repay us with an equal amount of pain. Universal law dictates that the universe has no choice but to reciprocate. Perhaps the event that angered us is solely meant to test our forgiveness. It is imperative that we learn to forgive, to release ourselves and our aggressors from our negative emotions that serve no other purpose than to keep us in bondage and give us ulcers.

Final Thoughts

Life is meant to be good, clean fun, filled with happiness and joy. Sure, we may have a few hurdles built into our scripts, but they are meant to make us stronger if they don't kill us, as some say. When we fully embrace the truth that this physical life is a temporary dream, then we realize that, no matter what happens, everything will turn out just perfectly anyway. Sure, I still have bad days, but I also know they will quickly pass, because I choose not to dwell on them and prolong the suffering. I know that God and Company will make my troubles evaporate, because They don't want me to suffer, any more than I do.

Life is meant to spark our ability to create. From the "image and likeness" of our Creator comes our desire and ability to create. We are creating many wonderful things that make life easier, more convenient, more fun and more exciting. Music is phenomenal and art has taken on many forms, from motorcycle "theme bikes" to a city's architecture. Watching our youth perform amazing athletic feats with everything from motorcycles to snowboards is inspiring. Humans, especially Americans, can turn anything into competition, thus driving us to achieve high levels of performance never before attained. And technology has created some wonderful gadgets that help us in every way imaginable to make life a little easier. An expression of our creativity can be seen in the many good and wonderful things we've accomplished. An easier life equates to more quality time for our friends and families, and more time to share, care and express our godlike Higher Selves.

Creating wonderful material goods and performing incredible athletic feats are not the only things we can create; we can also create joy, love, peace, sharing and caring, to name a few. By focusing on creating these characteristics in the lives of others, we can bring more of the same to our own lives, for it is through these actions that more joy and fulfillment reciprocates. In addition, we all have a talent or gift that is meant to be shared with the world. We all bring something here to share with others. Another of our goals is to discover that talent and share it.

If God is experiencing life through us, then it's imperative that we write a good story for Him, a story that He'll be proud to tell again and again, a story filled with love, hope, joy, accomplishment, creation, beauty, caring, sharing, smiles and lots and lots of laughter.

No one loves a good story more than God!

In closing, I would like to leave you with a prayer written by Saint Francis of Assisi. The prayer sums up many of the concepts contained within this book:

Lord, make me an instrument of thy peace.

Where there is hatred, let me sow love.

Where there is injury, pardon.

Where there is doubt, faith.

Where there is despair, hope.

Where there is darkness, light.

And where there is sadness, joy.

O Divine Master, grant that I may not so much seek to be consoled, as to console;

To be understood as to understand; to be loved, as to love.

For it is in giving that we receive, and it is in pardoning that we are pardoned,

And it is in dying that we are born to eternal life.

God Bless You. We Will Meet Again

Epilogue

A force I don't fully understand compelled me to seek the truth with unrelenting effort. A passion consumed me (probably more like an obsession) to understand life after death, the purpose of life, and the purpose of our relationship with God and the universe. So strong was the desire that I was willing to set aside my "normal" life and my favorite hobbies. An unseen energy I don't fully understand drove me to spend countless hours at a keyboard, typing my story and the conclusions of my research and experiences so that others on the same path might find answers. A sequence of connections and events occurred that were too uncanny to be coincidental. The development of intuition and spiritual communication was fostered to enhance "right discernment." An inspiring list of friendships, chance encounters, unexpected contacts and timely messages happened, just when I needed them most. A path of discovery too well-choreographed to be anything less than Divinely orchestrated occurred. All of this has led me to where I am today, a much happier person.

It is my sincere hope that I might help at least a few of you find your way home again. These pages were not written to bring fame and fortune. If I wanted that, I would have chosen a topic much less controversial. My career is doing fine, and my family lives very comfortably. I hope you can see that my reason for writing this book was my conviction concerning its message, and not financial gain. It's about the message, not about the money.

God Bless You

Acknowledgements, Suggested Readings and Listening

1. Balcombe, Betty F. *The Psychic Handbook*. Published by Samuel Weiser, Inc.
2. Berg, Michael. *The Secret*. Published by Kabbalah Publishing.
3. Borysenko, Joan. Audio series *The Power of the Mind To Heal*. Produced by the Nightingale-Conant Corporation.
4. Browne, Sylvia. *Journey of the Soul, Series*. Published by Hay House.
5. Chilton, Bruce. *Rabbi Jesus*. Published by Bantam Books.
6. Chopra, Deepak. Audio program *SynchroDestiny*. Produced by the Nightingale-Conant Corporation.
7. Edward, John. *One Last Time*. Published by Berkley Books.
8. Foundation for Inner Peace. *A Course in Miracles*. Published by the Foundation for Inner Peace.
9. Guggenheim, Bill and Judy. *Hello From Heaven*. Published by Bantam Books.
10. Hewitt, William W. *Psychic Development for Beginners*. Published by Llewellyn Publications.
11. Meyer, Marvin. *The Gospel of Thomas, The Hidden Sayings of Jesus*. Published by HarperSanFrancisco.
12. Moskowitz, Michael. Audio program *The Power of Kabbalah*. Produced by the Nightingale-Conant Corporation.
13. Murphy, Joseph. *The Power of Your Subconscious Mind*. Published by Bantam Books.
14. Padgett, James. Angelic Revelations of Divine Truth, Vol. II. Published by The Foundation Church of Divine Truth. (ISBN 1887621016)

15. Roth, Ron. Audio program *Reclaiming Your Spiritual Power.* Produced by the Nightingale-Conant Corporation.
16. Smith, Mark. *Auras, See Them in Only 60 Seconds!* Published by Llewellyn Publications.
17. Sutphen, Dick. Audio program *Mind Travel.* Produced by the Nightingale-Conant Corporation.
18. Schwartz, Gary E. The *Afterlife Experiments*. Published by Pocket Books.
19. Theresa, Mother. Audio program *Thirsting for God.* Produced by the Nightingale-Conant Corporation.
20. Van Praagh, James. *Talking to Heaven.* Published by The Penguin Group, New American Library.
21. Virtue, Doreen. *The Lightworker's Way* (©1997), *Healing With the Angels* (©1999) and *Archangels and Ascended Masters* (©2003). Published by Hay House, Inc. Carlsbad California. Virtue has a long list of books and audio programs worth checking out.
22. Walsch, Neale Donald. *Conversations With God, book 1.* Published by The Penguin Group, G. P. Putnam's Sons. Also consider the remainder of the *Conversations With God* trilogy and the many other books by Walsch.
23. Williamson, Linda. *Contacting The Spirit World.* Published by Berkley Books.

Please visit Joe's Website at www.joesawakening.com